Madhyānta-Vibhanga

Bibliotheca Indo-Buddhica Series No. 96

Madhyānta–Vibhanga

Discourse on
Discrimination between Middle and Extremes
ascribed to Bodhisattva Maitreya
and commented by
Vasubandu and Sthiramati

(Part I)

Translated from the Sanskrit
by
Th. Stcherbatsky

Sri Satguru Publications
A Division of
Indian Books Centre
Delhi-India

Published by :

SRI SATGURU PUBLICATIONS
Indological and Oriental Publishers
A Division of
Indian Books Centre
40/5, Shakti Nagar,
Delhi-110007
(INDIA)

First Edition : St. Petersburg 1936
Reprint Edition : Delhi 1992

ISBN 81-7030-301-X

Printed at:
D.K. Fine Art Press, Delhi-52

PRINTED IN INDIA

PREFACE

The **Vijñānavāda** school of Buddhism represents the latest and final form of that religion, the form in which, after having transformed India's national philosophy and leaving its native Indian soil, it spread over almost the whole of the Asiatic continent up to Japan in the East and Asia Minor in the West where it amalgamated with gnosticism.

The **Madhyānta-vibhanga-šāstra** (or sūtra) of **Maitreya-Asaṅga** with its commentaries, the **bhāṣya** of **Vasubandhu** and the **ṭikā** of **Sthiramati**, belong to the most fundamental works of this Vijñānavāda (*alias* Yogācāra, Vijñapti-mātratā or Cittamātratā) school of Northern Buddhism.

The till now unique MS of its sanscrit original has had the curious fate of having been discovered twice. The story of this double discovery and of the double text-edition which followed has been very pointedly narrated by the illustrious first discoverer, the much regretted late Prof. Sylvain Lévi. In his preface to the second (which really was the first) edition he *inter alia* writes: „il est fâcheux que l'édition concurrente, publiée en 1932 ne fasse pas mention (de l'autre édition) dans sa préface".[1] It seems that I have not been the only victim of this strange reticence. It is only much later that owing to the kind attention of Prof. L. de La Vallée Poussin and Prof. E. Lamotte I became aware of the second edition.

As soon as Prof. G. Tucci's edition[2] reached me I started on the work of translating this important text for the Bibliotheca Buddhica series whose publication was going to be resumed. Unfortunately I had no inkling of the existence of the other edition. My pupil, the late Dr E. Obermiller published a review of Prof. G. Tucci and V. Bhattacharya's edition[3] in which he suggested some corrections of those parts of the published text which represented

1) **Sthiramati. Madhyāntavibhāgaṭīkā**, édition par Susumu **Yamaguchi** (Nagoya, 1934).

2) **Madhyāntavibhāgasūtrabhāṣyaṭīkā** of **Sthiramati** edited by Vidhushekhara **Bhattacharya** and Giuseppe **Tucci** (Calcutta, 1932, Calcutta Oriental series № 24).

3) Indian Historical Quarterly, vol. IX, № 4, p. 1019 ff.

retranslations from the Tibetan to fill up the lacunae of the sanscrit MS. He also did not suspect the existence of the other edition which made some of his critical remarks superfluous.

My English version, besides the kārikā's of Maitreya-Asanga, contains a translation of Vasubandhu's bhāṣya in full as well as of the ṭikā of Sthiramati. For Vasubandhu I have made use of a very correct block-print executed in the printing office of the Aga monastery in Transbaikalia, its folios are marked in my translation by figures preceded by the letter V. The other figures in margin refer to the pages and lines in Prof. Tucci and V. Bhattacharya's edition. I am sorry I could consider Prof. S. Yamaguchi's text, as far as the first part is concerned, only in the notes. The division in chapters and sections, as well as their titles, are added by me.

It is a great pleasure for me to express my gratitude to my young friend Prof. A. Vostrikov, PhD with whom I discussed several hard passages of the text and to whom I am indebted for many valuable suggestions.

An analysis of the philosophy of this treatise and an appreciation of its value will be contained in a following volume of the Bibliotheca Buddhica series.

Anticipatively I subjoin the following remarks.

This translation aims at an intelligible rendering of Buddhist ideas; it therefore, with rare exceptions, avoids untranslated terminology, it tries to render Buddhist technical terms by more or less corresponding equivalents borrowed from European philosophy. This method seems to me not hopeless, because, in my opinion, Indian philosophy has reached a very high standart of development and the princinple lines of this development run parallel with those which are familiar to the students of European philosophy. India possesses parallels to our rationalism and to our empiricism, it has a system of empirical idealism and a system of spiritual monism, it has, first of all, a logic and, what is remarkable, an epistemology. In this epistemology Buddhist authors play a leading part. From the Indian standpoint Buddhism is a *šāstra* and what an Indian *šāstra* is Indologists well know from the example of the great grammatical *šāstra*'s of Pāṇini and Pātanjali.

Now it is a remarkable fact, which variously can be explained, but which is undisputable, that the Pali-school of Buddhologists entirely overlooked that *šāstra*, the system of philosophy which however is present on every page of the Pali kanon. An Indian *šāstra* first of all frames a special terminology for the concepts with which it operates and establishes clear-cut definitions of these concepts. The Tibetans, being the pupils of Indian tradition, have carried this care of minutely precise definitions to an extreme, almost artistic, perfection. Therefore the study of Tibetan sources has greatly contributed to our understanding of Buddhism. At the dawn of European Indology there has been a controversy between the great French scholar E. Burnouf and the great Russian scholar W. Wassilieff on the question whether Buddhism could be better understood from Indian or also from Chinese and Tibetan sources.

According to the first, only Indian sources provided evidence on genuine Buddhism, according to the second, Buddhism in the totality of its development could be understood only from Chinese and Tibetan sources in addition to the Indian ones. Wissilieff's standpoint enabled him to determine the exact meaning of the crucial term *śūnyatā* in which he discovered under a dialectical terminology an idea similar to the Absolute Idea of Hegel. The present translation brings an eloquent confirmation of Wassilieff's discovery made a century since, whereas the Pali-school discovered in Mahāyāna nothing but degeneration and nihilism. Working in the traditions of the school of Professors W. Wassilieff and I. Minayeff, my much regretted pupil Prof. O. Rosenberg in his „Problems of Buddhist Philosophy" and myself in my „Central Conception of Buddhism" and „Conception of Buddhist Nirvāṇa" established the exact meaning of the basic technical terms of the system: 1) the term *dharma* meaning Element of existence; 2) the term *saṃskāra* (= *sam-bhūya-kārin*) meaning cooperating Element of existence and 3) the term *pratītya-samutpāda* (= *saṃskṛtatvam*) meaning cooperation of the Elements of existence. The three terms refer to one and the same system of pluralistic empiricism which is the core of early Buddhism. Prof. O. Rosenberg has given to Buddhism the name of a *dharma*-theory and indeed Buddhism in the three main forms of its development is nothing but a theory of *dharmás*, i. e. a system of a plurality of ultimate Elements of Reality to which a monistic foundation has been added in the Mahāyāna. The recent capital work of Prof. de La Vallée Poussin „Vijñaptimātratā-siddhi" (here quoted LVP) which is a magnificent thesaurus of the most precious information on the ultimate phase of Buddhism contains among its 820 pages hardly a single one which would not be concerned with the elucidation and the profound implications of this or that *dharma*.

The term *śūnyatā* is an innovation of the Mahāyāna, an innovation made necessary by the course of philosophic development. Its germs are found in the Hīnayāna, but the Mahāyāna has given it a quite new interpretation, an interpretation in which the two main schools of the Mahāyāna radically diverged.

The whole chapter V of the first part of the treatise is devoted to the elucidation of the Yogācāra conception of this term as contrasted with the Mādhyamika view of it. It is there most clearly and emphatically stated that, for the Yogācāras, it means 1) *grāhya-grāhaka-abhāva* and 2) *tasya ca svabhāva*, i. e. 1) the (ultimate) non-reality of the relation of subject to object and 2) the (ultimate) reality of their (subjacent, monistic) Absolute. In other words the denial of Pluralism and the vindication of Monism, with the implication that this Monism has a superstructure of phenomenal Relativity or that the phenomenal Relativity has a subjacent foundation of Absolute, non-relative, Reality. The Absolute is thus the „Reality of Unreality" or as Prof. W. Wassilieff has expressed it—to quote the German version of his celebrated translator Th. Benfey (p. 121—2) „das mit dem Subject identische

Object, welches, so wie es in den Kreis unseres Denkens tritt, unmittelbar zu etwas subjectivem wird....... Affirmation und Negation werden identisch" (cp. below, p. 104). This Absolute represents the unique substance of the Universe *(ekam dravyam)*. There is no other substance. It embraces the totality of everything relatively real, but is itself the non-relative Absolute. It has, so to speak, a reflex on the opposite end of the scale, in the so called Thing-in-Itself (*svalakṣaṇa*) which is a point-instant of spiritual Reality. There are thus two Absolutes, the absolute Particular and the absolute Universal, the extreme concrete and particular and the extreme abstract and Universal, the limit, so to speak, from the bottom and the limit at the top. Between them we must locate the relative Reality of the phenomenal Universe. All phenomenal objects are interrelated and related to the two limits between which they must find their place. The one of them is the point-instant *(kṣaṇa)* of reality, the other represents its eternal *(nitya)* Whole; the one is particular *(sva-lakṣaṇa)*, the other Universal *(sāmānya-lakṣaṇa)*; the one is a single Element *(dharma)*, the other represents their totality *(dharmatā)*; the one is „the" Real *(vastu = sat)*, the other is the Reality *(satya)*; the one is interdependent *(paratantra)*, the other independent or Absolute (*pasinipṣanna*); the one is *paramārtha-sat*, the other — *paramārtha-satya*. Applying Kantian terminology we could perhaps say that the one is transcendental *(šuddha-laukika)*, the other transcendent *(parišuddha, lokottra)*.[1]

How are these two Absolutes related between themselves? They are, says the Yogācāra, neither different nor identical (p. 39—40), just as every other Universal: although it cannot be separated from its respective particulars, it is not identical with them. Each of them represents the „Reality of Unreality", the *paratantra* as *abhūta-parikalpa*, the *šūnyatā* as *abhāvasya svabhāva*. As such the *šūnyatā* can be characterized as being neither Affirmation nor Negation (cp. p. 78), or as Wassilieff puts it „Affirmation and Negation become identical".

Now the Mādhyamikas deny the ultimate reality of both these concepts. They neither admit the reality of the *paratantra* nor of the *parinișpanna* = *šūnyatā*. For them these two Absolutes are as relative as all the rest. They admit no exception from their principle of Universal Relativity, no *paramārtha-sat*, no Tning-in-Itself. They, of course, have a *paramārtha-satya*, or Highest Principle, of their own, but it consists just in the denial of the Thing-in-Itself, the denial of every ultimately real Element in existence. Tsoñ-kha-pa, a good judge, says in his Legs-bšad sñiñ-po that among all systems of philosophy, Buddhist as well as non-Buddhist, there is only a single one which denies every kind of an ultimately Real; and this is the system of the Mādhyamikas. According to the German expression, it represents „eine

[1] We thus can establish two corresponding series of equivalents — dharma = kṣaṇa = saṃskṛta-dharma = paratantra = svalakṣaṇa = paramārtha-sat. On the other hand — dharmatā = šūnyatā = tathatā = asaṃskṛta-dharma = parinișpanna = sāmānya-lakṣaṇa = paramārtha-satya.

Verabsolutierung des Relativen". From this universal Relativity there can be no exceptions. Neither the Buddha, nor the Bodhisattva, nor Salvation and Nirvāṇa are excepted. They are dialectical Ideas, not realities. As concepts they are constructions of our productive imagination, hence ultimately unreal, *bden-par med* as the Tibetan emphatically states. Highly instructive is from this point of view the division of *śūnyatā* into 16 varieties. Of these 16 varieties there are 8 which refer to the mahāyānistic Buddha and Bodhisattva. For the Yogācāra they represent Relativity also, inasmuch as they are objects of conceptual thought which distinguishes object and subject, but this Relativity has a subjacent Absolute Reality: for the Mādhyamikas it has none, for them it is mere *advaya* without any *eka-dravya* at the bottom.

But this does not at all mean that the Mādhyamikas are nihilists. They were accused of nihilism by the polemical fervour of the Yogācāras who imputed on them the principle *sarvam sarveṇa nāsti* (B. bhūmi, p. 44), as well as by the European scholars of the Pali-school. They however emphatically protested against that accusation. Relativism is not Nihilism. In Japan, where the Yogācāra tradition prevails, there is a tendency either to minimize the discrepancy of the two schools (Suzuki and others) or to accuse the Mādhyamikas of nihilism (Masuda and others). The Mādhyamika philosophy however is the doctrine officially professed by the Tibetan church. It would sound exceedingly strange if we would interpret the solemn and exuberant catholicism of that church as a disguised nihilism. This is the only point in which I would venture to diverge from the views expressed by Prof. L. de La Vallée Poussin in his capital work on the Yogācāra system. In accordance with some Japanese scholars, he is inclined to underrate the difference between the two main schools of Mahāyāna and to neglect the importance of the war which they were waging, whereas the whole of the Vijnaptimātratā-śāstra, as the title shows, is written with the aim of vindicating the Yogācāra views against the theories of the Mādhyamikas. He says p. 757 „il y a Mādhyamikas et Mādhyamikas, Yogācāras et Yogācāras". This is quite right in this sense that we have intermediate schools and subschools, but it is wrong when it tends to obliterate the difference between the main schools. It is also, in my opinion, not quite exact to say that Nāgārjuna „admet une réalité vide". The dictum of the „void vessel", the vessel which is void but real, is a characteristic Yogācāra dictum directed against the Mādhyamikas, as is clearly stated in the present treatise on p. 12.20 (transl., p. 22).

True is however that the Mādhyamikas have a *paramārtha-satya*, and that this *paramārtha-satya* consists in the negation of every *paramārtha-sat*.

The Discourse on Discrimination between Middle and Extremes is written with the same aim as the Vijñapti-mātratā-siddhi. It repudiates the Universal Relativism of the Mādhyamikas. It repudiates also the Pluralism of Hīnayāna. By a stricter discrimination between Appearance and Reality it establishes its own system of a spiritual Monism. There is a transcendent Absolute Reality subjacent to the Appearance of the phenomenal world, it is the reality of the Pure Spirit (vijñapti-mātratā), Hegel's Absolute Idea. The Mahāyānistic Nirvāṇa (the so called apratiṣṭhita) is nothing but this Absolute Idea in which the totality of life is merged.

PART I

THE DOUBLE ESSENCE OF ULTIMATE REALITY

CONTENTS OF THE FIRST PART

Chapter I

INTRODUCTION

Chapter II

THE UNIVERSAL CONSTRUCTOR OF PHENOMENAL REALITY

Chapter III

THE THREEFOLD ASPECT OF THE CONSTRUCTOR OF PHENOMENA

Chapter IV

THE DYNAMICS OF THE CREATOR OF THE WORLD-ILLUSION

Chapter V

THE ABSOLUTE

Chapter I

INTRODUCTION

§ 1. Vasubandhu's Salutation Stanza

[V. 1. b. 1.] *I fervently salute (Maitreya),*
That son of the Accomplished Buddha
Who has revealed to us this treatise.
And (Saint Asaṅga) I salute the teacher
Who has explained to us its meaning.
To analyse that meaning now
I will (myself) attempt an effort.

Sthiramati's Comment

[3. 1.] It is a rule[1] among educated men to salute their teacher and (to worship) their tutelary deity before beginning a work. Therefore this (our author Vasubandhu) wishing to intimate that he himself also follows this rule,[2] begins his commentary upon the „Discourse on Discrimination between Middle and Extremes" (viz. the Extremes of Scepticism and of Realism[3]) by an expression of devotion to its divine author[4] and to its (first) expositor[5] and then starts on the work of analysing[6] its meaning. He says:

[3. 5] *I fervently salute*[7] *(Maitreya),*
That son of the Accomplished[8] *(Buddha)*
Who has revealed to us this treatise[9]
And (Saint Asaṅga I salute, the teacher)
Who has explained (to us) its meaning.
To analyse that meaning now
I will (myself) attempt an effort.

[3. 6] What merit it attained by this salutation (of Vasubandhu)? The worship[10] of exalted[11] and benignant[12] persons is a meritorious act. When (one is equipped) with such accretion of moral merit, the right effort[13] will not be frustrated by accidents and obstacles,[14] it will be (crowned) by success without great worry.[15]

[3. 8] It is also possible to assume that, by proposing to give a thoroughgoing explanation[16] of what has been revealed by the divine author and commented upon by his expositor, the salutation stanza pursues in its totality[17] the aim of inspiring a reverential feeling towards both these authors, the author of the Revelation and the author of the Exposition, as well as to their works, the sacred text[18] and its commentary.

[3. 12] A reverential feeling is first of all inspired towards the sacred text, because it shows what has been revealed by its divine author.[19] Saint Maitreya has revealed this work in the form of stanzas. He is (a divine Bodhisattva) separated (from final Nirvāṇa only by his present) last rebirth (in Tuṣita heaven).[20] He is a being who has gone through all the consecutive stages of a Bodhisattva's career and has completely delivered himself in each stage from the respective defects of (a limited will and a limited knowledge).[21] He is thus a being who has attained the highest perfection (of all the miraculous powers of a Bodhisattva), viz. his (six kinds of) supernatural knowledge,[22] his unlimited memory,[23] his (four modes of) analytic insight,[24] his (proficiency in entering various kinds of) trance,[25] his (ten kinds of) supernatural powers,[26] his firm realization (of the Monistic idea),[27] and his (eight successive degrees of) complete liberation (from the illusion of materiality).[28]

[3. 17] Indirectly[29] a reverential feeling is also inspired towards this (second) commentary, because it is assumed that it contains the authentic explanations of the (first) expositor. This (first expositor) is Saint A s a ṅ g a. The revered teacher V a s u b a n d h u[30] has studied this sacred text under his guidance and, after that, has composed a commentary (of his own).

[3. 19] These two (great men) were in the highest degree endowed with an analytical understanding.[31] They were therefore capable of understanding (the sacred text) unmistakably, of retaining its meaning and of communicating it to others. Thus in the conviction that they teach the correct meaning of the sacred text, a reverential feeling is also produced towards this commentary (of Vasubandhu).

[4. 1] And thus it is that those who rely upon the personal authority (of great names)[32] will feel high respect to this sacred text and to its commentary. Those, on the other hand, who rely upon dogma[33] know (*a priori*) that the meaning of the sacred text and of its commentary are good, but when (by analysis) a definite (logical) knowledge will be produced[34] in them, they will realize that it is also due to the learning of the divine author and of his commentator, not alone to the dogma and its (understanding by) dialecticians. Thus a feeling of respect will be produced (in them also) towards both the divine author (of the Revelation) and to his expositor.

[4. 7]. Now, what is the nature[35] of Revelation and why is it designated by (the sanscrit word) *śās-tra*? Revelation proceeds from pure intimations appearing to us in the form of word-, phrase- and articulate-sound-complexes.[36] But (Buddhist) Revelation moreover[37] procedes from intimations appearing as special verbal (declarations)[38] conducive to supramundane (Absolute) Knowledge[39] (and the attainment of Buddhahood).

How can intimations (which are arising automatically out of the subconsciousness of the individual) be revealed and explained to him (by others)? This objection is futile, because the revealer and the explainer from which our intimations are supposed to arise are themselves nothing beyond our ideas of them.[40] (However that does not interfere with the fact that) a man training[41] on the Path towards Buddhahood attains special moral merits, special degrees of mental ecstasy and special direct intuition;[42] he abstains from deeds — corporeal, vocal and mental — which would be unfavourable (for attainment of Nirvāṇa) and attends to such actions which are favourable for it.

[4. 14] Further[43] (why is Revelation called) *šāstra*? It is so called because it conforms[44] with what this word *šāstra* (etymologically) means. It means („that what rules — *šās*, and what saves — *trā*"), what by repeated instruction in religion[45] r u l e s out all vices together with all their germs and s a v e s from a miserable rebirth (in hell), a rebirth which is frightful by long, uninterrupted, manifold and intense suffering.[46] Therefore by ruling out our enemies — the vices, and by saving from rebirth in hell it conforms with the definition of a work of Revelation.[47]

These two features (extinction of vice and salvation from rebirth) are characteristic of all Mahāyāna and all works devoted to its elucidation. They are to be found nowhere else.

Therefore this work is a work of Revelation. Accordingly it has been stated:

[4. 20] *That what controls our foes, the passions,*
What from rebirth and misery delivers
Is (our) Revelation, since it rules and saveth.
All other creeds do not possess it,
This double benefit (of Mahāyāna).[48]

§ 2. Every word of the salutation stanza singly explained

[4. 24] The word „this" (in the phrase „who has composed «this» treatise") is a direct[49] indication. (The author) has in his mind the stanzas of the work on Revelation called **M a d h y ā n t a - v i b h a n g a**, i. e. „Discrimination between Middle and Extremes". (This work) deals systematically[50] with seven topics (to be detailed later on) in order[51] to elucidate the three different Buddhist theories of Salvation[52] and is conducive to a complete extinction of all the moral and intellectual defects of (human nature).[53]

[5. 1] The words „who has revealed" (in the salutation stanza) mean „who has created". Although the root *nī* (from which *praṇita* is derived) means „to lead", this meaning is changed into „to create" by the addition of the preposition *pra.*[54] Indeed it is said:

> *Forcibly changed is the meaning of a root*
> *By the addition of a preposition,*
> *Just as the sweet water of the Ganges*
> *Mixed with (salt) water of the ocean.*[55]

[5. 5] „Having fervently saluted" means having directly worshiped, having saluted or worshiped directly as though (the Bodhisattva were personally present) standing before or near him; having saluted by gesture, speach and in thought.[56]

[5. 6] (Maitreya is called the son of the Accomplished Buddha in the sense of being) produced out of the essence of perfect Buddhahood. The Buddha is called the Accomplished,[57] because starting from[58] the limitations imposed (on all living beings) by desire and ignorance together with their seeds he well went (up to their complete annihilation and) the accomplishment of an Absolute Mahāyānistic Nirvāṇa.[59]

[5. 7] He indeed is the „Accomplished", because he has completely liberated himself from the limitations of a human nature;[60] because he has become identical with (Omniscience, i. e.) with the knowledge of all the Elements of existence, (their knowledge) in every respect;[61] because he has become the possessor of a (miraculous) body whose might is as inconceivably limitless as the might of the allyielding miraculous gem, (a body) through which he exercises all his wonder working powers;[62] because he has the faculty to contrive that all the aims of all the sentient beings (of the Universe) shall be fulfilled at once, automatically, by themselves; because he is identical with that special direct non-discursive highest knowledge[63] (which is Omniscience).[64]

[5. 11] The words „his essence" mean (the Absolute), the Ever-Self-Same[65] the (Transcendent) Pure Reality.[66] Since the direct[67] mystic intuition[68] (of the Absolute) is produced by this (transcendent Reality), therefore (Maitreya, i. e. his Omniscience) is said to be born „from", or born „in" (that Absolute). In this sense he is the son of the Accomplished Buddha.

[5. 12] (The words „produced from the essence of the Accomplished Buddha") also (carry the implication that Maitreya) is essentially identical with the Buddha. We find indeed in a scriptural work a passage which declares „he is born in the lineage of the Buddhas, (he is a Buddha by birth), because he possesses those miraculous powers which constitute the essence of Buddhahood". (Indeed the distance between him and a Buddha is insignificant). He is a Bodhisattva in the tenth (final) stage of his career and all things cognizable in every one of their aspects[69] are clear to him as though they were a myrobolan grain seen on the palm of his hand by a man whose eyes are covered by a thin veil of silk mousseline. With the Buddha this veil is as though withdrawn from his eyes and this is all the difference.

[5. 17] Here the words „born from the essence of the Accomplished Buddha" are an indication of the fact that the divine author of this treatise has attained to the highest pitch (of knowledge), the direct intuition of the Absolute. And since he has composed the treatise regardless of profit and honours (exclusively for the weal of mankind), he at the same time has proved that he equally possesses the highest degree of commiseration (for all living creatures) as well as the highest degree of knowledge.[70]

[5. 20] (The words „the teacher) who has explained" point to the author of the (first) commentary. They must be connected with the words „having fervently saluted" and also, according to other (authorities), with the words „produced from the essence of the Accomplished Buddha" (i. e. this teacher possesses likewise the essence of a Buddha). This author of the (first) commentary is Saint A s a ṅ g a. Having received the blessing of Saint M a i t r e y a and entering with his help (the trance called) „Intuition of the stream of the Elements of Existence"[71] he discovered this treatise and explained it.[72]

[5. 23] The word „and" (in the phrase of the salutation stanza — „and Saint Asanga I salute") either simply establishes the (grammatical) connection (of Asaṅga with Maitreya in this phrase) or (it may have no special meaning at all and is introduced for metrical reasons only), to fill up the verse.[73] It also may refer to an additional (number of saluted persons). Other Buddhas and Bodhisattvas, whosoever they should be,[74] are saluted, not alone that one who has revealed and that one who has explained this treatise.

[5. 25] To whom has he explained it? (It is said in the salutation stanza) „to us etc.". This means „beginning with us to other people also", to them, i. e. to us and to others (has he explained it). Being himself infallible (he possesses the authority) to give instruction (in the right comprehension of the text).[75]

[5. 26] In answer to the question what shall you do after having saluted the author and the expositor, it is said „I will strive", i. e. I will employ my efforts, „to explain its meaning". „To explain its meaning" means to disclose its intention or it also means to analyse its contents in separate (topics). The form of the locative case[76] indicates (here in the sanscrit original) the aim, it means „with the aim of disclosing the intention (of the work will I employ my efforts)".

As to the topics which here constitute the so called „body" of the work, they are seven; they are discussed in this treatise.

§ 3. The aim of the treatise and the topics discussed in it

[6. 5] Whatfore is this treatise revealed? It has been revealed in order to (teach) the production of that direct highest intuition (of Absolute Reality) which is (the exclusive property) of the Buddhas, our Lords.[77] By teaching that all (single) Elements of existence do not contain any absolute reality in themselves,[78] (that singly all are relative), a non-discursive direct intuition (of their absolute totality) is produced. By an intense concentration[79] of the mind upon this (intuition) a complete annihilation of the phenomenal mirage, of all its emotional and all intellectual obscurations with all their germs (lying hidden in subconsciousness)[80] is attained. (and the Gnosis is produced).

[6. 8] Thus this work is undertaken with the aim of establishing the (really) right theory of Absolute Reality, i. e. the theory of the relativity of every Element singly and the collective Reality of their sum-total. This is done by repudiating a double error, viz. 1) the error that the Relativity of every Element singly implies the unreality of all the Elements collectively (Nihilism) and 2) the error that the denial of a substantive Soul as an internal controller (of the personality) implies the denial of an Absolute (in the collective totality of the Elements of the Universe).[81]

[6. 11] However others maintain that the aim of the work is to repudiate ignorance and misconception by promoting the right comprehension on the part of those who are ignorant or are mistaken in regard of the (double) essence of Reality, of its illusive Appearance and all other (topics here discussed).

[6. 12] There also is another aim. The Bodhisattvas may think it very difficult to arrive (at Omniscience), because infinite are the particular objects contained in the five departments of knowledge, viz. the knowledge of the worlds, of the classes of living beings, of the elements of existence, of the rules of behaviour, and of the path towards perfection.[82] They can loose their energy and in order to combat this their mind-depression (Vasubandhu) quotes (the first stanza of the treatise, containing its table of contents, viz.) „Reality, its Essence and Appearance, the Absolute" etc.

§ 4. The seven topi[illegible]

[V. 1. B. 2.] (Vasubandhu introducing the first stanza says) — here, just at the beginning of the body of the work it is stated —

[Stanza 1. 1.] *The essence of Reality and its Appearance;*
The Absolute and its Unveiling
By Trance and Meditation;
Their Degrees and their Results;
Preeminence of Mahāyāna.

[V. I. b. 3] The following seven topics are discussed here, i. e. in this treatise, viz. 1) the (double) Essence of Reality, 2) its illusive Appearance, 3) the Absolute Reality, 4) its Purification (by ecstasy and meditation), 5) Degrees of Purification, 6) its final Result, 7) preeminence of Mahāyāna.

Sthiramati's comment

[6. 16] (Vasubandhu says) — „here, i. e. just at the beginning of the work, its body (i. e. its contents) will be established". „Here" means either in this analysis of the topics, or in this work. „Just at the beginning" means at first. What a Revelational work (*śāstra*) is, has been already explained.[83] „Its body" (is mentioned) either in the sense of a summary, or of its abbreviation, or of its foundation. Just as the carcas (containing the exterior and interior Elements[84] of an individual) is called his body, just so the body of a work consists of the topics which are discussed in it, which are its foundation. They are seven, viz. the Essence (of Reality, its Appearance etc.). Vasubandhu says — „they are established". This is (the predicate which) must be referred (to the seven topics), it means they are discussed.

[6. 23] It can be asked whatfore is this table of contents mentioned at the beginning of the work? Will it not be sufficiently known when the work itself will be gone through? No! the table of contents (stated at the beginning) is not useless! It is mentioned for the benefit of the student. Indeed a student who knows (in advance) what topics will be discussed will more easily follow the detailed exposition (of the subject), just as a horse running swiftly on a well known race ground.[85] Not otherwise![86]

[7. 1.] „These seven topics are discussed in this work" (says Vasubandhu), this means that they represent the complete work.[87] The word „these" refers to the topics indicated by the words Essence of Reality, (Appearance) etc. Seven is their number. This is mentioned in order to point out their inclusive number. „Topics" are the points that are aimed at, that are explained. „In this work" means in the work called „Discrimination between Middle and Extremes". They are „discussed", i. e. taught or definitely settled. „Thus" is a particle indicating that such is the meaning.

[7. 6.] (Vasubandhu) says „Essence" (of Reality). That by what something is essentially characterized is called its essence. Now the essence of Reality is double, impure and pure.[88] Of them the impure (or phenomenal) Reality is ninefold (it appears in nine different aspects), beginning with that (transcendental, but still phenomenal aspect which is the Constructor of phenomena, as stated in stanza 1. 1), „the Universal Constructor of phenomena exists", and ending (with stanza 1. 11 where it is stated) that „sevenfold are the phenomena proceeding from this Universal Constructor of phenomena".[89] The remaining part of the treatise, (of its first part, viz. stanzas 1. 12—1. 21) is devoted to an analysis of Pure Reality (i. e. of the Absolute).

[7. 9] If we understand by „essence" that through what something is essentially characterized, then it should be something different from both the phenomenal and the absolute reality?[90] But that is not so;[91] because the essence of a thing is just the thing itself.[92] E. g. density (or mass)[93] is the essential characteristic of a solid body,[94] but the solid element is not something existing apart from density (or mass).

[7. 13] (The word) „essential characteristic" can also be conceived (not as an instrument „through" which something is being characterized, but) as an object which itself is being characterized.[95] Thus indeed (Reality) impure and pure is essentially characterized (as such), i. e. as having the essence of Reality impure and pure (or Reality phenomenal and absolute).

[7. 15] (The division of Reality into impure and pure carries) still another (implication): in accordance with being either phenomenal or absolute[96] it also is either the Particular or the Universal (in the sense of the extreme concrete and particular, the Thing-in-Itself, and of the extreme abstract and universal, which is the Absolute Totality of all existence).[97]

[7. 16] (The second topic) is the Veil (of illusive Appearance covering Reality). It conceals the Elements propitious (to Salvation), by preventing them to appear. These Elements are concealed through it. In this sense Appearance is a veil. It consists of 53 varieties (of moral and intellectual defects which are obstacles on the Path towards the perception of Ultimate Reality).

[7. 18] (The third topic is) Absolute Reality. (When we think) „this is merely this", (i. e. the bare fact of the reality of something), the condition (of being merely this, „Thisness" or „Suchness") represents the Absolute; it can be nothing else (than merely this, nothing empirically definite). It can be considered from 10 different (viewpoints).

[7. 19] (The fourth topic) is the Antidote (against phenomenal impurity. It is so called because it represents) that part which annihilates the counterpart, (it is the enemy of impurity). It is the Path (of Purity, or Path to Salvation). It consists of Meditation (in rapturous trances). (The Path is Meditation, because its different stages) are created[98] by profound meditation.

[7. 21] (The fifth topic) is the Degree, i. e. the special degree of that very Path which is (gradually) developing in (uninterrupted) continuity. It has nineteen stages, e. g. the stage of „the Lineage", (i. e. that degree of trance when the certainty of belonging to the spiritual family of Buddhas is reached), and other stages.[99]

[7. 22] (The sixth topic is called) Reaching the Result, i. e. attaining the fruit. It has fifteen varieties, viz. the result of moral retribution etc.

[7. 23] (The seventh topic) is the unsurpassable preeminence of Mahāyāna (among all doctrines of Salvation). Y ā n a means a vehicle by which one moves, (by which one is carried). It is a progress and its excellency is unsurpassable in three respects,[100] the excellency of equipment, (of the start and of the result).

[7. 25] It is stated (in the stanza that the topics) are seven. The topics are just so many. This is said for the sake of limiting their number and for the sake of pointing to their consecution. They are specified as being just so many, not more (than seven). Their consecution is established in conformity (with the aim of the system) which is the attainment of (the Gnosis), the transcendent highest Intuition of the Absolute.

§ 5. The consecution of the topics

First explanation

[8. 3] The future Buddha at the beginning of his career (while still in the preliminary stage, the so called) stage of Faith,[101] chiefly attending to his duties of a (higher) morality, should nevertheless begin cleverly to distinguish between impure (or phenomenal) and pure (or absolute) Reality, since every Element of virtue propitious to Salvation is checked by some corresponding phenomenal impurity which must be known. If it is not cleared away, Salvation is impossible, but if it is not known, it cannot be extinguished, because its influence remains unnoticed. He then will realize that the object upon which he must concentrate in order to free his mind from impurity is (the pure or absolute) Reality.[102] With this object[103] he will then apply the method which extinguishes the cover (of phenomenal impurity). He will realize that (transic) meditation is the remedy (against the cover of phenomenal Appearance).

[8. 9] After that comes a process of concentration upon the Elements which counteract (the gloom of phenomenal Appearance), which annihilate the corresponding obscurations, which increase the force of the antidotes against them. (The future Buddha) must know the (respective) stage which he has reached in this process of meditation, e. g. „The stage of Certainty“ regarding his belonging to the Spiritual Lineage of the Buddhas.[104]

[8. 11] After that (the future Buddha) attains the result (of his career). The Elements of Transcendent (Transphenomenal) Reality clearly appear to him. (This first vision of Nirvāṇa is the so called) result of Entering the Stream[105] (attained at the 16th moment of the Path of Enlightment).

[8. 12] All these (six consecutive degrees in the moral and intellectual development of the future Buddha) are the common features of (the Path) of Bodhisattvas, Śrāvakas, (Pratyekas) and their novices,[106] i. e. of Mahāyāna and Hīnayāna and of all the three different Paths towards

Salvation). This agrees with Scripture (where we find the following injunction) — „this recluse is training for progress along the method of the Śrāvakas; he is also training for progress along the method of the Pratyekas; he also is training for progress along the method of the Bodhisattvas". (This proves that all the three methods applied on |the Path towards Salvation have common features). But the matchless preeminence¦ of Mahāyāna, which constitutes the seventh topic, deals with the special properties of a Bodhisattva which nothing can surpass.

Second explanation

[8. 17] But others maintain that the (double) Essence of Reality (the first topic) is mentioned at the beginning in order to produce a more clever (not naive) conception [107] of the (double) essence of Oppression and Deliverance, for. Oppression here means the veil (of phenomenal Appearance) and Deliverance means Absolute Reality. Through the knowledge of Absolute Reality the mirage (of phenomenal Appearance) is dispersed. Therefore (both) Appearance and Reality (are pointed out at the beginning).

[8. 20] After that (the next topic is the Path). In order to teach the expedient serving to annihilate the (mirage of phenomenality) its antidote, the Path (of Purity) with all attaining details, is mentioned.

[8. 21] The Path has beginning, middle and end. In each stage can it be lightly or middleway or intensely practised. This produces different varieties. In order to point to them the next topic are the (comparative) stages (of the Bodhisattva's progress).

[8. 22] Every stage brings a corresponding result. The next topic is therefore the Result (reached at each stage). All these six topics (are concerned with facts) which are the common feature of a Bodhisattva [108] with the Śrāvakas and other (Saints). But the last topic is the preeminence of Mahāyāna. It pursues the aim of indicating the non-common (special) features (of that religion).

Third explanation

[8. 25) Others again maintain that the (double) Essence of Reality has been given the first place because we cognize Reality either in its real (i. e. ultimate) essence or in its unreal (i. e. phenomenal) essence. After having realized this essential (difference), the mirage of Appearance can be rejected and Absolute Reality directly intuited. Therefore the next topics are Appearance (on one side) and Absolute Reality (on the other).

[9. 1] Next comes intense Meditation on the remedy against (the gloom of phenomenal Appearance), since this is the right expedient for both the rejecting (of the unreal) and the immediate realization (of the real).

After that comes the special stage which is but the comparative degree, high or low, which meditation has reached. The Result consists in the annihilation (of the mirage of phenomenal Appearance) through this intense meditation. After that the supreme vehicle of Salvation (Mahāyāna) is reached. The consecution of the seven topics has the aim of illustrating this process.

Fourth explanation

[9. 5] Again others think[109] that, since we are liable to be mistaken in regard of what Elements are real and what are unreal, the Essence (of Reality) must have been indicated (at first) in order to put an end to both an (exaggerated) denial and an (exaggerated) imputation (of Reality). (The doctrine of the origin of the phenomenal) mirage (should be then expounded) in order to promote its clever distinction on the part of those who strive to get rid of that illusion. But ultimate Reality is hidden under the veil (of phenomenal Appearance), therefore in order to promote a scholarly conception of Reality, the next topic is the (ultimate or absolute) Reality. The phenomenal mirage can be dispelled by a penetrating analysis of what is (essentially) real. Therefore after having given (the definition) of Reality, the counteracting (anti-phenomenalistic) profound Meditation (must be explained). The condition (reached in the progress of this Meditation must be next described in order to construct) a scholarly theory[110] of its different stages. Every stage produces its (corresponding) result,[111] therefore next to the theory of the stages their result must be (also) considered in order to produce a scholarly conception of what the Result is. (Finally), since all these topics (are here represented in that their aspect on which the Mahāyāna religion is founded), since they serve as an introduction to Mahāyāna,[112] therefore, as a concluding topic, the preeminence of the Mahāyāna (among all other religions) is discussed.

Chapter II

THE UNIVERSAL CONSTRUCTOR OF PHENOMENAL REALITY

§ 1. General Statement

With reference to the (double) essence of Reality we have the following statement:

[Stanza 1. 1]

The Universal Constructor [1] *of phenomena exists!*
(But he himself) does not contain any division [2]
In two parts, (the apprehended and the apprehending).
The Absolute [3] *however is contained in him,*
And in the Absolute again he is included.

Vasubandhu's comment

[V. 2. a. 1] Among them (i. e. among the seven topics) this stanza deals (with the first, viz.) the Essence (of Reality).

[V. 2. a. 2] Under „the Universal Constructor of phenomena" we here (must understand) our Productive Imagination [4] which constructs (the phenomenal world by splitting concrete reality in two parts) the one grasping the other. This duality is here just the relativity [5] of the grasped (objective) part and the subject grasping it. (He, the Constructor himself) is quite free of this (division).

[V. 6. a. 2] „The Absolute however is contained in him" (says the stanza). The Absolute is (here the Non-Relativity), it is this same (but universal) absence in every Constructor of phenomena of this (his constructed) division into object and subject.

[V. 2. a. 3] (The stanza further says) that „in this (Absolute) he is included". („He" means) the Universal Creator of phenomena. (Thus the Absolute is „devoid" of the relativity of subject and object, but this relativity is included in him as a phenomenal cover). Indeed the correct definition of the Absolute is given in the (following scriptural words): „when something is absent in a receptacle, this receptacle is then rightly regarded as «devoid» of it, such «devoidness» of the receptacle is the empty receptacle, the receptacle itself. It then represents reality as it really is (i. e. absolute reality), (because) what remains as existing (after the deduction of the thing absent) is rightly regarded as being Reality as it really is, (i. e. as the Absolute)".

Sthiramati's comment

[9. 12] With reference to the (double) essence of reality, (phenomenal and absolute), it is stated:

The Universal Constructor of phenomena exists!
(But he himself) does not contain any division
In two parts (the apprehended and the apprehending).
The Absolute however is contained in him,
And in the Absolute again he is included.

[9. 16] (Vasubandhu says) „among them", this means among the just mentioned seven topics, viz. the Essence of Reality, Appearance etc. etc. With reference to (the first of them, viz.) to the Essence of Reality, this stanza has been composed: „The Universal Constructor of phenomena" etc. (The order) of explanation follows (the order) of enunciation. Therefore the (double) essence of Reality being the topic mentioned in the first place, (it is natural) that its explanation is given before (all the others).

§ 2. The first meaning of the stanza. Repudiation of extreme scepticism

[9. 20] There are some (philosophers, viz. the Mādhyamika school, who maintain) that all the Elements of existence[6] are in no way realities. (In the early schools all existence was analyzed into Elements assumed to represent ultimate realities. But according to the Mādhyamikas) they are as unreal as a pair of horns on the head of a hare, (they do not exist at all).[7] Therefore, in order to repudiate this wholesale negation, it is stated — „The Universal Constructor of phenomena exists!" This proposition must be supplemented by the words „in itself". (It exists in itself, i. e. absolutely), it is the Thing-in-Itself.[8]

[9. 22] However is this not contradicted by Scripture? (Mahāyānist) Scripture indeed declares „all the Elements are devoid (of this absolute reality in itself)".

No! there is no contradiction, because it is (further) stated that „he contains no duality", (i. e. this constructor contains no division in two parts, the one grasping the other).

[9. 24) The Constructor of phenomena is devoid of the distinction into an apprehended object and an apprehending subject, in this sense (only) is he „devoid", but not in the sense of being deprived of all reality in itself. Therefore there is no contradiction with (Mahāyāna)-scripture. (The Constructor is devoid of empirical but not of transcendental reality).

[9. 26] But if that be so, then „duality", (i. e. every subject-object couple) will it not be totally non-existent, just as the hare's horns (which do not exist at all)? The Constructor of phenomena will then (alone) represent absolute existence (existence in itself). This would imply a denial (of the other, the ultimate) Absolute.

[10. 1] That is not so! because this (other) Absolute is contained in him. (What indeed is this other Absolute?) Just this universal non-existence of the division into object and subject in (every) Constructor of phenomenal appearance is the Absolute. Therefore it cannot be (deduced that the ultimate) Absolute does not exist.[9]

[10. 3] (Now) if this Absolute contains no duality (and if it is inherent in every Constructor of a phenomenon), why is it that we are not omniscient.[10] If it is present (before us) why is it not perceived? In order to solve this doubt it is stated (in the stanza) „and in this Absolute he is included".

[10. 6] (Because this Absolute is not pure), because the Constructor of phenomenal (illusion) is also found in it, therefore you are not saved (and omniscient). Just for this reason, just because the pure Absolute is covered by (phenomenal) impurity, it is impossible to perceive it, just as it is impossible to perceive the (genuine) purity of the water-element, when it is soiled by filth.

§ 3. The second meaning of the stanza. Repudiation of extreme realism

[10. 9] (The stanza) also aims at repudiating (the other extreme), the opinion of those who maintain that not only the Mind and mental phenomena exist as realities (or things by themselves), but that the (external) material objects likewise exist (as things by themselves).[11] (To their address) it is said that the Constructor (or the foundation) of phenomena (alone) exists.[12] He alone exists as a Thing in itself. There is no Matter outside him, i. e. Matter does not exist as a reality (or as a thing in itself, it exists merely as an idea).

[10. 12] Why is it that there is nothing (besides ideas)? (The answer is) „he contains no duality". (This means) that neither does this (Element which is) the Constructor of phenomena apprehend something, nor is he apprehended by some one. He represents (Monism, i. e.) pure (transcendent) Reality, the merger[13] of subject and object.

[10. 14] Indeed no sensible objects are at all perceived outside consciousness. (This is proved) by dreams and (hallucinations). Consciousness itself appears (in dreams) in the garb of external, sensible objects. Supposing „a" is the cause of „b", it is then impossible that „b" should appear in the absence of „a".[14] (If our ideas were produced by external objects, they could not arise in dreams). We therefore must know that consciousness containing ideas of objects arises without any external objects at all; just as it arises in dreams and (hallucinations) it also arises (in waking) and other conditions, it arises exclusively from a (subconscious) germ (which lays dormant in the Storehouse of subliminal consciousness and arises in due time to produce an idea) when it becomes ripe for that.

[10. 18] If there are no apprehended external objects, there (evidently) is no one who apprehends them. It is (absolutely) impossible that there should be an apprehending part where there is no (corresponding) apprehended part.[15] Therefore there are beyond the illusive constructions of our imagination[16] no (external) material objects[17] (and no consciousness apprehending them).

[10. 20] However, if there is absolutely nothing to be apprehended, Salvation (and omniscience) become impossible, because (this would mean that) there neither is any Pure Objectivity (transcending the limits of the phenomenal world).[18] That is not so, because (says the stanza) „The Absolute however is contained in him". The word „however" here replaces the word „because". This Absolute indeed constitutes the Pure (Transcendent) Object.[19] It constitutes that (Absolute) Universal Reality in which (empirical) subject and object disappear.[20] It is contained (hidden) in the Constructor of (the illusive) phenomena (of phenomenal worlds). Therefore Salvation (and Omniscience) are not impossible.

[10. 24] But if it really is contained in the Constructor of the phenomenal world, we should perceive it, since it is present (before us). Why then do we not perceive it? (We do not perceive it), because it is concealed by the Constructor of phenomena, not because it does not exist, just as the ether is not perceived because it is transparent, not because it does not exist.

§ 4. The third meaning of the stanza. The middle way between the two extremes of scepticism and realism

[11. 3] (The stanza) can also (be interpreted so that its first phrase is directed against radical scepticism and its second phrase against realism). Indeed (the phrase) „the Universal Constructor of phenomena exists!" has the aim of repudiating the total negation of every (ultimate reality by extreme scepticism). It is not true that all (the Elements) are neither unreal, nor are they real" (as maintained by the Mādhyamikas). (All Elements) are real, (but real only) inasmuch as they represent modifications (of the Element of pure) consciousness.

[11. 6] (The second phrase of the stanza) „he contains no duality" aims at repudiating a wrong imputation of reality.[21] It is directed (against dualism), against those who maintain that the external world exists just as it appears, namely as something real in itself, (both subject and object being ultimately real), independently from (that consciousness) which is the Constructor of phenomena.[22] The aim (of the text is to emphasize) that the Constructor of phenomena alone exists, (but not the illusive phenomena which are constructed by him).

[11. 9] However there are also some philosophers who think that the absence of both (a subject and an object) means an absolute blank,[23] such as the son of a barren women. On the other hand, there are others who think that the negation of all substance[24] (and its replacement by mere qualities — *dharmas*) refers only to the negation of a substantial Soul[25] regulating life from within (without affecting the full reality of all other Elements). Therefore, in order, on the one hand, to repudiate the negation of the Universal Absolute, and in order, on the other hand, to deny the reality of a substance in every single thing[26] it is stated that „the Absolute however is contained in him".

[11. 12] If the Absolute is contained in this Universal Constructor of phenomenal (i. e. in every real thing), then all living beings will perceive it and will easily attain (omniscience and) Salvation. However this does not happen, because (the stanza says) „And in the Absolute again he is included". (It exists under the cover of phenomena). As long as the Absolute is not disclosed Salvation is not possible. It is concealed[27] and a great effort is needed for purifying it.[28] Therefore there is no easy Deliverance.

§ 5. The fourth interpretation of the stanza. The contrast between Phenomenal and Absolute Reality

[11. 17] There is a further (interpretation, but as a matter of fact) it is not different from what has been stated above[29] regarding the essence of Reality. (Reality is double), impure and pure (or phenomenal and absolute). According to this interpretation the stanza „The Universal Constructor of phenomenal (illusion) exists, etc. etc." pursues the aim of calling attention[30] (to this aspect of the problem, viz.) the corruption (of pure Reality through the phenomenalizing forces) and its purification (on the Path towards Nirvāṇa). Phenomenal Reality (or the 12 stages of ever revolving life) is identical with the Constructor of illusion, because the essence of this construction is nothing but the (phenomenal) illusion[31] (of a mentally constructed *quasi* real world).

[11. 20] But how is this to be understood? How can the essence of the Constructor of phenomenal reality represent an illusion? (Was it not stated above that „he exists absolutely", being a reality-in-itself). He represents nevertheless an illusion, inasmuch as he does not really contain that duality (of subject and object as which he appears in phenomenal life). This subjective-objective form is Appearance, it does not exist (ultimately) in itself. (In itself ultimate reality is monistic). It is therefore evident that (from this point of view) the essence of the Constructor of phenomena is nothing but a (transcendental) Illusion.[32]

[11. 22] Now (the next words of the stanza, viz.) „The Absolute however is contained here (i. e. in him)" (according to this interpretation) refer to a consideration (of absolute reality) as a purifying (force counteracting the defiling forces of transcendental illusion).

[11. 23] The essence of purification consists in (the realization) of the Absolute, since (pure or absolute Reality) means non-duality (or Monism). We must moreover consider that (it is not Nirvāṇa alone which is here taken as the Absolute, but) Nirvāṇa as well as the Path towards it, because both Nirvāṇa and the Path (or, in other words, the Buddha and the Saint) are brought in full relief by (the idea of) the Absolute. The pure Reality (of the Absolute or of Nirvāṇa) must be converted into the Path towards Nirvāṇa (by the Saint) taking his stand in phenomenal reality. (Nirvāṇa) is not something existentially separate (from phenomenal reality). In order to point out (this relation between absolute and phenomenal reality), the stanza says „here" (i. e. in „him"), in the phenomenal reality, (sc. the Absolute is immanent in the Phenomenal).[33]

[12. 2] Now, if this division (of reality into object and subject) does not really exist, why is it that simple people are mistaken and think that (both the object and the subject) really exist? In answer to this question (the stanza states) — „and in the Absolute again he is included"; „he", i. e. the Constructor of the division [34] (of reality) into an objective, grasped part and into a subjective, grasping part, (he is contained merged in the monistic Absolute). It is just as the images of elephants and other (animals) which appear in a magically evoked phantom in which no real elephants [35] are contained. (The subject-object image of the world is a phantom concealing the absolute monistic world-reality).

[12. 5] The term „Creator of phenomena" means that one in whom this division does not exist or that one by whom it is constructed.

[12. 6] The word „phenomena" (or unreality, not-genuine reality) suggests that the form in which reality here appears to us, the form divided into an object grasped and a subject grasping it, does not (ultimately so exist).

[12. 7] The word „Constructor" suggests that the objects do not exist in that form into which they are converted (by creative imagination). We have thus emphatically stated that the essence of reality is something quite free from the division into two parts, the one grasping the other.

§ 6. The two Absolutes: the extreme concrete and particular and the extreme abstract and universal

[12. 10] This Creator of the phenomenal world who is he finally? (He is our consciousness!). The Mind and Mental phenomena in all the three spheres of existence (the sphere of men and gods of gross sensual desire, the sphere of ethereal beings with purified desires and the sphere of gods with no sensuous desires); the past, the present and the future, so far as they, being interconnected as causes and effects, agree as constituting phenomenal life, beginningless in time and lasting until the moment of Nirvāṇa — are each of them, without any difference, creators of phenomenal illusion. (They are the causally interrelated but mental Elements of the phenomenal world — s a m s k ṛ t a - d h a r m a). A difference between them (is introduced with) the separation [36] into an apprehended and an apprehender parts. The apprehended, objective part is constituted by the ideas representing (the external world), inanimate things and living bodies. The apprehending, subjective part is constituted by ideas representing the Ego and its sensations. Their duality consists of the apprehended and the apprehending parts, the apprehended is e. g. a coloured (surface), the apprehending part. is the (corresponding) visual sensation.

[12. 15] The fact of the unreality of the relation between a grasped and a grasping part, the universal fact of its unreality [37] (or relativity), this fact represents (the part) of the Absolute which is inherent in the Creator of the world-illu-sion.[38] But that does not mean that the Creator of this unreal relation, (of this relativity), is himself unreal.[39] (He is himself quite real, but he creates illusion). Just as when we mistake a rope for a serpent the rope is devoid of the reality of a serpent, devoid of it at any time, but it is not devoid of the essence of the rope; just so in the case under consideration (the moment which creates phenomenal appearance is itself devoid of this appearance, but it is not devoid of the nature of being its creator).

[12. 18] (The stanza says) „And in the Absolute again he is included", i. e. the Constructor of appearance is included. Thus (by these words) it is suggested that the (easy) cognition of the Absolute (i. e. easy Omniscience) is impossible, since it (i. e. the Absolute) lays (hidden and) oppressed [40] by accidental obscurations.

[12. 20] Accordingly it is said (in Scripture): [41] „he (the Bodhisattva) rightly perceives that if something is absent (from a receptacle, this receptacle) is then considered as „devoid" of that thing". And here, (in the case under consideration), what is absent? and in what (receptacle) is it absent? The division (of concrete reality) into two parts (is absent and it is absent) in the Creator of phenomenal illusion. Therefore (the Bodhisattva) intuits that (the Element which is) the Creator of the phenomenal world is „devoid" of the division into two parts. But that residue which remains after all duality has been rescinded is (ultimately) real. And what is it that here remains? (Two items remain, viz. the Element) which is the Creator of phenomenal reality and the Absolute,[42] (i. e. the extreme Particular and the extreme Universal). Both these items are (ultimately) real (the ultimate Particular and the ultimate Universal). This (the Bodhisattva) intuits (directly), without any wrong imputation of reality and without denying it where it exists. This he intuits according to reality as it really is.[43]

[12. 25] Indeed by intuiting that (the Element which is) the Creator of the world-illusion contains in himself no duality (of one part grasping the other), the imputation of a wrong reality is obviated. And by intuiting that (the particular moment) creating illusion, as well as the Absolute (or the totality of these moments both) really exist, an extreme scepticism is set aside.

[13. 1] We thus have elicited the correct definition (of that principle which conventionally is known by the name of) „Voidness", because (we have established) that the thing w h i c h i s d e v o i d of something, exists, but the thing o f w h i c h i t i s d e v o i d does not exist.

[13. 2] (This our definition of the principle of „Voidness" is the only right one. According to it one part of the Elements of existence are not ultimate realities, but the other, the part which „remains" after the deduction of the first, is absolutely real. Both the definitions of the Mādhyamikas and Sarvāstivādins, on the other hand, are) wrong definitions. (The first maintain that) not a single Element is real, (the second) that „every thing (i. e. every Element) really exists". The consequence of both these definitions would be to make impossible the principle of „Voidness" itself.[44] (Indeed if we with the Mādhyamikas declare that not a single Element is real, that) there is no such particular thing which we could characterize as the real thing which is „devoid" (of the object-subject relation,) then there can also be no general principle of „Voidness" (in that sense), because indeed a general principle is dependent on the reality of particular things, as e. g. the principle of „instantaneous being" (is dependent on the reality of particular instantaneous single things).[45]

[13. 5] (On the other hand if we with the Sarvāstivādins maintain that „every thing exists," i. e. that whatsoever is an Element is *eo ipso* real), then both (object and subject) will be ultimately real and there evidently will be no „Voidness" (in the sense of the ultimate unreality of this relation).

[13. 6] (The S a r v ā s t i v ā d i n objects). If the relation of object to subject is something absolutely unreal, unreal as the horns on the head of a hare, what does it then mean that the Constructor of phenomena is „devoid" of this division? (Does it mean that he is „devoid" of nothing?).

Experience shows that only a real thing can be deprived of another real thing, as e. g. a cloister can be deprived of monks (not otherwise!).[46]

[13. 8] (The Yogācara answers). That is not so! (It is just as in the case of illusions and hallucinations). Supposing a rope (lying on the road in the dark) is mistaken for a serpent, or (supposing we have) a magically evoked vision (of a man); supposing then somebody, in order to clear off the misrepresentation,[47] declares „there is here no serpent" or „there is here no (real) man"; just so, in order to induce naïve men to quit their (realistic) habits of thought (and in order to bring home to them the notion of the Absolute), it is declared to them „the Constructor of this phenomenal world is rid of the double form of subject and object, this form is Appearance, it does not exist in itself (it is not an ultimate reality at all)".[48]

§ 7. The Middle Path

[Stanza 1. 2]

Neither is it asserted
That all (the Elements) are unreal,
Nor are they all realities;
Because there is existence,
And also non-existence,
And (again) existence:
This is the Middle Path![49]

Vasubandhu's Comment

[V. 2. b. 1—5] „Neither unreal are (all the Elements of existence), because there are (two items that are real, viz. the eternal, all-embracing) Absolute and the (instantaneous) Constructor of phenomena. Nor are they not-unreal (i. e. not all are real). Inasmuch as there is separation into two parts (the one grasping the other) there is no (genuine) reality.

„All (the Elements)" means (the two main groups into which the 75 Elements of existence established in the Hinayāṇa are divided, viz.) the „caused" ones which are (also) the constructors of phenomena and the „uncaused" ones which is the Absolute.[50] „It is asserted" means it is established. „Because there is existence" — this refers to the real existence of the Constructor of phenomena; „and (also) non-existence", this refers to the division (into an object and a subject); „and (again) existence", this refers to the presence of the Absolute in the Constructor and of the Constructor in the Absolute. „This is the Middle Path", these words intimate that neither are all Elements exclusively unreal nor are they exclusively real.[51] Such an interpretation of the Middle Path agrees with (many) passages from the „Discource on Transcendent Intuition" and other (scriptural) works where it is stated that „all this is neither unreal, nor is it real". (This means that there are some Elements that are real and others that are unreal).

Sthiramati's comment

[13. [15] With what aim has this stanza been composed? Its aim is to declare that all (the Elements of reality), the caused (or instantaneous) ones and the uncaused (or eternal) ones are (in their ultimate essence) not affected by the division into one part grasping the other. This indeed also appears as the real meaning of the passages from the „Discourse on Transcendent Intuition" which declare that „all this is neither unreal nor is it real". It repudiates the radical (theories of extreme scepticism which declares that not a single Element is real, and of extreme realism which maintains that whatsoever is an Element is *eo ipso* real). Otherwise the first half of this text („not unreal") would stand in contradiction to the other half („not real").

[13. 19] (The stanza) moreover has the aim of establishing (the doctrine of) the Middle Path — otherwise either the unreality or the reality (of all Elements) would be onesidedly asserted — and also of making a conclusive statement regarding the repudiation of an exaggerated denial of reality, as well as of an exaggerated assertion of it. (Asserted is as real first of all) the causally interdependent Element,[52] which is the Constructor (or the basis) of phenomena, because it obtains its own realization in strict dependence on causes and conditions. (Asserted is as real) also the Absolute, the uncaused Element, since it does not depend on (causes and possesses an independent, absolute reality of its own). „This is asserted" sc. in the „Discourse on Transcendent Intuition" and similar works.

[13. 23] (The words of the stanza) „because there is existence" refer to (that Element of existence which is) the Constructor of phenomena, (they mean that all Elements cannot be unreal, because admitted must be the reality of the Constructor of the phenomenal worlds). That essence of every causally interrelated Element of existence which is the Constructor of the (corresponding) phenomenon, (it alone) is not unreal, (it is absolutely real as a Thing-in-Itself). But that other essence of this Element which converts it into either an apprehended object or an apprehending subject is (a construction of our productive imagination), it is not ultimately real. (This is expressed in the further words of Vasubandhu) „because there is non-existence", non-existence namely of this duality.[53]

[14. 1] (The repetition in the stanza of the words) „and again because of existence"[54] refers to the presense of the Absolute in the Constructor as being its universal property[55] and (*vice versa*) of the Constructor in the Absolute as being the possessor[56] of that property. Thus it is that the „uncaused" (i. e. the eternal Element or the Absolute) is not unreal, (not relative), inasmuch as it represents the „Elementness" (o. absolute totality of all the genuinely real Elements of existence).[57]

[14. 3] When (the Scripture) maintains that it is not real (in saying that it is „neither not devoid nor devoid"), this should be interpreted so that in itself it is essentially devoid, (but devoid only) of the division in two parts, (the one grasping the other).

[14. 4] (It is said in the stanza) — „And this is the Middle Path". Indeed in the Ratnakūṭa[58] and other (scriptural works) we find the following deliverance: „O, Kāšyapa! It exists" is one extreme, „it does not exist" is another extreme. The intermediate attitude between these two extremes, O, Kāšyapa! is called the Middle Path. It represents the (deepest) intuition of that reality (which is hidden at the bottom) of every Element of Existence. This is the Middle Path. In this manner the Middle Path is made to agree (with our System).[59]

[14. 7] The word „all" (used in the sacred texts in such phrases as „all is real" — *sarvam asti*, and „all is unreal" — *sarvam šūnyam*) refers to (both categories of the Elements of existence as established in the early schools, viz.) the causally dependent (or instantaneous ones — *saṃskṛta*) and the causally independent (or eternal ones — *asaṃskṛta*). The Elements are not all exclusively (relative and) unreal, because there are among them two Elements that are (absolutely) real; they are the (instantaneous) Constructor lying at the bottom of every phenomenon and the (eternal Element) of the (allembracing) Absolute.[60]

[14. 9] „Nor is it exclusively real",[61] since (their appearance, viz. their division) into two parts (the one grasping the other) does not (in ultimate reality) exist at all.

[14. 10] Whether we assume that all the Elements (into which reality has been analyzed in Buddhism) are real or that all are unreal, in both these cases, we shall have extremes, but not the Middle Path.

§ 8. The categories of ideas in which the Creator of the phenomenal worlds manifests himself

Vasubandhu's Comment

[V. 2. b. 5.] After having thus characterized (our Productive Imagination), as the Creator of phenomenal reality from the positive side (as existent) and from the negative side (as the absence of a real division into Mind and Matter), its particular essence (i. e. the different categories of ideas in which he manifests himself) will be now[62] indicated:

[Stanza 1. 3] *The Mind itself appears to us*
As a projection of things (inanimate),
As well as living bodies,
(As the ideas) of a Self and his sensations.
Their objects do not exist however,
And without them unreal are also
These (ideas).

[V. 2. b. 6] (There are four categories of ideas, ideas of inanimate things, of living bodies, of a Self and of his different sensations). Among them the ideas of things (inanimate reduce) to sense-data, such as coloured (surfaces and different shapes) etc.: they are projections appearing to us as real (external) objects. The ideas of animate things (or living bodies reduce) to the five organs of sense which appear as projections connected with one's own or with another man's continuity of life (in some bodily frame). The idea of the Self is the Mind (itself, but not the pure Mind of the Absolute), it is the phenomenal Mind intimately connected with egotism. The ideas of sensation are the six kinds of sense-perception (including the perceptions, or apperceptions, of the internal sense).

[V. 3. a. 1] The stanza says „their objects do not exist", because the things inanimate and the living bodies are projections of nothing, they do not exist at all;[63] and the ideas of a (phenomenal) Ego and of sense-perception are (perceptive ideas, but) wrong ideas, (inasmuch as the external objects corresponding to them do not exist). And since these (external) objects do not exist the perceptions apprehending them do not (really) exist likewise.

Sthiramati's Comment

[14. 12] (Vasubandhu says) „after having thus characterized the Creator of phenomenal reality from the positive and from the negative sides" — (these words have the following meaning). A „positive characteristic" means here a characteristic through reality, to wit „The Constructor of phenomena exists". The (ultimate) reality of the Creator of the world-illusion is thus indicated, such is the meaning.

[14. 15] In the same way is he characterized by non-existence. The non-existence of something is a negative characteristic. (This non-existence here refers) to the non-existence in the (double) form of an apprehended object and of the subject apprehending it. Because this double form does not really exist in the Creator of phenomenal reality, therefore this Creator himself also does not exist, (i. e. he does not exist) so far this his double form is concerned. This is asserted.

[14. 18] (Vasubandhu says) „now the particular essence will be indicated". What indeed is (here) the difference between „real essence" and „particular essence"? (Is not the particular essence of a thing its real essence?)[64] The real essence is here the general, the particular essence is the special. If the particular cases (in which the Constructor manifests himself) will not be indicated, what will happen? The „body" (or the compass) of the Constructor of phenomenal reality will not be indicated. Therefore, in order to indicate that compass, the following stanza has been composed:

The Mind (itself) appears to us
As a projection of things (inanimate)
As well as living bodies,
As the ideas of an Ego

And of his sensations.
Their objects do not exist, however,
And without them
Unreal are also these ideas.

The first meaning of this stanza

[14. 24] (This stanza has) also[65] (the following meaning). It has been here established that the Mind, undifferentiated into subject and object, is the unique (Reality), it is the Constructor of the phenomenal worlds. (However formerly the Elements of Reality have been distributed in 18 different groups, viz. six sense-organs including the internal sense, six kinds of corresponding sense-objects, including the internal objects of the internal sense, and six kinds of sensations including the internal apperceptions or reflections of the Mind upon himself).[66] It remains unknown how are these groups to be rightly redistributed (in order to tally with the new conception).

[15. 1] In order to declare that (the items of the old division) can be systematized under the head of the Mind-Constructor as special categories of ideas in which he manifests himself, the particular items of the Constrution of the phenomenal world are indicated. (The Category of the ideas of things corresponds to the six categories of sense-objects; the category of the ideas of living beings corresponds to the six categories of sense-organs; the category of the ideas of sensations corresponds to the six kinds of sensations in the old division, and the category of the ideas of Ego is an additional item absent in the old classification).

A second interpretation of the stanza

[15. 3] There also is (another interpretation of this stanza). (The initial stanza, in the words) „The Universal Constructor of phenomena exists" merely asserts his existence, but says nothing about his essence. Nor is the reason indicated why notwithstanding the unreality of the division into object and subject, there is an inveterate belief in its reality. Neither has the reason been indicated why (instead of believing in the reality of the external world) we should believe in the unreality of the division of existence into an objective part and a subject grasping it.[67] Therefore in order to indicate all this, the stanza says:

The Mind itself appeurs to us
As a projection of things and living bodies
And as ideas of an Ego and Sensations.

[15. 8] The essence of the Creator of the world illusion is the Mind (himself, his creative imagination). The Mind is here understood together with the mental phenomena inherent in him, but predominantly[68] the Mind himself (the pure Mind) is here referred to.[69]

[15. 9] The cause of our inveterate belief in the real existence of a subject and his objects (consists in the character) of our ideas of inanimate and living things (which always appear as projections into the external world).

[15. 11] The reason why we should believe in the unreality of the division into object and subject is stated (in the words of the stanza):

Their objects do not exist however
And without them unreal are also these ideas.[70]

§ 9. Another division of ideas in three, resp. eight, classes. Mind-store ideas, Ego-ideas, six kinds of sensational ideas[71]

[15.12) Among these four classes, the two first classes, viz. ideas of things inanimate and of animate bodies constitute the Mind-store together with its satellites of mental phenomena.[72] It consists (exclusively) of the process of maturation in the Subconsciousness (of the influence of former good or bad deeds) and has therefore no outspoken moral character of ist own.[73]

[15. 13] (The second class is constituted by) the idea of a Self (or Ego), it represents the phenomenal Mind with the inherent satellites (of egotistic feelings). Since it always possesses the vices (of Egotism), it is morally not quite indifferent, it is an element (always) slightly vicious.[74]

[15. 14] (The third class is constituted) by sensation ideas. They are the six classes of sense-perceptions (inclusive of the apperceptions by the inner sense), perceptions visual and others with their satellites[75] (of feelings and volitions). (From the moral point of view) they are either good (i. e. propitious to Nirvāṇa) or bad (unfavourable for Nirvāṇa) or indifferent, (accordingly as they are associated with a good, bad or indifferent volition).

[15. 16] Thus we have (in our system together) eight categories of ideas, viz. 1) ideas of things inanimate and animate, (or of the external world), 2) ideas of a Self (or Ego) and 3—8) six kinds of perceptive ideas (inclusively of the apperceptions of the inner sense). They are accompanied by their satellites (of feelings, ideas and volitions). They all arise out of the subliminal Mind Store (the Psyche) under the influence of cooperating forces (which bring their germs to maturity). They manifest themselves in the five modes of phenomenal existence (as infernal beings, as ghosts, brutes, men and gods) in accordance with the possibilities (of each individual being). (The subconscious Mind-Store-theory thus represents) the second (of the four) great principles (intuited by the Saint directly at the moment when he attains omniscience, viz. the so called) Truth of the Origin of Phenomenal Life.[76]

[15. 18] (The difference in the fate of all the classes of living beings is conditioned) by a difference[77] which is produced in the subliminal Mind-

Store in accordance with the influence of former moral, immoral or neutral deeds, owing to which ideas arise of mutually discrepant character, (these ideas constitute the whole of all the manifold, phenomenal individual existences in all the spheres of life).[78]

[15. 21] How is it that our ideas take the form of external objects if there are none in existence? (We sometimes mistake at a distance a post for a man), but if there were altogether no men in existence, never would a post appear to us in the form of a man. This objection is futile! (Whether known or unknown the object always appears as something external to consciousness). Indeed when an idea of a thing arises there is in the mind of simple people[79] an inveterate habit of thought to believe in the real existence of the object outside our consciousness; e. g. people suffering from eye-disease have a constant vision of flying locks of hair, (they naturally perceive them as external to their consciousness). In order that they should quit this their belief (in the reality of things existing outside their consciousness), it is said to them „it is a mere idea, it only has the form of an external thing or of a living body,[80] just as with ophthalmic people the vision of flying hair (has the appearance of an external thing) without the reality".

15. 26] Thus it is that the interdependent Elements[81] of the phenomenal world are (nothing but ideas), mental realities of eight different kinds.[82] It is here asserted that they represent the Constructors of phenomenal reality (i. e. they represent our Mind or its creative imagination).

Vasubandhu's Comment analyzed by Sthiramati

[16. 1] (Vasubandhu says that „the ideas of things inanimate reduce to sense-data), such as coloured (surfaces and shapes appearing as external) things", i. e. they (the inanimate things) in their essence represent coloured (surfaces), sounds, smells, tastes, contacts[83] and objects of the inner sense.[84] They are „projections" because they are produced as images having such forms.

[16. 2] „Ideas of animate things are ideas of one's own or another one's continuity of life superimposed on the five sense-organs" says (Vasubandhu), (i. e. superimposed) on the five sense-organs which are the indication of animal life, because they represent the places to which (the beings) are extraordinarily attached.[85] Sticking to them or attached to them is the living organism. On the basis of the production of such images (of organized bodies) we have ideas which are their projection (into the external world).[86]

feelings are directed towards the Self, it is quite all right (to consider) the phenomenal mind as the idea of the Self.

[16. 9) The six sense-perceptions (five according to the number of outer senses and one apperception by the inner sense) are ideas (founded) on sensations (says Vasubandhu). They are sensation-ideas because they appear in the form of apprehender-ideas. On the basis of their production in this active form of an apprehending (consciousness) they are (called) sensation (or intimation) ideas.

[16. 11] „Their objects do not exist however" (says the stanza), i. e. there are no external objects corresponding to these four classes of ideas.

[16. 12] (Vasubandhu says) „because there are no (separately)-formed ideas of things inanimate and living bodies (beyond the ideas which appear as apprehending them); and because (the ideas apprehending them as external objects, viz.) the ideas of the Ego and his sensations, are wrong perceptions, (since they represent to us as existing in the external world things that do not exist there at all)",[88] (therefore there are no external objects at all).

[16. 13] This means that the ideas (of external things), of inanimate things and living bodies, since they represent the objective (passive) part (of cognition), cannot be said to represent wrong perceptions. (They are no perceptions at all). Just their deficiency in having a separate form of their own,[89] (their coalescence with the ideas apprehending them), proves that there are no external objects (separate from the ideas grasping them).

[16. 15] But other philosophers maintain that the external object is not altogether formless, since it has that form which the perceiver imposes on it. However the unreality of the external world is sufficiently established by the illusive character of these ideas.[90]

[16. 16] (But what indeed is the form of an object?) It is either the manner[91] in which it is conceived, e. g. as being something instantaneous. This (perceptive character) the external object does not possess, since it represents an apprehended, (but not an apprehending) part. This means that if something is not an apprehender, (i. e. is not a perceptive idea), it can have no form (and therefore does not exist at all). Or the „form" of an object, may mean (its projection, i. e.) the distinct feeling of the presence of the object in the ken.[92] This the two categories of external things, inanimate and animate, do not possess, (because they appear as the objective part lying outside consciousness). Hence the formlessness (which we are obliged to ascribe to the external object) establishes its non-existence.[93]

[16. 19] (Now, we have established that inanimate things reduce to sense-data and the animate ones to the presence of sense-organs). If both these categories are formless, how is it that they are different, (their difference is it not a difference of form?) Indeed on the one side we have colours and other sensible qualities, on the other the organ of vision and other sense-organs. Under these conditions it must be asked what is the advantage of idealism (over the old realistic conceptions) equally admitted in life and in science. These establish the separate existence of sensible qualities, on the one hand, and of sense-organs on the other. Why should we reject them and replace them by (the reality of the Mind alone), the Mind which is supposed to be not different from them in his essence, (under the pretext that) there are altogether no objects outside the Mind?

[16. 23] This must be explained on the following (analogy). Although our consciousness does not contain in itself a real plurality of different objects, it has the capacity of producing a manifold of ideas. Each is produced from its own germ (which lays dormant in subconsciousness) and is strictly peculiar to the respective continuity (of conscious moments constituting a given personality).[94]

[16. 25] Thus e. g. the pretas (ghosts) imagine that they perceive rivers filled with putrid stuffs, excrements and urine garded on both sides by men armed with sticks. However other men perceive these same rivers as filled by transparent fresh water which has nothing repulsive, (the difference is not produced by external reality which is the same, but from the germ of ideas strictly peculiar to every being).

[17. 2] The yogins again, when plunged in transic meditation, being engaged in the concentrated contemplation of the horrible, perceive whole areas[95] completely covered, without a free place, by skeletons. The same happens in the so called kṛtsnāyatana exercises when the yogin concentrating his attention on a piece of earth perceives the whole of the horizon filled up by it.

[17. 4] Now, it is quite impossible that, if the appearance of ideas were strictly conditioned by the presence of corresponding external objects, they could arise independently from the latter; nor is it possible that these ideas should represent something quite different from the external objects which are supposed to have produced them.

[17. 6] Therefore it cannot be doubted that all perceptions, which represent external inanimate and animate things are produced without any presence in the ken of such objects. And therefore (the two other categories of ideas), those which represent the Self and those which represent its sensations, are wrong ideas, since they represent an apprehending part where there is altogether no corresponding apprehended part.

Another interpretation of stanza 1.3

[17. 9] Or (the meaning can also be the following one). (The words „their object does not exist" mean) — the object does not exist in that form which is constructed by the Mind, (by its creative imagination). (The object is wrong and) a wrong idea is produced by a wrong object, as

e. g. (the wrong idea) of a tiger is produced (when a noise is mistaken) for his roar.[96] (The object accordingly will not be altogether non-existent, but it will be immanent to consciousness).

[17. 11] However it is our principle that (an idea cannot be divided in two parts, the one grasping the other, because if we reduce cognition to a moment of simple awareness, this) awareness (is pure), it is devoid of another part (i. e. an objective immanent part) constructed by a second act of awarenes.[97]

Therefore just as there are no external inanimate and animate things corresponding to their ideas, there also is no objective Ego and no objective part immanent in the ideas of perception.[98]

[17. 13] And since there are no objects (says the stanza) „their ideas are likewise unreal". An idea is something that apprehends.[99] If there is no apprehended part there can be no (corresponding) apprehender part.[100] Therefore, since there are altogether no objects, the ideas in their rôle of apprehenders[101] of reality do not exist (they are not ultimate realities), but they are not unreal in so far as they are mere imagination of things, of living bodies, of Ego's and of perceptions (they have the reality of mental facts).

[17. 16] If we would deny also the reality (of these mental facts) we would run into the (Mādhyamika) theory of universal negativity, because with the only exception of the reality (of ideas quà ideas), we do not assume any other reality (in them).

[17. 17] On the other hand if we assume (in the idea itself an objective part) which is different from it, how is its apprehension to be accounted for? How is this splitting (of one idea into two parts) possible?[102]

[17. 18] Consequently finally established is the principle which we have asserted at the beginning, i. e. the apprehended part and the apprehending part do not separably exist, but that consciousness which wrongly represents them as existing in the shape of separate realities, actually exists. Therefore (as it is stated in the stanza):

The Universal Constructor of phenomena exists!
But he himself does not contain any division
In two parts (an apprehended part
And an apprehending one).

§ 10. The Postulate of Buddhism

[17. 21] (The next stanza) begins by emphasizing that this (principle, the principle namely that a real consciousness constructs an unreal phenomenal world must be regarded as firmly established).

[Stanza 1. 4] *Established have we therefore this*
That our (consciousness) creates illusion.

(Reality) is not such (as it appears),
Nor is it a total blank
Because extinguished can be that Illusion,
And this extinction means Salvation.
Such is our Postulate.

Vasubandhu's comment

[V. 3. a. 2] Therefore, in the shape in which (the world) appears to us, in that shape does it not really exist. But this does not (mean that in the phenomenal world) there is absolutely nothing real, because this Universal Illusion (has a real cause) which produces it. Why is it that we do not admit (the world) to be an absolute blank? Because we maintain that

Extinct Illusion means Salvation.

Otherwise (without admitting the reality of consciousness itself) there neither could be a real Bondage nor a real Salvation and we would bring upon ourselves the blame (of being Materialists) who do not recognise the difference between phenomenal impurity and the purity of the Absolute.[103]

Sthiramati's comment

[17. 23] Established is therefore the illusive character of these four categories of ideas. „Therefore" means in accordance with the reasons given above in the stanza:

And without them
Unreal are the ideas.

[17. 24] In order once more to emphasize the reality (of the Mind although he) creates mere illusion and to prove the illusory character of the division (of concrete reality) into an apprehended objective part and an apprehending subjective one; (the stanza) says:

It is not such (as it appears),
(Nor is it) a total blank.

[18. 2] We can also explain the word „therefore" (in the first line of the stanza) as referring to the reason which will be indicated later (i. e. in the second half of the stanza). In pointing to it (the stanza) says:

It is not such (as it appears),
(Nor is it) a total blank.

[18. 4] (Reality) is not such as it appears (in the phenomenal world), nor is it an absolute non-Ens. Indeed it appears as divided into a cognized part and a cognizer part. But of them, first of all, the cognizer part is evidently unreal, because from the four categories of ideas (which represent the totality of our mind) two are not cognizers at all, and two are wrong cognizers. (The categories of things inanimate which reduce to sensible qualities and the category of living bodies which reduce to sense-organs are exclusively objective, they are not cognizers; the categories of the Ego and of our sensations are wrong cognizers, since they project into the external world things which do not exist there at all). But the (immanent) cognized part of our consciousness also does not really exist, because (there can be no immanent object). (Pure consciousness) is absolutely devoid of every (second) essence imposed upon it by another special mental act. (Thus the immanent object is an illusion, pure consciousness is neither a cognized nor a cognizing part). But it neither is a total blank.

[18. 8] (Vasubandhu says „that does not mean that behind the phenomenal illusion) there is absolutely nothing real, because although being a mere illusion (it has a real cause) by which it is produced". This means that although a reality by itself, the shape in which it appears is an illusion,[104] (but this illusion is a real fact) just as a magical vision (is a real fact although it represents an illusion). The word „mere" (in the phrase „mere general illusion") has the aim of excluding anything else, (the whole phenomenal world itself is nothing but illusion).

[18. 10] The meaning is here the following: since the illusive ideas really exist, it is impossible to assert that nothing exists. However the non-existence of the object and of the subject of cognition are asserted, why is it then that the non-existence of the illusive ideas cannot be likewise asserted? (When such a question is asked) the implied meaning is that such a topic as the absolute reality (behind the illusive ideas) transcends all possible cognition, nobody can realize it, (since that Pure Awareness which produces mere illusion is in itself uncognizable).

[18. 14] (The answer then is stated in the stanza) —

This is our Postulate,
Extinct illusion means Salvation.

That is the reason why simple non-existence cannot be admitted. On the contrary. Its reality is inferred indirectly (through the dialectical opposition) of the parts of phenomenal impurity and of the purity of the Absolute.

[18. 17] „Otherwise, (says Vasubandhu) — i. e. if we admit the absolute unreality (of illusion) — there will be neither Bondage, nor Final Deliverance". If this trascendental illusion (this wholesale error) did not really exist, there would be no obscuration of reality and consequently also no Bondage, (no phenomenal life). And since Salvation means salvation out of a preceding bondage, there equally would be no Salvation.

[18. 20] But then indeed, on the one side, you do not admit the reality of that shape of the world in which it appears to us and, on the other side, you do not admit its total unreality, (what do you admit then?) In order to answer such a thought of the opponent (the stanza says):

This is our Postulate,
Extinct illusion is Salvation.

It follows by implication that as long as this (transcendental illusion) is not extinct Bondage (will prevail).

[18. 22) „Otherwise, (says Vasubandhu) there will be neither any Bondage nor any Final Deliverance". We would be rightly accused of denying both the impurity (or phenomenalization) and purity (or sanctification of Reality).

[18. 23] But if it is so, (if the bifurcation of reality into one part grasping the other is not ultimately real), how are we to explain that all living beings beginning [105] from brutes (up to the higher classes of gods) perceive the world in apparent (division)? However if this division would represent absolute reality, in this case the impurity (and oppression of phenomenal life) would last eternally. There consequently never [would be any Nirvāṇa]

[19. 1] And likewise (on the other hand) if we admit no transcendental illusion at all, there could be no (phenomenal) wretchedness; absolute purity (and bliss) should be existent in all eternity. In both these cases the struggle for Final Deliverance would be senseless.

Consequently it must be necessarily admitted (what was stated at the beginning):

The Universal Creator of the world illusion exists,
But he himself does not contain any division
(Of one part of reality grasping the other).

Chapter III

THE THREEFOLD ASPECT OF THE CONSTRUCTOR OF PHENOMENA

§ 1. General statement

Vasubandhu's comment

[V. 3. a. 4] After having thus indicated the „particular essence" of the Constructor of Phenomena (i. e. after having mentioned the four categories of particular ideas in which he manifests himself) his „inclusive essence" will be explained (i. e. it will be indicated) how in him alone, in him exclusively[1] (i. e. in every particular Ens) a threefold aspect is included.

[Stanza 1. 5]

As an objective (part)[2] t'is totally imagined,
As the Constructor of that thing imagined
It is (reality) interdependent,
And as the merger of the subject with the object
T'is called (the Absolute)
The non plus ultra of Reality.[3]

Among these (three aspects) the one which represents (reality) as an „object" (in contrast to the subject) is entirely a construction of our imagination. The Constructor of this (constructed) phenomenon (is a moment of pure consciousness) „dependent" on other (preceding moments). The merger of this (constructed) object with the subject is called the Ultimate, the Absolute Reality.[4]

Sthiramati's comment

[19. 5] (Vasubandhu says), „the inclusive essence will be indicated". This either means that just[5] the inclusion (of the three aspects) constitutes the essence (of the Constructor), or it means that (this Constructor) possesses an essence which is characterized through the inclusion of these three aspects.[6]

[19. 6] Now why is this (inclusive character) indicated? (The reason is the following one). It has been stated above that the Constructor of phenomena (i. e. the Creator of the illusion of phenomenal reality) alone exists. He is free (of the relation) between an apprehended object and a subject apprehending it. However other scriptural works declare that there are (in him) three different essences (viz. an imagined one, a real one and an absolute one). Therefore in order to show that there is no contradiction with these works the inclusion (of the three essences in the one) is here indicated. The Expositor (Vasubandhu) therefore (emphatically) states „alone in the Constructor of phenomenal Appearance, in him exclusively“ [7] (are the three aspects included). (This is expressed in stanza 1. 5):

As an objective part t'is totally imagined,
As the Constructor of the thing imagined
It is reality interdependent,
And as the merger of the object with the subject
T'is called (the Absolute),
The non plus ultra of Reality.

[19. 13] The object and the subject of cognition (are correlative). They are devoid of proper reality (each in itself, separately from the other). Although not (ultimately) real, they are imagined as being real. Therefore this their aspect is called „totally imagined“. It does not exist in ultimate reality,[8] but in every day life (it is supposed) to be real and is spoken of (as if both parts were) realities by themselves.

[19. 15] (The second aspect is the aspect of causal) dependence. Since the origination of every real thing is strictly dependent on (a complex) of causes and conditions (the real thing, the Thing-in-Itself) is called the Dependent.[9]

[19. 16] With reference to it the following stanza has been composed:

(By creative imagination) not constructed,[10]
From cooperating causes originating,
(Connotatively) unutterable at all,
The thing's own essence is Dependent;
T'is the domain of Pure Reality,
But it is yet phenomenal.[11]

[19. 20] The (non-phenomenal), the ultimate aspect of Reality consists in its „non-duality“ (i. e. in Monism, in the Universal character of the absence of a division into object and subject as inherent in every single Constructor of a phenomenon).[12] It is not dependent on causes, (eternally) immutable and therefore Perfection (of Reality). With regard to it the following stanza has been composed:

Perfection of reality consists
In the full absence of reality imagined.
Of non-discursive[13] *(direct Enlightment of the Saint)*
T'is the domain exclusive.[14]

[19. 24] (The stanza says) „on behalf of object", i. e. (it is totally imagined) as an objective part. In the same manner (the words of the stanza) „as the Creator of the thing imagined" and „as the merger of the object with the subject" must be interpreted (namely as definitions of the second and the third aspect of the Constructor).

[19. 25] (Vasubandhu says) „object here means the totally imagined form of it". Objects are here[15] of four kinds, 1) the sense-data, 2) sense-organs, 3) the Ego[16] and 4) its sensations. These four kinds of objects are (mere ideas), they are not to be found in the Constructor of phenomena (i. e. in reality) in that form in which they are imagined. Thus it is therefore that the first aspect which is entirely constructed by imagination has no reality (at all).

[19. 27] There is also (another stanza) on this (subject):

Imagination (is the Mind),
T'is not itself created by imagination.[17]
But by another mental act.
T'is split in two, (an object and a subject).
No ultimate reality obtains
In this dichotomized form.[18]

[20. 3] (Vasubandhu says) „The creator of this thing imagined (is a moment of consciousness) dependent on other (preceding moments). It is called „dependent-on-other (things)", because it is not self-existent (not *causa sui*), since it depends on, or is produced by, causes and conditions.

[20. 4] (Vasubandhu says) „the merger of the object with the subject is the ultimate, (the Absolute Reality)". It is called „the ultimate" because (of a double kind of perfection), 1) the perfection of immutability (as the absolute whole of existence), and 2) the perfection of Truth (as cognized by the mystic omniscience of the Saint only).[19]

[20. 6] (It should be noticed) that when we here assert that the Constructor of phenomena contains no duality (i. e. no object-to-subject relativity) this refers to the division (of reality) into an objective and a subjective parts, but not to the absence of every relativity. It is just in this Constructor of phenomena that Causality (i. e. causal relativity) prevails. For this reason it is called the Dependent. This same (Dependent Element), but having a (superinduced) object-subject form constitutes the (first), the totally imagined aspect (of the Constructor). Again this same (Dependent Element), but layed bare of the object-to-subject (and effect-to-cause) relativities is the Absolute. Thus it is that the Constructor of phenomena (i. e. the Thing-in-Itself) includes in himself all three aspects.

[20. 12] And thus it is that (the idea) of the Constructor of the phenomenal (worlds) points to that Pure Reality which at first must be thoroughly investigated, (then) must be layed bare (of all superinduced illusion) and (finally) intuited directly by the Saint in a moment of mystic enlightment when all illusion has been cleared away (and Omniscience attained).[20]

§ 2. The unreality of the external world

Vasubandhu's comment

[V. 3. a. 6] We will now demonstrate the essence of that expedient through which the negative characteristic[21] of the Creator of Illusion (i. e. the ultimate unreality of the division into object and subject) can be realized.

[Stanza 1. 6]

When (the Pure Spirit) is considered
All other objects disappear
When disappeared have all the objects
Their apprehender also disappears.

This means that when Pure Awareness[22] is intuited (as the unique ultimate reality by the transic enlightment of the Saint) the perception of the objective world disappears and, when the perception of the (pluralistic) objective world has disappeared, then, taking one's stand on th s non-perception of all objects, the perception of Pure Awareness itself (in the rôle of a perceiving subject) likewise disappears. Such is the method of (gradually) realizing the (ultimate) reality which represents the merger of the apprehended object and the apprehending subject.[23]

Sthiramati's comment

[20. 14] As long as this (ultimate reality which is) the Constructor of the phenomenal world is not thoroughly investigated, as long as attributes (are to him ascribed) which are not (ultimately) real, he presents himself as a (pluralistic) world of Appearance with its illusion, (moral and immoral) deeds and rebirths.[24] Therefore in order thoroughly to know that the world of Appearance is an illusive attribute (of Absolute Reality) and in order to show the expedient through which this can be known (the following stanza) has been composed:

When the (Pure Spirit) is considered
(All other objects) disappear;
When disappeared have (all the objects)
(Their apprehender) also disappears.

[20. 17] (This means that) such is the essential feature of the Constructor of Apperance, or that this absence of the object-to-subject relation is itself the negative essence (of the absolute reality of the Constructor). (Vasubandhu says) „can be entered", i. e. cognized. (The words) „its expedient" refer (to that mystic intuition of Monism) after attaining which the Saint realizes that this (division of reality into an apprehended object and a subject grasping it) is an illusion.[25] It refers to the double proficiency (of the Bodhisattva to get rid of the belief in the existence of an external world, and to get rid of the belief that there is a consciousness really apprehending it). It begins to be reached on the Path of Training (preparatory to the Path of Vision) when all objects wheresoever they might exist will appear as fully absorbed in the (unique, undifferentiated) Absolute.[26]

[20. 20] The aim of the stanza is indirectly to point to this (Mahāyānistic Path of Illumination of the Bodhisattva). (Vasubandhu explains) „when Pure Awareness is intuited (as the unique ultimate Reality), the perception of a (real) objective world disappears". Pure Awareness means non-existence of external objects. A representation which exhibits the form of a patch of colour or any other (external thing) arises out of a germ which having attained maturity appears (from one's Subliminal Mind-Store), but the patch of colour as an external object does not exist. (The Bodhisattva thus begins) by realizing the non-existence of the apprehended object in founding himself at the same time (provisionally) on the existence of the apprehending subject.

[20. 24—21. 1] Indeed (in order to arrive at the conviction that the external world does not exist) he should argue thus. A representation can depend on an external object either at the moment when it arises or (at a subsequent moment), when it has already arisen. But at the moment when it arises (being in *statu nascendi*) it does not yet exist and cannot therefore apprehend the object. Neither can it do this (at a subsequent moment) when it already has arisen, because when arisen it already contains the (ready) image of the object. A representation indeed has no other function to fulfil as to appear in projecting the object into the external world. A representation has not to take action in order that we may say „it perceives the object".[27]

[21. 5] But supposing an object is employed about simultaneously existing representations, not about nascent ones; however under these conditions[28] the production of the representation will not be owing to the external object. The whole hypothesis of such an origin becomes senseless, because the perception of a simultaneously existing object is excluded (by our fundamental theory) of the instantaneous character of every reality (the object, if it represents a cause, must precede the representation, but being instantaneous it will exist no more at the moment when its cognition will be produced, thus the simultaneous momentary existence of the objective cause and of the representation produced by it are impossible).[29]

[21. 8] According to the same[30] (principle of instantaneous reality) an object cannot be apprehended by a representation as long as it has not undergone some change of its own condition. (There are some philosophers who therefore) surmise that the object undergoes a change of condition just at the moment when it is grasped. (A new quality, viz. „cognizedness", is produced in it). But then we nevertheless will be obliged to face the consequence that a changed condition of the object will (really) be grasped, and therefore an object will be perceived which (as a matter of fact) has become a different object.[31]

§ 3. Repudiation of the Sautrāntikas

[21. 11] There is another (philosopher) who professes the following theory.[32] (All existence being instantaneous), it is just the disappearing thing that is the object and the cause of our cognition which arises (in its track in the next moment). It is its (special) cause which is distinguished from all its other causes and conditions by creating the image of the object and projecting it (into the external world).[33] This same philosopher assumes that either the atoms of colour or of some other stuff, themselves or their assemblages, are thus the (real) objective cause (of the image).[34]

[21. 15] (We answer.) In either case there is an impossibility, (neither the single atoms nor their assemblages) can be objects. Indeed every perception arises as representing either a jar or a cloth or such sort of thing, it never represents an atom. It is however impossible that our cognition should contain the image of one thing while its object would be a thing quite different.

[21. 17] (We must moreover consider that if we establish the principle that the cause producing a cognition is its object, the causes are many, all will be objects.) The organ of sight and all other sense organs (are also causes producing sense-perception). We will arrive at the absurd consequence that they will be (not organs), but objects.

[21. 18] When another philosopher[35] maintains that only aggregates of atoms become objects of perception, not single atoms separately, this his objection is futile. Although the atoms be assembled[36] they can be admitted as objects of perception only singly, not as aggregates, but such a perception of atoms, one by one, never arises. They always appear as aggregates. Just for this reason the atoms cannot be the real objects of perception.[37]

[21. 23] Moreover an aggregate of atoms cannot represent a (real) object (as the real cause of its perception for the following reason). (An aggregate is always a nominal Ens) and a nominal Ens can never be the cause (of whatsoever). Indeed when (we speak) of a cause producing cognition (a real, efficient cause is meant), just, as the immediately preceding moment in the stream of consciousness is a real efficient cause (of the following moment). The object-cause should also be assumed (as a real cause, but being a nominal entity it cannot be a cause).

Thus it is that (the theory of the Sautrāntikas maintaining that an instantaneous object produces) just at the moment when it disappears a cognition (arising in the following moment) cannot be admitted.

§ 4. Repudiation of the Sarvāstivādins

[21. 25] (Remains the theory of the Sarvāstivādins who assume) that an extinct thing can (nevertheless) be an object of cognition. But if this were so, then a past thing and a future thing could be the object of a (present perception). (However this hypothesis is quite unnecessary), since it is an undisputable fact that in dreams and (in hallucinations) we have perceptions without any (corresponding external) object at all.

[22. 1] There are some (realistic philosophers) who maintain that even in dreams and hallucinations our representations are not altogether without any external object, since their object is a mark[38] (left by the object). Such a mark is a reflection (coming from it), it has the nature of an energy (being neither a physical nor a mental object, but a force).[39]

[22. 3] However it is quite impossible to assume the existence during dreams of such marks (or reflections) when the objects themselves are absent, just as it is well known that e. g. the reflection of a face (in a mirror) never appears if there is no face actually present.

[22. 4] (But even if we admit the existence of such an external force, we must face the former dilemma, viz.) the representation will be either nascent or ready produced; neither the one nor the other, as has been stated above, could apprehend an object (the nascent because it does not yet exist, the ready produced, because being produced, it has nothing more to do and disappears at once).[40] Consciousness itself, since it contains the image of the object, represents its reflection, there is therefore no need to assume the existence of a specific energy (for the sake of explaining the presence of ideas in dreams).

[22. 7] That consciousness itself contains representations, this must be necessarily assumed.[41] If it did contain in itself no images (if it were imageless pure consciousness) it would be quite impossible to establish a definite correspondence between the object apprehended and the cognition apprehending it (since the apprehending pure consciousness would be always the same).

[22. 9] There is another (philosopher) who thinks that in dreams as well as in the yogi's meditation, (viz. when the yogi concentrates all his thoughts on the mental contemplation of the disgusting and horrible condition of a putrified dead body), there necessarily is some kind of penetrable (transparent, subtle) matter representing the external object. However such an object (if it were real) would possess real colour, figure and other (physical qualities) and this contradicts the permeable character of this (supposed) external object cognized (not by the senses, but by the Mind only). And indeed with the only exception of the „latent matter" (of the Vaibhāṣikas) no other kind of permeable[12] matter has been assumed in science.[13] Therefore this is a mere (futile) hypothesis.

[22. 12] There are other philosophers[14] who maintain that only such objects can be perceived in dreams of which we have had a former experience, because a blind-born man cannot in his dreams perceive e. g. the colour blue.

[22. 14] But (we reply), it is not true that a blind-born man does not perceive colours in his dreams.[15] He only does not know them by name, because their names have not been taught to him, and he therefore cannot talk of them to others. (Even if we assume that we can see in dreams only such things which we have had some previous experience of), why should we deny that a blind-born can perceive colour in dreams? He certainly has seen colours in some of his former existences. Dreams are not restricted to objects experienced in the present life. There is no difference between a waking and dreaming man in regard of whether their ideas refer to the past, the future or the present. It is therefore pure fancy to maintain that dreams can refer only to some actual experience (of the present life).

[22. 20] (But even admitting that only past experience can be the object of a dream), since the past experience (is an experience which) exists no more, we should be certain that the images we see in dreams are purely mental without any corresponding external objects. Thus it is that by obsering (in these cases) that Mind alone exists, we become engrossed in the idea of the unreality of the external world.

[22. 23] (Vasubandhu says) „basing oneself on the non-perception of any objects the non-perception of Pure Awareness (in the rôle of a perceiving subject) is likewise produced". Just as the object, which our productive imagination constructs as apprehended outside our consciousness, does not exist and (the Bodhisattva) thus enters in an objectless domain (of thought) in basing himself on the principle of Mind only; just so (vice versa) in basing oneself on the strength (of the principle) of the unreality of the apprehended object, the unreality of the subject apprehending it, (the subject) of that pure intimation which apprehends, is likewise realized. Indeed (these notions are correlative), the apprehending part exists only as dependent on the apprehended one. If the apprehended part does not exist, neither does the apprehending one exist.

[23. 2] It is therefore established that (the Bodhisattva) thus cognizes the unreal essence of the object and the subject, (these object and subject) being in their essence mental constructions. But that does not at all affect (the ultimate reality of the underlying Element) which is the Constructor of the (imagined) phenomenal world.

[23. 3] Now (since object and subject are correlative and equally unreal in a monistic universe), why does the Bodhisattva not begin by first establishing the unreality (of the subject, i. e.) of pure sensation itself (in the rôle of the cognizer of an object in the ken)? (Why should he begin by repudiating the reality of the object, i. e. of the external world?) (The reason is the following one.) The reality of the subject which apprehends the external objects depends upon the real existence of these objects. But when (it is proved that) there is (absolutely) nothing which could be an external object, that reality which represents the objective part of cognition disappears and the Bodhisattva is easily at home (in a purely spiritual Universe). But if, on the contrary, he would have begun by denying the reality of the apprehending subject, this would have meant (Nihilism), a total denial of every reality (whatsoever it might be), since the relativity of the apprehended and the apprehending parts would not have been (rightly) understood.[46]

[23. 7] And the Bodhisattva attains this stage of (monistic) intuition which lies passed the spheres (where reality) is distinguished into object and subject at the close of the first period of incalculable eons, if he has practiced the Path of Accumulating Merit[47] without interruption.

[23. 9] Thus taking his stand on the conviction that all is Mind only, the Bodhisattva realizes (a world) in which there is no Matter. He enters the trance called the Stage of Warm Belief[48] — this being the first degree of the Transcendent[49] Mahāyānistic Path of Training (when the unreality of the Elements of the external world reveals itself to him, though but slightly).

[23. 11] Next to this he enters the condition called the Headway-trance,[50] (the second degree of this Path, the degree where the light shed on the unreality of the external world is intensified). After that he (becomes absorbed) in the trance called the Persevering[51] one, (being the third degree of this Path) where the representation of the objective world has completely vanished and the idea of the unreality of the subject who was perceiving it dawns unto him.

[23. 13] Next to it (the Bodhisattva, as Vasubandhu puts it,) „taking his stand on the non-perception of objects, creates a non-perception (even) of that simple awareness" (of the presence of an object in the ken, which represents the Mind in its rôle of an apprehending consciousness). He is then absorbed in the trance called the Highest Worldly Condition" (the last degree of the Path of Training) which is associated with a Gnosis and all those mental phenomena which are its satellites.[52]

[23. 15] After this comes the Path of Transcendent Enlightment. There only the all-pervading (Absolute, the foundation) of the miraculous powers of a Bodhisattva becomes visualized. The Bodhisattva enters the first stage of Saintliness. It is a mental act (of undivided, monistic cognition) of Absolute Reality, it is not an emotional act as the acts of (undivided) overwhelming feelings (of the Bodhisattva, his feelings of Love, Commiseration, Sympathy and Equanimity which although being meritorious do not lead to the cognition of the Absolute).[53]

§ 5. Cognition of the Monistic Absolute

[Stanza 1.7]

It is thus proved that (the Absolute's) perception
Is in its essence non-perception.

Vasubandhu's comment

[V. 3. b. 2] Since there are no objects which could be perceived, (real) perception is impossible.

Sthiramati's comment

[23. 18] (The author, Maitreya goes on) to show that the essence of the intuition (of the Absolute) consists in a non-perception (of the pluralistic phenomenal World) and says:

It is thus proved that (the Absolute's) perception
Is in its essence non-perception.

[23. 20] This also (means) that our initial thesis, (the thesis namely) that the Creator of the phenomenal world (i. e. the Thing-in-Itself) can contain no duality (of an apprehended object and a subject grasping it), this thesis becomes established in this (other) formulation (inasmuch as the monistic principle can be) introspectively realized by every individual (in the depths of his own consciousness when concentrated in the deepest transic meditation).[54] (The non-perception of the pluralistic world is a non-perception of duality, or Monism).

[23. 22] In order to point this out (the stanza) says:

It is thus proved that this perception
Is in its essence non-perception.

This means that, since there are no (real) perceivable objects, there can be no (real) perception of them.

[23. 24] The word „perception" can be interpreted either as a process, or as the agent or the instrument (of perception). All the three meanings require the complement of an object and are not possible without it. But (since the object does not really exist) it becomes proved that its perception is in its essence non-perception. Therefore (Vasubandhu) the author of the commentary says „since there are no (real) objects that could be perceived their (real) perception is impossible".

[24. 3] (The stanza 1. 7 further states):

It should be known therefore
That equal are perception and non-perception.

Vasubandhu's comment

[V. 5. b. 3] (Phenomenal perception is equal to non-perception), because it is not proved that this perception is a (real) perception. But although in its essence it is a non-perception, it nevertheless is called perception, in that sense namely that it represents to us (as real) such objects which ultimately prove not to be real.

Sthiramati's comment. *First explanation of the semi-stanza*

[24. 4] Their equality should be known, because there is no difference between not perceiving (the manifold phenomenal world) and perceiving the (monistic) Pure Awareness (of the Absolute). The first does not (separately) exist at all, there is therefore (between them) no difference, (the Absolute is immanent in the Phenomenal).[55]

[24. 6] In order to remove the contradiction of the terms perception and non-perception (Vasubandhu says) „it is called perception in that sense that it represents to us (as real) such objects which (ultimately) are not real.[56] But (as a matter of fact) nothing is perceived by such perception, since its objects do not exist. Therefore there is here no contradiction, because from the standpoint of absolute reality „this perception is in its essence non-perception".

Second explanation of the semi-stanza

[24. 10] But others maintain that equal are the perception of simple people mistaking things not really existing for realities and the non-perception by the Saints of (external) objects. Both (this perception by simple men and this non-perception by the Saints are the same thing), just as the illusion (representing a rope as a serpent is in its essence) a non-perception of the serpent.

[24. 12] (Vasubandhu) therefore says „it nevertheless is called perception in that sence (namely) that it represents to us (as real) such objects which (ultimately) are not real".[57] (He a'so says), „although in its essence it is a non-perception", i. e. just as the illusion of a snake (in the place of a rope) is called „non-perception", (since a mistaken perception is in its essence a non-perception).

Third explanation of the semi-stanza

[24. 15] Others again give (the following explanation). Simple people assume that there is a perceiving subject. But the Saint knows that this is an error: there can be no perceiving subject, because there are no objects to be perceived. We therefore must conclude that both these views, the (wrong) assertion of the existence of a perceiver and its (right) denial, are identical (at the bottom), because in both cases invariable is (the fact) that if there are no objects, there can be no perceiver of them. (Vasubandhu) therefore says „because it represents to us (as real) such objects which (ultimately) are not real".

Fourth interpretation of the semi-stanza

[24. 19] Others again maintain that (the dictum) „it must be known that equal are perception and non-perception" should be interpreted as directed against both the realism (of the Sautrāntikas) and the Scepticism (of the Mādhyamikas, i. e. both are equal in the sense of being equally mistaken and equally not appreciating reality where it really is). Indeed, there are no external objects. Their perception is no real perception, since it lacks the essential feature of real perception, (the feature namely of perceiving reality). (We, Y o g ā c ā r a s) do not take away from perception its real essence (of being a perception of reality).[58] But we neither impute on it the character of being no knowledge at all (as the Mādhyamikas are doing). What is then (our attitude)? They are equal. Both (perception and non-perception) are equal as regards that non-discursive perception (of Pure Reality which underlies them both).

[24. 24] Therefore it must be known, that non-perception and perception are each in itself identical (with the other), if we leave alone both the ascribing (of unreal attributes to pure Reality) and the denying (of this Reality itself). Hence it is stated (in the **A b h i s a m a y ā l a ṅ k ā r a**):

Nothing from it to be taken away,
Nor anything at all to be added,
The Absolute should be regarded as it really is.
Who knoweth Absolute reacheth Salvation.[59]

[25. 3] If that is so, why then do we call our awareness (of the existence of something in the ken) perception, (but not non-perception)?
Although (as Vasubandhu says) „in its essence it is a non-perception" inasmuch as it represents a projection (into the external world) of things which do not exist (there), it is nevertheless called perception, because in common life as well as in (profane) science it is known (under this conventional name).

§ 6. The hells, the earth and the heavens are the phenomenal Worlds created by the Constructor of Appearance

V a s u b a n d h u's c o m m e n t

[V. 3. b. 4] That aspect of the Constructor of phenomena will now be indicated which (manifests itself) in a differentiation in various modes (of phenomenal existence).

[*Semi-stanza 1. 8*] *(Ideas) are Constructors of Appearance*
In all Three Realms of Being,
They are the Mind and mental derivates.

These three Realms of Being are 1) the Realm of Carnal Desire (or of gross bodies, embracing the hells, the earth and the lower heavens), 2) the Realm of (transparent, ethereal bodies, possessing) forms (but free of gross carnal desire, they are the residents of the seven higher heavens) and 3) the Realm of Formless Existence (not attached to a body or a place, embracing four different modes of illimitable existence).

Sthiramati's comment

[25. 6] (Vasubandhu says) „that aspect (of the Creator of Appearance) will now be indicated (which manifests itself in a) division". There are indeed (three) different ways of constructing phenomenal life. They constitute the Realms of Carnal Desire, of Pure Forms and of Formless (Existence). This division itself is (most) essential, (it is called) essential division, because the essence of the Constructor of phenomenal life is characterized by it.

[25. 8—9] Now, what indeed is the aim of dwelling upon this essential division? (The aim is the following one). We have established that the Creator of Appearance is the only reality existing.[60] (There is no real external world). Under these conditions the existence of worlds inhabited by living beings possessing gross bodies and of the worlds of (transparent) forms is not possible. (The immaterial worlds alone would be real). However (the Buddhist religion) is a religion which establishes different degrees of Saints in accordance with different impediments (to saintliness) and different remedies against them. (The system of these impediments and remedies is founded on the system) of the various modes of existence in the different Realms of Being. The denial of their reality would mean a catastrophe for Buddhism as a religion. In order to clear away this contradiction, the true import of the division in different modes of existence is explained.[61] (The phenomena in the realms of both gross and refined matter are ideas constructed by imagination, just as the formless existence is also mere imagination, but these ideas are not devoid of reality as ideas).

A second explanation of the existence of different worlds

[25. 12] There is also (another theory against which our stanza is directed. Some philosophers maintain namely that not all mental phenomena are Constructors of Appearance, but only some of them. They maintain that the supposed Constructor of Appearance is nothing but the subconscious operation of the Mind preceding the production of every definite idea), it is the operation of running through a manifold of sensation and the operation of fixing the attention on one point of it. These two operations of the Mind are the Constructors of phenomena, but not the other mental faculties.[62] Therefore in order to repudiate this wrong theory the stanza indicates the real import of the division into various modes of existence:

(Ideas) are Constructors of Appearance
In all Three Realms of Being
They are the Mind and mental derivates.

[25. 16] By no means the „running" and the „fixing" operation alone represent the Constructor of phenomena. But just as Matter is assumed to consist of primary as well as of secondary qualities [63] just so (the Mind or) the Constructor of Appearance consists of the Mind itself (the pure Mind) and of its mental derivates (all mental phenomena), but not of the (pure) Mind exclusively. They constitute the essence (of reality) in all the three Realms of Being. (Every existence is mental, all ideas are creators of phenomena, the running and fixing operations are present only in a non-concentrated mind and in the first degree of concentration, the three following degrees are free of them).

[25. 18] (Vasubandhu says) „the three Realms of Being are the Realm of Carnal Desire, the Realm of Form and the Realm of Formless Existence.

[25. 19] Among them the Realm of Carnal Desire (or of gross bodies, i. e. of the ideas of such bodies) is represented by classes of living beings, beginning with the denizens of the hells, (including human beings and the gods of the lower heavens), they are (all created) by this World Constructor.

[25. 20—21] The Realm of (Transparent) Forms (or of ethereal bodies) is constituted by seventeen classes (of gods), the Brahma deities and others. The Realm of Formless Existence consists of four classes of (abstract) deities merged in the contemplation of four kinds of Infinity, of infinite Space etc.

A third explanation of the division

[25. 22] Others again give the following explanation. The sphere of Carnal Desire (or of gross bodies) consists of such living beings who have not extirpated in themselves all carnal desire and are endowed with a (gross) body, (i. e. with the ideas of gross bodies). The sphere of (transparent) Forms is constituted by such beings who have extirpated in themselves all gross carnal desire, but are still endowed with a (transparent) Form, (i. e. with the respective imagination). The sphere of Formless Existence is constituted by such beings who have extirpated in themselves every carnal desire and possess no material form (even) in idea." (They have no distinct non localized existence)

A fourth explanation of the division

[25. 26] Others again give the following (simple explanation). The sphere of (Gross) Desire is constituted by such living beings whose life is controlled and shaped by the instinct of attachment to gross enjoyment. The sphere of (Transparent) Forms is constituted by those (heavenly) beings whose life is controlled and shaped by an attachment to (pure, subtle, transparent) Forms of Matter. The sphere of Formless Existence is constituted by such living beings whose life is the realization of their attachment to amorphous (ubiquitous) existence.[65]

A fifth explanation of the division

[26. 2] Others again maintain that the sphere of Carnal Desire consists of such beings whose minds are never pacified and who always are in a condition of mental uneasiness. The sphere of (Pure) Forms is constituted by beings whose minds are steady-concentrated and who are free from the condition of mental uneasiness. The amorphous sphere consists of beings whose minds are steady-concentrated and are free of all kind (of emotion), suffering as well as joy.

A sixth explanation of the division

[26. 5] There are some philosophers who think that the sphere of gross bodies consists of beings (composed of the full list of the 18 kinds of component Elements of existence). They have not extinguished round themselves neither the phenomena of odour and taste, nor their corresponding sensations. Those who have extinguished the phenomena of odour and taste, as well as of the corresponding sensations, belong to the sphere of (purified transparent) Forms. (These individuals consist of only 14 classes of Elements). Those who have extinguished in themselves the fifteen classes (of sensuous component Elements) belong to (the transphysical, amorphous sphere).[66] (They consist only of the three classes of Elements purely spiritual and are ubiquitous).

[26. 7] Among all these definitions what are the best ones? Necessarily to be mentioned is only that one which has been quoted in the first place, the other explanations are all dependent (on the first).[67]

(Although the term „Constructor of phenomena" (quoted in stanza 1. 1) is the general title of the whole first chapter (and must be understood by implication in all the following stanzas), its repeated mention (in stanza 1. 8) is justified, because (the running exposition of this subject) has been interrupted[68] (in stanza 1. 7) by a discussion of non-perception (and real perception).

§ 7. The other name of the Constructor of the phenomenal worlds

Vasubandhu's comment

[V. 1. b. 4] (The Creator of phenomenal Appearance) is also characterized by another name which is indicated (in the next half stanza):

[Stanza 1. 8. c—d]

The Mind perceives the Thing,
Its evolutes perceive the qualities.

This means — the Mind (itself, i. e. pure sensation) apprehends the Thing alone, (i. e. the Thing-in-Itself, the pure object). The mental phenomena, such as e. g. feelings (pleasant and unpleasant) etc., apprehend its qualities, (i. e. the qualities of the Thing, pleasant or unpleasant).

Sthiramati's comment

[26. 10] (Vasubandhu mentions) „a characteristic by another name"; this means that by pointing to the Mind (itself) and to its different evolutes, (i. e. mental phenomena), another characteristic name of the Creator of phenomenal Appearance is elicited. Why is that? Because engaged in the construction of the thing which is being constructed and of its qualities are (just) the Mind and the mental faculties.[69] The perce vers of the Things themselves and of their qualities are (on the one side) the Mind and mental phenomena, (on the other, the same is done) by the Creator of phenomenal worlds. Therefore it happens that the Mind and the Creator are the names of one and the same thing.[70,71]

[26. 15] (Vasubandhu says) „among them the Mind apprehends the Thing alone". Here the word „alone" serves to exclude (every kind) of definiteness. The meaning is (that we call Mind itself nothing but pure sensation, i. e. the perception of the mere presence in the ken of something quite indefinite), the perception of the Thing-in-Itself layed bare of all its qualities.

[26. 17] „The mental phenomena, such as e. g. feelings etc., apprehend its qualities" (says Vasubandhu). This means that they are employed about cognizing this or that thing in this or that of its special functions. Supposing a thing has the peculiarity of being delightful or painful. Such a thing is the source of pleasure or pain. The apprehension of this (its quality) is called feeling. Supposing further a peculiar thing can be designated as being a woman, or a man or anything else, the apprehension of this its quality is called idea (or concept). All other (mental phenomena) must be respectively interpreted according to these patterns.

§ 8. Controversy between the Pluralist and the Monist on the reality of separate mental phenomena

[26. 21] And such is (the character) of these (mental phenomena) that they are all (separate only in abstraction), in reality they are intrinsically united: by the unity of their residence (in the same sense), by the unity of the same object (to which they refer), by the unity of the time (in which they appear) and by the unity of that reality, (i. e. that mental thing which they represent); but not by the unity of their (abstract) form, since otherwise we would have the absurd consequence that they would coalesce and would be not different from pure Sensation.[72]

[26. 24] There are however some philosophers (who favour a pluralistic doctrine and) maintain that every mental phenomenon, (a feeling, an idea, a volition, a pure sensation) is a separate mental (reality). (For them) this our consciousness is a manifold of separate Elements appearing to us as a (thinking) substance and (its inherent attributes), just as the eye in a peacock's tail (appears to us as a unity, but consists of an assemblage of differently coloured points inhering in some material substance).[73]

(The Yogācāra). But how can a unity be at the same time a plurality?

(The Vaibhāṣika). (This is just as in common life), people assume that one and the same reality can possess a variety of attributes. Thus the absurdity of one reality being at the same time many realities is obviated.

[27. 1] (The Yogācāra). Your objection would have been quite all right, if the essence of an existential Element (a *dharma*) were (for us just as it is for you) a final and absolute reality. But since (for us) it is a mere illusion of reality, your critique misses the point. We have stated above (in stanza 1. 4), that reality „is not such as it appears, nor is it an absolute blank,[74] (i. e. there are Elements which are unreal, but there is one Element which is absolutely real; the Mind alone is ultimately real in a monistic universe, its different attributes are all illusive appearance).

(The Vaibhāṣika). That is not so! Scripture contradicts this. (We read in Scripture): „The Element which represents a feeling, the Element which represents an idea, the Element which represents a volition, the Element which represents a pure sensation, all these Elements are united, they are not disunited". However what is here called „union" is nothing but (simultaneousness), the simultaneous appearance[75] of many different realities.

[27. 6] (The Yogācāra). (The scriptural text quoted by you) does not suggest for us the meaning which you put into it, because we do not admit that all the Elements of reality (which were established by the early schools) are absolute and final realities.[76]

Chapter IV

THE DYNAMICS OF THE CREATOR OF THE WORLD ILLUSION

§ 1. The Subconscious Mind-Store or the Psyche

Vasubandhu's comment

[V. 3. b. 5] The dynamical aspect [1] (of the Constructor of phenomenal illusion) is (now) indicated —

[Stanza 1. 9]

(The Mind is double),
The one is the Foundation-Mind, [2]
The other one is actual sensation. [3]
The mental evolutes (contained in it)
Are (feelings, [4] *ideas* [5] *and the will* [6]
Respectively) they enjoy, [7] *cognize* [8]
And activate [9] *sensation.* [10]

The subconscious Mind-Store (or the Psyche[11]) is the foundation, since it is the source of all other sensations. Produced from it the actual sensation is experience. Feeling means experiencing (pleasant and unpleasant retribution for good or bad former deeds). An idea (or concept) means a thorough experience (or knowledge of what a sensation refers to). The will, attention and other mental faculties activate (such) sensations, (i. e. convert them into actions).

Sthiramati's comment

[27. 7] The only (reality which is assumed in this system is the reality of the Creator of phenomenal Illusion). There is no other (reality). Thus there (seemingly) is no room for a (real) distinction between cause and effect[12] (in such a monistic universe). In order to show (the place of phenomenal causality in it) „its dynamical aspect is indicated" (says Vasubandhu).

[27. 9] Thus we will have the following definition: „The Creator of the phenomenal worlds is Causality".[13] Motion alone constitutes its essence, it is essentially a process.[14]

[27. 11] This process however can be envisaged from two different points of view, (as a consecution of moments and as a change of life). Motion regarded as a consecution of moments is that process in which we experience the present moment of phenomenal life. Motion regarded as the change (from one life) into a future life is that process through which life develops (in twelve consecutive stages) with its vices, moral resp. immoral deeds and life-continuity (from birth to death and from death to a new birth).[15]

[27. 13] (The essence of the first, i. e.) of the Constructor of the world as he appears in a single moment of the process has been described above. In the sequel the process leading to a future life will be described through a description of the (twelve so called) great „oppressors" (i. e. twelve factors converting the pure reality of the Creator into an impure phenomenal existence).[16]

[27. 15] (The stanza says—) „(The Mind is double), the one is the Foundation-Mind". The word „the one" refers here to the subliminal Mind-Store, (or the Psyche). It represents the source of all the other seven kinds of sensation in that sense that it is their] efficient cause.[17] It is therefore called the (primary) cause-sensation.

[27. 18] „The other is an actual experience". („The other"), the word „sensation" is understood. We must supplement the words „it is the result of the (first category)". The seven different kinds of sensation [18] (constituting the second general category) represent its kinetic aspect. (It is called) actual experience, since its *raison d'être* [19] consists in experiencing (the retribution for former good or bad deeds).

[27. 22] (The stanza says) —

> *The mental evolutes (contained) in it*
> *Are feelings, ideas and the will.*
> *(Respectively) they enjoy, cognize*
> *And activate (sensation).*

[27. 23] Those mental evolutes which are contained in it, i. e. in a pure sensation, represent at the same time its products. Such is the meaning.[20] The reality of a sensation and the pleasure produced by it are ultimately one and the same thing, (they are not two things).[21]

[27. 24] The (subliminal) Mind-Store is indeed the cause of all other sensations, it is therefore the (efficient) cause-sensation.[22] All the Elements of phenomenal life are hidden collected in it as its (future) results and it is also hidden in them as their cause. Thus it is the Store, (the mutual hiding place).

[28. 1] (It is also called „sensation". Sensation is that mental Element which suggests the presence of something in the ken). This sensation suggests the existence of living beings and of the world in which they live.[23] It is the projection of their appearance (into the external world).

[28. 2] Being exclusively (an automatic) result (of good or bad deeds), the subliminal Mind (or Psyche) represents itself consciousness in its morally-indifferent (neither good nor bad) condition,[24] but it is charged with the germs of all the Elements of (future) phenomenal existence[25] (good and bad) and it is also the cause of all future actual sensations, therefore it is called the (fundamental) causeofensations.

[28. 4] „Produced from it the actual sensation is experience", i. e. it is produced (not by an external object, but by a germ lying dormant in this subliminal store of consciousness, i. e. in the Psyche). This means that it arises out of this sensation-store, it arises as something having its origin in that (store).

[28. 6] How does it arise out of it? (It arises in the following manner). The Mind-Store contains the undeveloped germs of all future life. Actual experience develops them. When developed, these germs again give rise to actual sensations homogeneous with them. Thus the actual sensation has its cause in the subliminal (dormant) one.[26]

[28. 10] However does it not follow (from the definition we have given that causality between subliminal and actual sensation is reciprocal). Subliminal consciousness can then also be represented as an experienced result and actual sensation as its cause? (It cannot be objected that subliminal sensation is latent): it is also the seat of a feeling, (a feeling, which is neutral), neither pleasant nor unpleasant, and it is also charged with some biotic force.[27] (It is therefore a cause), since it is impossible to be a cause without being charged with some force. This is stated in a stanza of the Abhidharma Sūtra:

All Elements of life
In the (sub)-consciousness are hidden,
As well as consciousness in them
They always mutually are
Effect and cause of one another.

[28. 17] (Answer). No! This deduction is wrong. (It cannot be followed that subliminal consciousness is accompanied by a kind of feeling and that this feeling is actually experienced as a retribution for former deeds), because such feeling is hardly noticeable, (it is latent). It is in any case not noticeable in the same degree as actual sensation is, nor can its existence be ascertained inferentially, as e. g. the upward movement of the sun, (being not perceived directly but inferable).

[28. 21] (There is indeed a general dependence of our subconscious store of ideas upon our previous conscious deeds).[28] Under the influence of good or bad deeds our fundamental subconscious Mind stores up the seeds of future experience which will contain their retribution;[29] under the influence of our indifferent (neutral) deeds it (stores up) the seeds of such future events which will contain the automatic continuation of preceding conditions (and no noticeable change in them). Thus[30] it is that the subconscious Mind-Store is the immediate efficient cause of all the (conscious) events of phenomenal life, but our actual (conscious) deeds [31] are only the general (remote) condition, not the immediate cause (in regard of our subconscious store of ideas). Therefore the deduction that our actual conscious deeds are the cause of the subconscious store (in the same degree as the latter is the cause of actual sensation) is wrong.

[28. 26] „Feeling is experiencing (of retribution)" (says Vasubandhu). It is being experienced in all its three varieties [32] (of pleasant, painful and neutral experience, being always the retribution for some former good, bad or indifferent deed respectively); in this sense it is experience. Life has a flavour; to relish the essence of this flavour in a corresponding experience is feeling. That is the reason why unsophisticated people are so attached to sense-objects and try exhaustively to enjoy them.[33]

[29. 2] Others maintain (that the term „experience" is wider in connotation, it embraces) not only feelings (enjoyed as retribution for former deeds), but also ideas (and sensations).

[29. 3] This is wrong. The comment (of Vasubandhu) denies it (in stating) that „feeling means experiencing (of retribution)". But the cognition of the object, (of the object itself, layed bare of all its qualities), does not differ from pure sensation. It is not at all right to represent this (pure sensation, which is the fundamental Element of existence, the Mind itself) as a mental evolute (or a mental phenomenon).[34]

[29. 5] (Vasubandhu says „an idea is thorough experience" this means e. g. that) an idea (or concept) is the condition of being further engrossed [35] in an emotion, e. g. of pleasure, in that sense that an abstraction is made of its characteristic features (and a concept is produced).

[29. 6] „The will, attention and other mental faculties urge our (nascent) consciousness" (says Vasubandhu, e. g. they urge it to proceed) to an experience or to (the formation of) a concept.[36]

[29. 7] We may also (explain the definitions of Vasubandhu in the following way. He says) „feeling is experience" because it experiences the object according to its (pleasant or unpleasant) nature and because it experiences the results of former deeds with a feeling of pleasure or (of pain). (He says „an idea is a thorough experience" meaning by this) that an idea (or concept) means definite knowledge,[37] because it makes definite that feature of the object which is the cause of our purposive action (about it). (He says that „the will, attention and other mental faculties activate sensation" meaning by this that these) faculties direct our cognition towards this or that object. Thus owing to the force of our will [38] our (nascent) consciousness adheres to this or that object.

The word „etc." (in Vasubandhu's expression „the will, attention etc.") refers to such mental faculties as desire etc.

§ 2. The dynamic aspect of the Creator of the World-Illusion. The 12 stages of the rotation of phenomenal life

Vasubandhu's comment

[V. 4. a. 2] That aspect of the Constructor of Appearance which manifests itself in the welve impediments (to Absolute Reality) will now be demon strated.[39]

[Stanza 1. 10—11]

Affected is the world by twelve Great Impediments:

1) By being „covered" and
2) By being „forestalled";
3) By being „conveyed" and
4) By being „determined";
5) By being „completed" and
6) By being „trebly definite";
7) By being „experienced" and
8) By being „summarized";
9) By being „fastened" and
10) By being „realized";
11—12) By „suffering", (by birth and death)
(Is this world tormented).
From the Constructor of Appearance
(These twelve impediments proceed).
They are divided in a group of three:
A group of two and a group of seven members.

So it is! (i. e. so does the Creator of the Wor'd-Illusion proceed in creating the illusion of a world living in the misery of ever reverting twelve stages of development).

Among these twelve Great Impediments 1) the one called „the cover" means (that the living world is affected) by a Transcendental Illusion which is an impediment to the perception of Absolute Reality, (because it makes us mistake phenomenal Appearance for Absolute Reality); 2) by being „forestalled" (or forecasted) means „through casting the germ-force left behind by former deeds into the run of a (present) consciousness; 3) „by being conveyed" means „by conducing consciousness to the place of rebirth"; 4) by „being determined" means that the (fate of) the new being is totally included in the embryo; 5) „by being completed" means (by the complete development) of the six sense-faculties; 6) „by being trebly defin.te" means by sensation (which is made definite by three elements, viz. consciousness, sense-organ and object); 7) „by being experienced" means „by feeling"; 8) „by being summarized" means „by the sexual desire" (of procreating) a new existence which was forestalled by former deeds; 9) „by being fastened" means „by attachments to cherished objects which are suppo;ed to be propitious (to the new existence)"; 10) „by realization" means that the deeds committed during a former existence are now producing their manifest retribution in a new existence; 11—12) „by suffering" means that the living world is tormented by birth, old age and death.

[V. 4. a. 6] Further:

These twelve impediments proceed
From the Constructor of Appearance.
They are divided in three groups:
A group of three, a group of two
And a group of seven members.

The three groups are 1) the Impediments of vice, 2) the Impediments of former deeds, 3) the Impediments of a present life. Illusion (1), Sexual desire (8) and Attachment (9) are the Impediments of vice. Former deeds (2) and fully developed present existence (with its willful deeds) (10) are the group of deeds. The remaining seven members are the impediments of a present life.

However they can also be divided in two groups of impediments, the one are causes and the other are results. (The first comprises the two first groups of the former division together, i. e.) the vices and the former deeds. Impediments which are results are the remaining seven members.

Divided in seven groups (the twelve Impediments) represent seven (different) causes, to wit 1) Transcendental Illusion is the cause of error; 2) the former deeds are the cause forecasting (a new existence); 3) (the intermediate run) of consciousness is the cause conveying (to a new place of existence); 4) the embryo and the six senses are the cause determining (the character of a new existence); 5) the cause of experiencing (retribution) is sensation and feeling; 6) the cause of the full realization of a new life are sexual love, attachment to cherished objects and (the responsible deeds) of a new existence; 7) the cause of suffering are birth, old age and death.

Sthiramati's comment

[29. 13] (The evolution of the Constructor of phenomena has been examined). It has been examined 1) wherefrom the evolution starts (i. e. from the subconscious Mind-Store); 2) what is its character (i. e. it is a process of causality); 3) what is its aim (i. e. exhaustive experiencing of retribution for all former deeds).

(This is its kinetic aspect as far as it represents a continuous run of conscious moments. Its kinetic aspect as far as it represents a continuous run of rebirths will be now examined). (Vasubandhu says, that the author here) proclaims the (doctrine of the twelve) Great Defilers (or Impediments to Pure Consciousness). The essence of that doctrine consists (in showing) how the (three kinds of) Great Impediments,[40] to wit 1) the fundamental vices (of human nature); 2) its (prehistory, i. e.) its former deeds and 3) the different stages in the development of life (from birth to death and from death to a new rebirth), produce, in a process of constant evolution, nothing but great suffering to the living beings.[41]

[29. 15] This (process) is not a manifestation of an (eternal) Soul.[42] It is the phenomenal outgrowth[43] exclusively from (that Element of Pure

Awareness which is) the Constructor of the world of phenomena (or our Productive Imagination). In order to demonstrate this, it is said:

(Tormented is the living world) —

1) by being covered and 2) being forecasted, 3) being conveyed and 4) being determined, 5) being completed and 6) by treble determination, 7) by being experienced and then 8) summarized, 9) being attached and 10) being realized, 11—12) by suffering it is tormented.

(What these terms mean will be now explained).

§ 3. The root cause of phenomenal life. Transcendental Illusion

[29. 19] The doctrine of the twelve members of Dependent Origination (or of the ever reverting life-rotation) is here represented as an aspect of the evolution (of the Constructor of phenomena). By his „being covered" is the world tormented (or affected). The words „tormented is the living world" though mentioned at the end refer to the whole series.

[29. 21] By what is it „covered" and how by being covered is it tormented? The answer is—it is covered by (Transcendental) Illusion. Illusion is a cover, because it is an impediment to the perception of reality. Indeed the essence of illusion is always non-perception (of reality). When (ultimate) reality is under cover, its perception cannot arise. (It cannot arise) in that domain of knowledge which is the domain ruled by (illusion).[44] Therefore (Transcendental) Illusion is an impediment to the perception of (absolute) Reality; it prevents the production of the Absolute knowledge (or of the Gnosis).

[29. 25] The Gnosis (or the knowledge of the Absolute Reality) is in first line[45] a supernatural (mystic) Intuition[46] (of the Saint in a moment of transic vision when he has reached the Path of Illumination). But when the trance is over, he retains a subsequent[47] conceptual knowledge of it, if it was (previously) prepared by learning, thought and profound meditation (while abiding in the Paths of Accumulating Merit and of Training). This is also called a knowledge of Absolute Reality, (because it follows in the track of its direct intuition).[48] Since illusion is an impediment to the perception of reality, it becomes the (root) cause of those prenatal biotic Forces which produce phenomenal life. Thus it is that the living world is tormented by this „cover", i. e. by Transcendental Illusion.

§ 4. The second member of Dependent Origination. The prenatal Biotic Forces.

[30. 5] „By forecasting" says the aphorism. We must connect it with the words „the living world is tormented". By whom is it „forecasted"? Where and what is „casted"? The answer is (as follows). By (prenatal)

Forces the seed (of a future life) representing a residue of former deeds (is „casted") into the Psyche (or into the run of subconsciousness).[49] The „Forces" (*saṃskāra*) here mean former deeds (*karma*), corporeal, vocal or mental, (of uncertain or) of absolutely certain retribution. (Etymologically the word *saṃskāra* means) „working together", i. e. „striving to compose a new life".[50] It casts (or composes) the not yet composed (new life). The word *saṃskāra* means here only this, all its other meanings (are not implied).[51]

[30. 9] And this (Force of former deeds needing retribution) is capable of composing a new life (which will be the retribution for them) only when it is swayed[52] by Transcendental Illusion. The mere existence (of former deeds cannot necessitate retribution in a new life). In this sense it is said (in the formula of the 12-membered Dependent Origination) that „prenatal forces are dependent on Transcendental Illusion". They indeed produce a new existence (of the simple man) who has not attained the Gnosis. They never can produce the rebirth of a Saint who has attained Omniscience.

[30. 12] However Transcendental Illusion is not only the fundamental condition of the efficiency of prenatal forces in composing a new life, (it also is a direct cause); the origination of a new life is produced by a combination[53] (of a fundamental condition and an efficient cause).

[30. 13—14] Indeed Transcendental Illusion is intimately associated with all phenomenalizing forces, and just as it is the associate cause[54] of the primary phenomenalizers, it also is the immediate cause of all volitions and actions produced under their influence.

[30. 16] It is (also) the (general) cause of all virtuous deeds which have been committed in the hope of receiving for them some mundane advantage, since, when they are produced, Transcendental Illusion (mistaking phenomenal for absolute reality) is their (inevitable) proximate satellite.

[30. 17] It is likewise the (general and proximate) cause (of all solemn resolutions of a Bodhisattva to devote all his life to the final Deliverance of all creatures, these resolutions having an absolutely certain) „immovable"[55] retribution (in a heavenly existence). (They nevertheless are products of Illusion, because they are) accompanied by a belief of quitting one's high position (for a still higher one).

[30. 18] In this sense is it stated that Transcendental Illusion is the cause of prenatal forces producing a new life.[56]

[30. 19] When it is here said (by Vasubandhu) „in consciousness" (i. e. prenatal forces throw the germ of a new existence into the run of a consciousness), what is meant is the (subliminal) Mind-Store (the Psyche), but not the actual run of consciousness, because (during a swoon etc.) there always can be a brake[57] in the run of actual consciousness, (a brake which) would prevent it to be transferred from one place into another. (This can be achieved only by the Psyche which never has a brake).[58]

[30. 21] Moreover the prenatal Forces cannot cast a seed into (the actual run of consciousness) because this actual run (having always the character of definite, either virtuous or bad deeds), cannot be associated with seeds having the contrary character.

[30. 22] (Vasubandhu) says „the germ-force of a new life is the residue of former deeds (wanting necessary retribution)".

[30. 23] What is indeed this germ-force produced by former deeds? It represents the seed of a future life, its cause. Just as a (proper) soil, (suitable) air etc. (are the necessary special conditions for raising a crop), (just so the seed of a new life develops under suitable conditions). (It has the character of an evolutional cause)[59] producing through a process of change and maturation,[60] in dependence on these conditions, a new life, (just as a rice-seed produces) at first the plant and then the rice crop.

[30. 25] (Vasubandhu) says „by depositing". Depositing is (here) a synonymous expression for „developing". Depositing (with reference to the seed of a new life is here) applied to the first moment of the development of the seed in this new section. (It cannot refer to the creation of an unprecedented seed).[61] Since there can be not a single new Element, neither in the life of the worldling nor in the pure life of a Saint, whose seed could be added (to the run of his subliminal consciousness, since the latter contains all seeds).[62]

[31. 2] Thus it is that prenatal Forces by developing in the Psyche the (old) seeds of future existencies (by this constant rebirth) torment the living beings.

§ 5. The third stage. Intermediate existence

[31. 4] (The aphorism says) „By conveyance", i. e. the world of the living is tormented by being (constantly) conveyed (to a new birth-place). Since it is not clear by whom and whereto it is conveyed, (Vasubandhu) says „(it is tormented) because consciousness leads it to a (new) birthplace". (This means)[63] that consciousness (of the moment of death) is followed by an uninterrupted run of conscious moments which, being influenced by (the moral character of) former deeds convey, or lead, the germ-force of a new life from the place of death to the place of rebirth.[64] Indeed thus exactly is it shown that the immediate cause (producing rebirth) is the consciousness of intermediate existence and not the former deeds (directly); the former consciousness is alone charged with the efficiency of former deeds, but a cause which has disappeared can impossibly produce any result,[65] (an intermediate existence must therefore necessarily be assumed).

[31. 10] However those individuals who are candidates for rebirth in the highest, immaterial worlds are reborn at that very place where they have died. How is it then to be understood that they are „conveyed" to the place of rebirth through an intermediate existence? (They are not subject to an intermediate existence since they have liberated themselves from the influence of former deeds. The necessity of intermediate existence) must be understood according to the requirements of each case separately, just as the necessity of (the next), the embryonic,[66] stage (which also does not exist for rebirth in the highest immaterial worlds).

§ 6. The fourth stage. The Embryo

[31. 13] (The stanza says) „By being totally enclosed", i. e., the living being is tormented by being „totally enclosed".[67] By whom, where and who is enclosed? It is answered — „by the fact that one's own future existence[68] is totally enclosed in an embryo."[69] (The embryo contains) mind-and-body or all the five groups (of the Elements of phenomenal life). Having been produced from the intermediate existence they pass through the first, the second, the third and the fourth phase of the development of the foetus up to that phase when hands and feet begin to appear,[70] but the six sense-faculties have not yet evolved. (This is the embryonic condition) of „Mind-Body as produced from (intermediate) consciousness" (says Scripture).

[31. 17] The difference of the class of beings (into which the embryo develops) is produced by the difference of the germ-force (contained in each embryo).[71] When the being is born[72] the individual existence is different according to whether it appears as a human being[73] or as a brute or as some other (class of being). Therefore it is said that the expression Mind-Body completely embraces an individual existence.

[31. 20] Further (the expression Mind-Body thus refers not to the embryo alone, but) it encloses also the whole of an individual's existence (from birth up to the moment) of death, since all its Elements from the beginning are potentially determined (in the embryo).[74]

[31. 21] (The expression Mind-Body can also be taken either collectively or partitively). Collectively it means all Elements of an individual existence indiscriminately. Partitively it points to the difference between its mental and physical Elements. In the same manner the expression „the causally interdependent Elements of existence" takes all these Elements collectively. The expression „the five groups of Elements" (takes them partitively).[75]

[31. 23] As regards supernatural rebirths (the stage of the developed) six sense faculties is then directly produced from (the last moment of) the consciousness (of the preceding existence). Therefore we must know that the rule according to which life begins with an embryo is conditional, i. e. (subject to exceptions).[76]

§ 7. The fifth stage. The Sense faculties

[32. 1] (The aphorism says) „By completion", i. e. the living being is affected „by becoming complete". (What does that mean?) By whom, when and who is becoming completed? (The answer is —) the body which was forecasted in the embryo becomes complete through (the development) of the six sense-faculties. Indeed the living being in the embryonic condition, since the organ of vision and other organs do not yet exist, is not quite complete. Albeit[77] the tactile sense exists even in this (embryonic) condition, it is by no means quite complete, since as a place[78] (upon which other sensations) are based it does not yet exist. But at that stage (of development when all) the six sense-faculties are present, since the organ of vision and the other sense-organs have fully evolved, their places[79] are also completely developed, and thus the tactile sense becomes quite complete, because the organ of vision and the other sense-organs which are based on it are quite developed.

[32. 8] How is it that the organ of vision and the other sense-organs are based on the tactile sense? (They are indeed based on it) since their activity is entirely dependent on the presence of the tactile sense (in these organs also).

[32. 8] The inner sense is also included among the six sense-faculties, (it is the sixth sense-faculty). Then the living being becomes complete, because all the places of sensation are completely developed in him. Since at the stage of the developed six sense-faculties, the main members[80] of the body, as well as the minor ones, are completely evolved,[81] inasmuch as all the places (where the organs are located) are fully developed, the living being becomes affected by (the completeness) of his six sense-faculties.

§ 8. The sixth stage: Sensation

[32. 13] (The stanza) says „By (the anticipation) of a perception through (the concurrence) of three (elements)".[82] The words „the living world is tormented (or affected)" must be connected with this. The three (elements) are the sense-faculty, the object and consciousness; their concurrence is meant. The process which is then started in the sense-organ and which anticipates the production of a feeling, either pleasant or (unpleasant or indifferent), which is the presentiment of its apprehension, (this process of a presentiment) is here called „sensation".

[32. 15] Just therefore[83] this process in the sense-organ is (metaphorically) called „contact" since there is some similarity between (the procedure of a physical) contact and a (mental) sensation.

[32. 17] Or this can also mean that when the six sense-faculties have evolved on this basis, a threefold procedure in our sensibility is started which is the presentiment of a feeling, either pleasant or unpleasant or indifferent.[84]

§ 9. The seventh stage. Feeling

[32. 19] (The stanza says „through experiencing". Vasubandhu comments) „through experiencing means „by feeling" (is the living world affected)".

First explanation. Experiencing means feeling, because feeling is emotionally experienced, i. e. enjoyed.

Second explanation. Feeling means experiencing, because (the consequences) of former good or (bad) deeds are experienced through a (pleasant or unpleasant) feeling.

Third explanation. Feeling is not the expedient through which the consequences of former deeds are being experienced, but feeling is itself experienced. Pleasant or (unpleasant) feeling is being experienced, (not the former deeds are being experienced). Engrossed[85] by pleasant (or unpleasant) feelings the living world is tormented (i. e. disturbed) by hatred, passion and infatuation.[86]

§ 10. The eighth stage. Sexual desire

[32. 24] The living being becomes affected „by summing up" (the preceding development). We however do not know (what that means), by whom and what is summed up? (The answer is —) „by sexual desire" (is it summed up). That new existence which was forecasted by the deeds of former births is thus summed up (when sexual desire arises).

[33. 1] Indeed (we have seen that prenatal biotic) forces develop in the (intermediate) consciousness[87] a new life by fostering its germ, and just as a corn-seed is moistened by water, so is this seed of a new life (as though moistened) by sexual desire. There is indeed in all classes of living beings a desire for the continuation (of the kind). When it is fixed upon the production of a new life and its definite realization through sexual love, this is here called „the summing up" (of the preceding development).[88]

§ 11. The ninth stage. Attachment to cherished objects

[33. 4] (The living being is tormented) „by being bound up". It is the place to ask by whom, who and to what is it „bound up"? (Vasubandhu) himself answers: „by attachments of that conscious (life which was forecasted) to cherished objects and other (ideas) which are favourable to (the continuation) of life". The essence of such attachment is natural inclination.[89] There are four kinds of attachments: attachment to cherished objects, to (habitual) views, to the belief in the efficacy of religious rites and to the belief in the existence of a (personal) Soul. To these (ideas which are believed) to be favourable to (the continuation of) existence the individual gets attached. Indeed consciousness following its natural inclinations abides by them.[90]

§ 12. The tenth stage. The full realization of a new life

[33. 9] (The aphorism says) „by turning its face". Since it is natural to expect from the hearer the question (what does that mean, Vasubandhu) himself answers, („it means that the living being is affected by the fact) that the deeds committed during a (former) existence are (now) producing their manifest retribution in (this) new existence".[91]

[33. 11] Indeed the former deeds (good or bad) are the cause producing a new life. The intermediate existence contains the germ-force which develops into a retribution-result (for these deeds). When this process is realized, the new existence, since it actually exists, is „manifesting its face" in the direct realization of what was merely forecasted. Thus (it is said that the living being) is affected (by the fact that the forecast is realized) in an actual existence, it is showing its face", (i. e. becoming manifest).[92]

§ 13. The eleventh and twelfth stages. The sufferings of a new birth on which a new death follows

[33. 14] (The aphorism says) „by suffering", this means that the living being is tormented by a (new) birth and by a (new) old age and death. Thus when from a (present) existence a new birth is produced the living being suffers, because his consciousness is swooned in the semen and in the blood during pregnancy. The mother suffers by the difficulty of digestion,[93] by the anxiety (of eating unsuitable) food and by (the restrictions) of cohabitation, by never being free from trouble (during pregnancy).[94] The offspring suffers also when it passes through this narrow and impure passage (out of the womb).

[33. 20] After being born the living being suffers again by a new old age indicated by baldness and grey hair, by death consisting in the dissolution of his mind and body, by the loss of his cherished youth and life.

[33. 22] (What does it mean when a being is called „living"?). Living means moving. It moves towards an evanescent state from a homogeneous (equally evanescent) condition.

[33. 24] (What does it mean when it is said that the living being is „affected"?). Affected means oppressed, (tormented). It is tormented by birth, old age, disease and death, tormented in all the three spheres of being (in hell, on earth and in the heavens), coming and going, in constant instantaneous change.[95]

[33. 25] Others again interpret the term „affected“ (tormented) as meaning „impure“.[96] It represents a twelve-membered (wheel) of interdependently originating (impure phenomena). Its essential aim is to indicate the state of complete (phenomenal) depression (in which the pure reality of the Absolute appears to us). By its eleven characteristics of illusion, („forecasting“ etc. up to the characteristic of final „misery“) it constitutes the direct counterpart of the pure (Reality of the Absolute). The consecution of the (twelve) items (of phenomenal oppression) indicates that every preceding member is the cause of the following one.

§ 14. The twelve members of Dependent Origination united in groups and regarded from different standpoints

[34. 4] (It is now asked) how many are the groups of impediments (which oppress the purity of Absolute Reality) as indicated by this twelvemembered Dependent Origination? The twelve members can be distributed— in a group of three, a group of two and a group of seven (members).

[34. 8] (Vasubandhu says) „So it is“ (i. e. so does the Creator of the world-illusion proceed in creating the illusion of a world living through twelve ever reverting stages of development). The word „so“[97] has the meaning of summarizing (a group) and opposing it (to the sequel).[98] (The first group contains the first, the eighth and the ninth members, viz. transcendental illusion, sexual desire and attachment). They are vices which are impediments, i. e. they are vicious impediments. (The second group contains) the impediment of prenatal forces (and the third group contains) the impediment of (all the stages of a current) life (i. e. the second and the tenth stages refer to prenatal forces of the present and of the future life, the remaining seven members refer to different features of the current phenomenal existence).

[34. 9] Indeed (as regards the first group) a vice when it is practiced is an impediment, since it produces depression in oneself and in others. Accordingly it is said in Scripture — „Influenced by passion, overpowered by passion a man commits willful actions which are hurtful for himself, he commits willful actions[99] which are hurtful for others, he also commits willful actions which are hurtful for both sides“. This refers also to actions committed under the influence of hatred and infatuation.

[34. 13] Prenatal forces (k a r m a) and the different phases of a present existence are also impediments, because, (even if they are not vices by themselves), they produce impediments (on the path towards the moral perfection of a Saint).

[34. 14] Indeed (we have seen that) under the influence of vices man commits actions which (necessarily) forecast a new existence (in which they must be retributed). But a Saint who has intuited the Absolute Truth, even if he commits some actions, is free from projecting rebirth (and retribution). With an ordinary man whose mind is subject to vices the rising passions convert the germ of a future life into actual existence and thus his rebirth, through the bond of an intermediate existence, becomes the cause of a great impediment (on the path towards the attainment of Final Deliverance). Therefore the life of a Saint, his mind being liberated from the influence of vice, will not be continued in an intermediate existence (or in a new birth, which would be objectless).

[34. 18] Thus it is that the actions (of the ordinary man) whether good or bad, since they require his mental and corporeal efforts and must be retributed in a future existence, are impediments.

The (run of a present) existence, (its seven different stages), is also an impediment (for the prospective Saint), since it makes him subject to all kinds of misfortune (and disturbs the quiet concentration of his mind).

§ 15. The division of the twelve members in three and in two groups

[34. 20] Since those impediments which have the character of causes constitute two groups, the group of vices and the group of former deeds (and since all the remaining ones have the character of their results, we have together) three groups.[100] The impediments having the character of vices are illusion, love and attachment. They all have the character of vice. The impediment of willful deeds (requiring retribution) are prenatal forces and (the willful deeds) of a current existence. Both have the character of being willful. The difference between them however is the following one. Actually committed actions of a past existence are real prenatal forces. The deeds of a current existence are only potential causes (of a retribution in a future life).[101] The remaining (seven) members; to wit, the intermediate life, the embryo, the six sense-faculties, sensation, feeling, a new birth, (new) old age and death, since they constitute the run of a current existence, are the impediments (of a present life).

[35. 1] The impediments are double when regarded as causes and results: impediments having the character of causes refer to those members which have the character of vices and actions (requiring) retribution; impediments having the character of results refer to all the remaining (seven) members. [102]

[35. 3] Between them the class of willful deeds (requiring retribution) and of vices has the character of a cause, since its function is to produce a rebirth consisting of a life which, starting in an internediate existence culminates in an experience (pleasant or unpleasant, the retribution), (but finally always contains) old age, death and lamentation.

The impediments having the character of a result consist of the remaining (seven) members, viz. intermediate existence etc., because they represent the result of former deeds requiring retribution and of vices.

§ 16. The division in seven groups

[35. 6] This same (twelve-membered) Dependent Origination (which has been interpreted above as the phenomenal counterpart of pure Absolute Reality) can be reduced to a series of seven causes which will represent 1) the cause creating the error (of phenomenal reality), 2) the cause forecasting (a new life), 3) the cause leading to it, 4) the cause determining it, 5) the cause experiencing it, 6) the cause bringing it (to full eclosion), and (finally) 7) the cause exhibiting the lamentable misery (of the whole job).

1) The cause creating „the error" of phenomenal reality is Transcendental Illusion. In the grips of this illusion ordinary men are mistaken in regard of Absolute Reality and consider evanescent things as eternal substances.

2) The cause „forecasting" a new life consists of prenatal (biotic) forces, since they throw into a consciousness the seed of one of the four modes of procreation.

3) The cause „leading" (existence from one place to another is the intermediate run) of consciousness, since owing to it the being which died in a certain place is transferred to the place of rebirth.

4) The cause „determining" (the new existence) embraces the embryonic state of mind-body and the development in it of the six sense-faculties. (It is so called because) the being which has been transferred into the place of rebirth becomes now „determined" in regard of the class of beings in which he is going to exist.

[35. 14]. In the preceding (classification of the twelve members) the cause called „determination" referred only to the embryonic condition of life and its viviparous or other mode of procreation. But now (in this classification of seven causes) it embraces also the next condition, viz. the development of the six sense-faculties, because it takes in consideration the supernatural mode of birth, (where there is no embryonic condition in the womb, but beings appear straight off with all their developed sense-faculties).[102]

[35.16] It is also possible that in the former classification the mere determination (of the class) of being is taken in consideration, whereas in this (classification) the incomplete embryonic state as well as the complete condition of developed sense-faculties, both are considered (as representing „determination"). There is no contradiction (between the two classifications).

[35. 18] 5) The cause consisting in „experiencing" the new life consists of (the two items), sensation and feelings, because the retribution which is being experienced consists (of two items), feeling and its cause (sensation).

[35. 20] 6) The cause „bringing" (the full realization of a new existence) consists in love, attachments and new full life. Every ordinary man experiences the result of his former deeds and strives for enjoying some (pleasant) feelings. When his desires are in full swing he becomes attached to his cherished objects with a passionate reaction to their acquisition or loss. Being (reinforced) by these attachments, his former deeds, those that must be retributed in the (present) new existence, being in the condition of a germ-force and being gradually transformed, take a course of development towards receiving their forstalled retribution. This constitutes the full realization of a new existence. It thus „brings" (to full eclosion) that existence which has been forestalled (and made necessary) by former willful deeds. „Brings" (into realization) means the same as „manifests its face" (in a realization). Thus (the three items of) love, attachment and fully realized existence are together called the „realization" cause.

Another explanation

[36. 1] The three members — sexual desire, attachments and a full life — are a „realization" cause (not because they realize a forestalled existence, but because), in accordance with the inclinations (of this new existence produced) from sexual desire, they realize a new k a r m a, (they become charged with a new force which will reap retribution in a next following existence).[103]

[36. 3] 7) The cause creating despondency (and lamentation) is (constant) new birth, old age and death. Indeed a rebirth among this or that class of beings is (necessarily) forecasted, and thus in every new existence the sufferings of birth, old age and death are being experienced, as well as all sorts of other misery and grief, and an infinite variety of corporeal and mental sufferings and (unpleasant) efforts.

[36. 5] By pointing to the threefold division of all impediments, (the impediments of (vice, of prenatal forces and of life stages) it is shown that phenomenal existence has a general and a special cause. Indeed vice (and illusion) are the general phenomenalizing cause of existence, just as the soil is the general cause of all growing plants. The influence of the biotic force of former deeds, on the other hand, is the special cause (determining the class of beings), just as the seed determines the kind of a future plant. The new existence always agrees in kind with its seed.

§ 17. Other meanings of the twelve-membered formula of Dependent Origination

[36. 9] (The twelve-membered formula of Dependent Origination) also shows (that the process of phenomenal life) should not be divided in three sectors, to wit, life past, future and present,[104] but it represents (one continuous beginningless run) of deeds, vices and their results.

[36. 10] When the series is divided in two sectors, (the sector of causes and the sector of results, the aim is to emphasize that the world-process is quite impersonal), there neither is any active agent who produces it nor any passive being who (enjoys it or) suffers from it, (it merely is an impersonal beginningless run of causes and effects).[105]

[36. 11] But (the formula) can also have moreover (the following meaning). Former deeds and vices (necessitating retribution) are here the unique source of phenomenal life, since we see that their presence or absence is always followed by the presence or absence of rebirths. (The Saint is never reborn.) Therefore rebirth (or phenomenal existence, the whole of it, all the 12 members) is only a result. We cannot distinguish here between cause and result. Every member contains (potentially) all the five groups, (i. e. the totality of the Elements of life).

[36. 15] However (when the twelve-membered formula is regarded as referring) to the seven causes (of phenomenal life), we again can distribute it in two parts, the essence of the one will be forecasting, the essence of the other — realization. (The former embraces the first seven members of the series, the latter the remaining five ones). In the (first) seven members, it is shown, by whom is the new existence forecasted, how is it forecasted and what is (really) forecasted. The realization part, on the other hand, shows in its five members, by whom is the forecasted existence realized, how is it realized and what is (at all) realized, as well as the lamentable misery of the (whole job).

[36. 20] Indeed, by whom is it forecasted? By former deeds dependent on a transcendental illusion. How is that? (Ordinary humanity) being ignorant in regard of the Absolute makes efforts to perpetrate deeds either good or bad or prayers for final retribution.

[36. 22] How is a life forecasted by former deeds? By fostering its seed in consciousness und by determining (the character) of its future development.

[36. 24] What is (really) forecasted? The embryo of a new life, its sense-faculties, sensations and feelings respectively (are forecasted).

[36. 25] The thus forecasted existence by whom is it realized? It is realized in the manner stated above, by the „attachments" (of phenomenal existence) i. e. prenatal (forces) produce the experiences (pleasant or unpleasant) of a current life. Dependent on them a sexual desire is produced (and a new existence), dependent on which (the „attachments" realize a new full life).

[36. 27] How is it realized by this (attachment to cherished things)? By converting to actual existence the (latent force) of former deeds which is present in consciousness[106] in the potential condition of a germ-force.

[37. 1] Manifold indeed are the forces of reproduction which are (latent) in our consciousness, because it is influenced by various prenatal forces und because it is determined in its character by that kind of attachment which is natural in it. An existence is here called fully realized existence only because it will have a continuation in a next following one.

[37. 4] Now, what does this realization (at all) represent? It is the final appearance of that existence which was forestalled in the embryonic condition and (its further development).

[37. 5] When this existence is arrived at, why is it a cause of lamentable misery? It contains old age and death, the loss of the cherished youth and life.

[37. 6] But is not the cause „conveying" (life from the place of death to the place of rebirth, i. e. the intermediate existence between two rebirths, the third member of the series) superfluous? No! it is not superfluous. It repudiates the belief that life being annihilated in death a completely new existence is produced at birth, (whereas life is beginningless, every birth is really a rebirth).

§ 18. Summary of the theory of the Constructor of Appearance

[37. 8] Now, all these (twelve) Impediments, (the phenomenalizers of the Absolute) spring up from (that unique Element which is) the Constructor of the world of Appearance, because they all depend on consciousness and its evolutes. Indeed it has been already stated that „consciousness and its evolutes (our ideas) are the (real) constructors of Appearance in all the three spheres of existence". (Everything depends on consciousness and is mental). Such is the summarized meaning (of the theory) of the Constructor (of the world of phenomena). Its detailed explanation has the aim to facilitate comprehension. Its succinct formulation has the aim to assist memory. Both therefore have been here given.

[37. 13] (Thus nine chief characteristics of the principle of the Constructor of Appearance have been here given). 1) Its positive characteristic is given in the words (1. 1) „the Constructor of phenomena exists". 2) Its negative characteristic is given in the words (1. 1) „it does not contain" the duality (of subject and object). 3) Its particular essence, (its essence so far as transformed in particular things) is expressed in the words (1. 3) „consciousness appears as transformed in ideas of things, of bodies, of Ego's, and of sensations". 4) Its general essence (consisting in the three aspects of every thing cognizable) is expressed in the words (1. 5) „imagined (essence), interdependent (essence) and the Absolute". 5) The essence of the expedient which leads to the realization of the unreal character (of the phenomenal world) is given in the words (1. 7) „basing on the perception (of reality) the non-perception (of the phenomenal) is produced". 6) The essence of its division is given in the words (1. 8) „all consciousness and all ideas in all the three spheres of life are nothing but Constructors of Appearance". 7) The indication of the synonym (of the term consciousness) is contained in the words (1. 8)

„what in respect of the (pure) thing itself is called consciousness (i. e. pure awareness) is called in regard of qualified objects ideas (or mental phenomenons". 8) The definition of its dynamical essence is contained in the words (1.9) „the one is fundamental (static), the other experiential (kinetic)". 9) Its essence as containing (the twelve) Impediments (on the Path towards the Absolute) is contained in the words (1.10) „By a cover, by being forecasted, by being conveyed, by being determined etc.".

Chapter V

THE ABSOLUTE

§ 1. The five topics to be considered in connection with the problem of the Absolute

Vasubandhu's comment

[V. V. a I.] After having thus examined (that Element which is) the Constructor of phenomena, (Maitreya) declares how the Absolute [1] should be conceived.

[Stanza 1. 12]

The Absolute, its essence and its names
Their meanings and its division
The proof (of its existence),
(Five topics) must briefly be examined.

Sthiramati's comment

[38. 1] (Vasubandhu says) „after having thus examined (the Element which) is the Constructor of phenomena", (after having examined namely) its nine characteristic aspects, „(Maitreya) declares how the Absolute should be conceived". What indeed is the narrow bond [2] between (the two conceptions) here (alluded to)? He (Maitreya) has started by postulating (the reality of two great principles), a Constructor of phenomena and an Absolute. And just as pure (Absolute Reality) [3] is preceded by impure (phenomenal reality),[4] just so the knowledge of the absolute Totality [5] of all Elements of existence reposes on a knowledge of the particular Elements [6] (which are the Constructors of phenomena). That is the reason why after having thoroughly examined the Constructor of (particular) phenomena, the author immediately goes over to a thorough examination of the manner in which the Absolute should be conceived. He says „its essence and its names", etc.

[38. 7] Its „essence" consists in the denial of the (ultimate) Reality (of one thing and in the denial of the ultimate) Unreality (of another thing); (it denies the ultimate Reality of the division into subject and object, by maintaining their Relativity, and it denies the Unreality of their subjacent monistic Absolute, by maintaining its ultimate Reality). By such a Relativity (and subjacent monistic Reality) all its different varieties are embraced.[7]

[38. 8] (The second topic are its synonyms). A synonym is another name. (The third topic is the special meaning of every synonym). The „meaning of a synonym" is the reason for using a special name (in a special context) according to (the shade) of meaning connoted by it.

[38. 9] (The fourth topic is „division"). The Absolute is like empty space, it can have no essential division,[9] (it is unique), but nevertheless, although undifferentiated[10] (in itself), it can assume and reject occasional impurities[11] (and thus be differentiated indirectly).[12]

[38. 11] Another (explanation of the „division" is the following one). (Sometimes an eternal) Soul (and sometimes a plurality of ultimate) Elements are erroneously assumed (as absolute Realities). (All such theories are here rejected and replaced by two theories, the theory of the Relativity of all the supposed ultimate Elements of existence, and the theory of the really ultimate monistic Absolute subjacent to them). (The rejected realities can be arranged in) a system of sixteen items. (They can be regarded as representing indirectly a system of 16 varieties of the Absolute Reality subjacent to a system of 16 varieties of Relative Reality).[13]

[38. 11—12] (The fifth topic is the „proof" of the existence of the varieties of the Absolute). It represents the argument which establishes these varieties of Relativity (and the unique ultimate Reality subjacent to them).[14]

§ 2. Another explanation of the five topics

[38. 13] What is the further reason that the Absolute should be considered from these (five) points of view? It is as follows.

1) Those who aspire to become omniscient Saints[15] must know the essence of Absolute Reality, because the Absolute represents the pure object, (purified from all the filth of phenomenal existence, the object which they strive to cognize).[16]

2) They must know it by its names, in order not to be led astray when in different scriptural works it is alluded to by different names.

3) They must know it according to the (precise) meaning of these names, because when the identity of the meaning of all these names is realized,[17] we will know with precision that the Absolute is the absolutely pure objectivity of the transcendent world.

4) They must know it according to its „division". (The division really affects only the phenomenal aspect of reality, but) its absolute purity is attained by removing all the influence of phenomenal impurity. Therefore in order to stimulate the effort for the (gradual) extinction of (all vestiges of) phenomenal impurity, the Absolute must be known according to its (indirect) division.[18]

5) They must know the argument establishing the division, because when this argument will be well known it will be easy to understand that the Absolute, although it represents an undifferentiated unity, is nevertheless divided (indirectly, through the degrees of its attainment by the Saint).

§ 3. The definition of the Absolute

Vasubandhu's comment

[V. 5. a. 2] How is the essence of the Absolute to be conceived?

[Stanza 1. 13]

The unreality of both
(The object and the subject),
And the reality (subjacent) of this unreality,
(This is the essence of the Absolute).

T'is neither (exclusively) assertion,
Nor is it (exclusively) negation.[19]

(And the Constructor of phenomena)
Is neither different from it
Nor is it quite the same.

„The unreality of both", i. e. of the apprehended object and the apprehending subject. The real existence of this kind of unreality, (i. e. the merger of the object and the subject) constitutes the essence of the Absolute. It is thus precisely established that the Absolute is (Monism, i. e.) that (ultimate) reality which excludes (every dialectical duality).

[V. 5. a. 3] (Now) the reality (subjacent) of this unreality is —

Neither an assertion nor a negation.

Why is it not a mere assertion? Because it is a negation of duality. Why is it not a mere negation? Because it is an assertion of the (monistic) reality subjacent to the negation of duality. This is the essence of the Absolute.

From the Constructor of the (particular) phenomena it is —

Neither separate
Nor is it essentially the same.

If it were separate, then the universal would be separate from its particular and this is an impossibility.[20] Indeed (e. g.) the universal instantaneousness of all the real Elements of existence which is inherent in every single instantaneous Element (is not something separate from the latter).[21] Neither is the general phenomenality (inherent in every particular phenomenon something separate from the latter).[22] But if the Constructor of phenomena would be quite the same thing as the

Absolute, the latter would not represent that (transcendent) Pure Reality (which the Superman alone can cognize directly in a moment of mystic intuition), nor would it be a Universal Ens (and therefore eternally the same). It is thus very clearly established that the essence of the Absolute is something quite free of being either identical or separate from the Constructor of phenomena.[23]

Sthiramati's comment

[38. 20] (Vasubandhu asks) „how is the essence (of the Absolute) to be conceived?" The „essence" has been mentioned in the first place, therefore the first question concerns the (essence of the Absolute). It must be conceived as —

The unreality of both,
(The object and the subject).
And the reality (subjacent) of this unreality.
This is the essence of the Absolute.

„Of both", i. e. of the apprehended (part) and of the apprehender (part). (Their unreality) in the Constructor of phenomena, or (their unreality) owing to (the unique reality) of the Constructor of phenomena, means that they do no exist as (two separate) realities, since (their relation) is constructed by productive imagination. And the reality of this (double) non-existence (the reality subjacent to the non-existence of separate Matter and to the non-existence of separate Mind is the reality of Monism), the essence of the Absolute.

[38. 25]. Owing to the requirements of prosody (the abstract term **ś ū n y a t ā** meaning the „foundation" of the Relative i. e. the Absolute) appears here (in the stanza) without the generalizing abstract suffix (tā). (It should be regarded as understood, although) not expressed.[24]

[38. 26] (Vasubandhu says) „and the reality of (this) unreality". What are they both (this reality and this unreality?). The non-existence of duality is necessarily itself a reality. If this were not the case, the duality would exist (and there would be no Monism).

[39. 3] Therefore (Vasubandhu) delivers himself in the following way [25] — „It is thus precisely established, that the Absolute is (Monism, i. e.) the ultimate reality (underlying) the absence (of every duality)". Its essence excludes the reality (of the subject-object Relativity).

[39. 4] **A n o b j e c t i o n.** Since the term „non-existence" means denial of existence, the word „reality" (in the phrase „the reality of this unreality") is superfluous. The meaning would remain just the same if this word were omitted, („unreality" simply and „reality of unreality" mean quite the same).

A n s w e r. No, it is not superfluous! Because if it were simply said „the unreality of two things" [26] constitutes the essence of the

Absolute (without adding the words „and the reality of this unreality") it would mean the non-existence of two things, as e. g. the non-existence of two horns on the head of a hare; it could not follow (that the unreality of one thing *eo ipso* means the reality of the other), as e. g. the unreality of the phenomenal world *eo ipso* means the reality of the Absolute.[27]

[39. 8) Thus it is that we maintain that the Absolute is absence of duality; and that this absence (of duality) is present in (the Thing-in-Itself which is) the foundation of all phenomena. The Absolute is a positive concept, the counterpart of a negation. It is clearly shown that it means the sum total of all the Elements of Reality.[28]

[39. 11] (The following explanation is) also given. The word „non-existence" has many meanings. When it is therefore maintained that Absolute Reality is absence of Duality, we do not know in which of its many meanings the term „non-existence" should be taken, (whether it means the preceding non-existence of a thing before its production, or its subsequent non-existence after its destruction, or mutual non-existence of two things the one in the other, or absolute non-existence in every respect). In order to show that it here means absolute non-existence[29] it is said that the Constructor of phenomena (i. e. the Thing-in-Itself) contains the non-existence of duality, (its absolute nonexistence).

Second explanation

[39. 13] Indeed neither the previous non-existence of a thing before its production, nor its following non-existence (after its destruction) can be said to exist anywhere except in the substratum (of this production or destruction). Nor could the mutual non-existence of two things the one in the other be said to reside in one substratum, since it (always) resides in two different things.

[39. 15] (Remains total non-existence). Indeed since reality[30] assumes (in our system) a negative essence, what is here declared is this, that just total non-existence of (the division into) object and subject constitutes the (monistic) Absolute.

[39. 17] But if the essence of the Absolute is thus a negation, how can it be called the Highest Object?[31] It is so called because it is the object of a Gnosis (of the highest mystic intuition of the Saint in trance), not because it is a real thing (v a s t u).

[39. 18] Be it so![32] This „reality of unreality"[33] however does not exist (at all), because it is —

Neither an affirmation, nor a negation.

[39. 21] Why not an affirmation? Because it denies duality. If it were a (simple) affirmation it would not be a „total non-existence" of duality, we would not have the principle[34] of „unreality imagined as reality".

[39. 22] Why is it neither (exclusively) a negation? Because it is an affirmation of that (monistic) reality which is subjacent to the dualistic unreality. The denial of this duality is not a denial of the subjacent reality.

[39. 24] Without this (reality of negation of duality) we would have an affirmation of duality,[35] and we would not have (vindicated our) principle of unreality imagined as a reality. Just as the principle of Impermanence and the principle of phenomenal Misery (the first Truth of Buddhism) is neither affirmation nor negation,[36] since their essence consists in this, that human beings erroneously imagine momentary things as stable and miserable things as blissful.[37]

[40. 2] (Now, if the Absolute is nothing but the reality subjacent to unreality and the Constructor of phenomena is also nothing but a point-instant of reality subjacent to the construction of an unreal phenomenon), if the Absolute is thus an attribute of the Constructor of phenomena, is it something separate from the Constructor, or is it identical with him?

[40. 3] (Having also this question in his mind) Vasubandhu answers „T h i s i s t h e e s s e n c e o f t h e A b s o l u t e", n a m e l y „t h e R e a l i t y o f U n r e a l i t y".

[40. 4] On the other side (as an answer to the same question may be quoted the general proposition that) affirmation itself is nothing beyond the negation of a negation, (it is a double negation, i. e. it has a dialectical structure, being both positive and negative).[38] Therefore in regard of the (single) Constructor of unreality the Absolute (being the universal principle of all such constructions) is —

Neither a separate thing
Nor is it essentially the same.

[40. 7] „If it were a separate thing (says Vasubandhu) then the Universal would be separate from its particular (and) this is an impossibility". Why is it an impossibility? If the Universal were a separate reality, different from the particular (under it), then the Universal would be a reality (by itself), just as every other reality. If then the Universal and the particular were two separate realities, the one could not be the attribute of the other, and we would be obliged to find[39] for this second reality (i. e. for the Universal) a further reality (in guise of its respective Universal) and so on *in infinitum.*[40]

[40. 10] „Just as instantaneousness or phenomenality" (says Vasubandhu), i. e just as instantaneousness is not separate from a particular instantaneous Element, and just as phenomenality is not separate from a particular phenomenon, just so (is the universal „Elementness" of all Elements of reality not separate from the particular Element and) the universal foundation of all things relative is not separate from the particular relative Element.[41]

[40. 12] But if the (particular) Constructor of phenomena (says Vasubandhu) would be quite the same thing as the (universal) Absolute, the latter would not represent that (transcendent) Pure Reality (which the Superman alone can cognize directly in a moment of mystic intuition), nor would it be a Universal Ens (and therefore eternally the same).

[40. 13] Purification is that through what something is made pure, (the instrument of purity), it is the Path towards the attainment of Buddhahood. If it were not different from the particular Thing(-in-Itself), it could not represent the aim of the Path, just as every other particular Thing (does not represent it). Neither could it represent a Universal Ens, if it were not different from the particular Thing. If that were the case, it would then be mutually different with any other particular thing, as it is the essence of particular things (to be mutually different from one another). Its Universal character would then be lost.

[40. 17] We can also[42] (argue thus): if the particular Thing-in-Itself (i. e. the particular Absolute) were not something different from this (Universal Absolute), the character of reality (in the particular things) would not be differentiated and consequently there would also be no Universality, because the existence of Universals depends upon the existence of (respective) particulars.

[40. 19] We further[42] can (argue thus): if we will concentrate our mental efforts on the particular Thing-in-Itself, (although it be transcendental), we will never attain the Pure (Transcendent Reality). This Pure Object is so called because it must be made pure (by the efforts of the Saint on his Path of Purification). Otherwise (if the knowledge of particular things could produce saintliness) every living being would be a Saint.[43]

[40. 21] Objection. (We thus maintain that the Absolute, being the Universal Thing-in-Itself, is neither separate nor is it quite the same as the Constructor which represents the particular Thing-in-Itself. Now the Jaina philosophers are known by their theory of universal indetermination which allows them at the same time to affirm and to deny every predicate in regard of every subject). When we maintain that (the Absolute) is indeterminable as being at the same time neither separate nor identical (with the Constructor), do we not side with the Jainas? Indeed that philosopher who maintains that a thing which is a reality (a real Element) is indeterminable as to whether it is the same or not (in regard of another real thing) has embraced the Jaina view.[44]

[40. 23] Answer. The accusation (of Jainism) is not founded, since our Absolute is not a thing, (it is a Universal and we only maintain that a Universal is neither quite the same nor is it separate from the particular under it).[45]

[40. 24] Conclusion. We have thus elucidated the essence of this our Absolute from all (kinds of view-points, viz.) 1) it has a negative essence (as a negation of duality), 2) it has a positive essence (subjacent to) the negative one,[16] 3) it has a monistic essence (as the merger of object and subject), 4) it has an (undefinable) essence, being neither identical nor separate (from the Thing-in-Itself).[17]

§ 4. Other names of the Absolute and their meanings

Vasubandhu's comment

[V. 5. a. 6] What terms must be considered as synonyms (of the term Absolute)? (The stanza 1.14 says) —

Reality Self-same, the Highest Truth,
Reality Undifferentiated, the Ultimate Pure Object,
The foundation of (the Buddha's) powers,
These are in short the synonyms of Absolute.

[V. 5. b. 1] What is to be considered as the (precise) meaning of these terms:

[Stanza 1. 15] They mean in order quoted:

1) Never different and 2) never wrong,
3) (All difference) extinguished,
4) The object by the Saint intuited,
5) Foundation of his (mystic) powers.

1) It is Self-same Reality (or Suchness), because not being subject to change it remains eternally the same. 2) It is the Highest Truth in the sense of not being an object of (Transcendental) Illusion, (being cognized by non-discursive, direct, mystic intuition). 3) It is (Reality) undifferentiated because extinct in it are the distinctive marks (of all objects), and differentiation exists no more. 4) It is the Ultimate Pure Object, (it is the Transcendent World) because it is the object known to the Omniscience of the Saint (alone), it is the object of his highest mystic intuition. 5) It is the foundation of his (miraculous) powers, because it is the cause producing them. Indeed the (wonder working) attributes of the Saint arise on this foundation (of absolute knowledge).[18] The term dhātu in this passage means „cause".

Sthiramati's comment

[41. 1] Now, after having finished with the definition of the Absolute, its different names must be considered —

[Stanza 1. 14]

Reality Self-same, the Highest Truth,
Reality undifferentiated, the Ultimate (Pure) Object,
The foundation of the Buddha's Powers,
These are in short the synonyms of Absolute.

[41. 4] A synonym is (another) name, the designation[19] of the same thing through another word. (It really means) „a turn" of names, because all these names can „in turn" be used for the designation of the same thing. This same Absolute is designated in different scriptural works by these (five) different names.

[41. 6] These five names are (however only) the principal designations arranged in metrical form. There are other names not mentioned in this list. They can be supplemented from Scripture,[50] e. g. Non-duality (or Monism), the (Transcendent) World (mystically cognized) in direct intuition, „Elementness" (or absolute whole of all the Elements of existence), Reality Unutterable, Reality Undistroyable,[51] Reality Uncaused, Nirvāṇa etc. etc.

[41. 8] How are we to understand the meaning of the term „synonym" (in this context)? (Synonyms are different words having one meaning, but here it is assumed, that each has its own different sense?) This is to be explained in the following way. All these terms are not metaphors,[52] but the words themselves have all the same general meaning and each term at the same time expresses a different shade of it.[53] (This is shown in the next stanza, 1. 15).

They mean in order quoted:

1) Never different, 2) Never Illusion,
3) (All difference) extinguished.
4) (Transcendent) object by the Saint intuited,
5) Foundation of his (mystic) powers.

[41. 13] (Vasubandhu explains) „it is (Reality) Self-same (or Suchness) in the sense of (never) being „other", i. e. of (never) changing. This means that being the expression of the core of the reality (in every thing), it remains „eternally self-same". „Eternally" means in all times. It does not change, because it is not produced by causes, (it is eternally the same).

[41. 16) It is the Highest Point of Truth, because it „never is Illusion". Truth is the exact[54] (knowledge of reality), the non-Illusion. The highest point means the limit. The highest point of truth, the limit of truth, is that point beyond which there is nothing to be cognized.

[41. 18] In what (sence) does Self-same Reality (or Suchness) represent the limit of the cognizable? In the sense of being cognized (by the Omniscient only), by that (supra-mundane) intuition[55] of the Saint which is quite pure of all (mundane) illusion.[56]

[41. 19] (Vasubandhu's words) „in the sense of never being illusion" (also mean) „in the sense of neither assuming any reality[57] (where it is not), nor denying it (where it exists)".

[41. 20] (Vasubandhu) indicates the cause of just this (feature viz.) „it is not a point of (Transcendental) Illusion".[58] Indeed (what is) Transcendental Illusion? It is conceptual thinking (or logic in general). Since (the Absolute) cannot be cognized by conceptual, (logical methods), it is a point free from Transcendental Illusion. (It can be cognized only by the direct mystic intuition of the Superman).

[41. 22] (Vasubandhu says) „because extinct are (all) distinctions".[59] The extinction[60] of all distinctions means non-manifoldness (or Monism). In order to point it out it is said „(it is the non-manifold) because there is in it at all no differentiation". The Absolute Reality is „devoid" of alltogether every differentiation, e. g. the differentiation into realities caused and uncaused,[61] therefore it is called („devoidness" or) differencelessness. It is differenceless, because every differentiation is absent. Undifferentiated means just (this feature) of the absence of differentiation (or Monism).

[42. 2] (Vasubandhu says, „the Absolute is called the ultimate, pure object), because it is the (transcendent) object intuited by the direct intuition of the (omniscient) Saint". There is a highest, supra-mundane direct intuition, its object is the ultimate pure object. Pointing to it (Vasubandhu) says „it is the ultimate (pure) object, because it is the object intuited by the direct intuition[62] of the Saint, (the Omniscient)".

[42. 4] (Vasubandhu further says) „it is the source of Buddhas powers, because it is the cause producing the (miraculous) faculties of the Saint". (The term d h a r m a-d h ā t u is here used in a special sense). The term d h a r m a „attribute" refers to the special attributes (or powers) of the Saint, beginning with his powers of rightly intuiting[63] (the Buddhist theory of the Elements of existence) and other attributes up to his eight degrees of Liberation[64] (from the bonds of Materiality) and (final) Omniscience.[65] Their d h ā t u means their cause. By way of explanation[66] he says „because the powers of the Saint arise from that source".[67] The word d h ā t u is also used in the sense of an Element of existence serving as a support for its own particularity and for the secondary Elements (evolved from the primary ones), therefore (says Vasubandhu) „this word has here the meaning of a cause",[68] as e. g. when the expressions the „cause (or source) of gold", „the cause (producing) copper" are used in the sense of a „mine" (producing these metals).

[42. 9] All other names of the Absolute found in different scriptural works can be explained as to the identity of their import according to the method here indicated, (i. e. they express the main idea of Monism each in its special way).

§ 5. The varieties of the Absolute

V a s u b a n d h u's c o m m e n t

[V. 5. b. 4] The Absolute is unique, there are no various Absolutes. In what sense can we speak of its varieties? (The answer is given in stanza 1. 16):

It either is phenomenalized
Or it is the Pure Absolute.

These are the two (main) varieties of the (unique) Absolute. When is it phenomenalized, when is it the real Absolute? (In answer to this the stanza states):

It either is impure or it is pure.

It is impure when regarded as situated behind phenomenal reality. It is pure, when this impurity is cleared away.

[V. 5. b. 6] If it can change into impure and change into pure, it then possesses changing qualities. It then cannot escape from being impermanent. How can it then remain (eternally the same)? It is so (i. e. eternally the same and changeless) because —

Its purity is admitted,
As we admit the purity
Of (elementary) water,
Of gold or ether.

When cleared of accidental impurity its essence never changes.

Sthiramati's comment

[42. 12] Since the essence of the Absolute consists in this that there is no difference between the apprehended object and the apprehending subject, it is impossible to imagine how indeed can a division (of that unique Absolute be produced)? Therefore a question about this is raised. It has also been stated above that after the synonyms the varieties must be indicated. That is (also) the reason why (Vasubandhu) asks „how is the possibility of varieties in the Absolute to be understood?" (The answer is the following one). The Constructor of phenomenal Appearance, (the Thing-in-Itself, represents the Absolute) as manifested in the phenomenal world.[69] When it is removed remains the pure Absolute. In both these conditions, of phenomenal impurity and purification, there is nothing but the Absolute itself which is being either phenomenalized or purified.[70]

[42. 16] Therefore, in order to declare[71] that although there are two conditions, the one of oppression (by phenomenal impurity), the other of purification (from the bonds of phenomenality), there nevertheless exists but only one unique Absolute Reality which is being oppressed and purified. (In order to declare this, the stanza 1. 16 says):

Oppressed and purified,
These are its varieties.

[42. 19] But this is not enough in order to know when it is marred and when purified. Therefore it is asked, when is it marred, when purified? The answer is in the next half stanza 1. 16 b):

It is either impure or it is pure[72]
Its purity is like pure water,
Like unalloyed gold or pure ether.

[42. 22] (This means that when a Bodhisattva has attained Omniscience a complete revulsion in the foundations of his personality has taken place, he is another being, a Superman). In accord with this Fundamental Transsubstantiation,[73] (in accord with) whether it has not yet taken place or already taken place, the Absolute is distinguished as being either impure or pure.

[42. 23] (Ordinary men) are bereft of (transcendent) knowledge, they are in the grips of the habit of distinguishing object from subject, their mentality is infected by emotional and (intellectual) blemishes, they fail to understand or they misunderstand (the problem of the Absolute). To them the Absolute is not revealed. For them it is distinguished as being impure.

[43. 1] But in respect of the Saints who have attained Omniscience, whose intellect is infallible, the Absolute Reality appears (eternally) without any interruption as pure, as dustless pure ether; for them it is declared to be free from all (phenomenal) impurity.

[43. 2] Thus it is that the Absolute can be impure, but not in itself. By its nature it is **resplendently pure**. Its impurity or purity are relative, (depending on the category of beings contemplating it).[74]

[43. 4] „But, (says Vasubandhu), if it can be either impure (or pure, it evidently possesses changing qualities)". Indeed (experience) shows that a change of condition is never possible without (some kind) of evolution and evolution is always connected with a process of creation and destruction. (Vasubandhu) therefore asks „how does it then (escape) from being impermanent, since it possesses changing qualities?" (The answer is the following one). The pure condition of the Absolute does not represent a new transformation different from its impure condition; its condition of being the Absolute cannot change in whatsoever any essentially different condition. (What happens is only this) that accidental impurity is removed, because —

Its purity is admitted
(As we admit) the purity
Of water-element,
Of gold or ether.

Therefore it is not impermanent. Just as elementary water, gold or ether cannot be impure in their essence, because this impurity does not belong to their nature; and just as this their nature is not changed when some accidental impurity is removed from them and they become quite purified without a change in their nature; just so the pure Absolute can become infected by the accidental impurity (of phenomenal existence), albeit in its genuine nature it has never changed; it can be purified, when the impurity (of the veil of phenomenal appearance) is removed.

[43. 15] Indeed those (who do not admit that phenomenal appearance is only an accidental veil of ultimate reality), who maintain[75] that the same reality is at first phenomenal in its essence and then becomes absolute in its essence; they never will be able to explain the disappearance of one condition and its replacement by another.[76] Neither will those who maintain that both (the phenomenal and the absolute) are accidental be able to explain (the cessation of the phenomenal life and the attainment of eternal Nirvāṇa). Therefore (this our Absolute) is not touched (even in the slightest degree) by impermanence.[77]

§ 6. The sixteen modes of Relativity-Reality

Vasubandhus comment

[V. 6. a. 1] There also[78] is another division. The Absolute Reality is sixteenfold, (since it is subjacent to sixteen modes of Relative Reality) viz. — (The Absolute subjacent to) —

1) the Relativity of the internal Elements of life;
2) the Relativity of the external Elements;
3) the Relativity of our body (which is the residence of both) the internal and external (Elements);
4) the Relativity (of Space), i. e. of the world which is the residence of that residence;
5) the Relativity of (the knowledge) of Relativity (itself);
6) the Relativity (even) of the Highest Truth;
7—8) the (mutual) Relativity of both the conditioned and unconditioned Elements of life;
9) the Relativity (of that Element of the Bodhisattva) which is supposed never to have an end;
10) the Relativity (of that feature of the Bodhisattva) which is supposed to have neither beginning nor end;
11) the Relativity (of the resolution of the Bodhisattva) never to forsake the living beings;
12) the Relativity of the permanent nature of a Bodhisattva;
13) the Relativity of the (beautiful) tokens on the body of a Buddha;
14) the Relativity of the miraculous powers of a Buddha;
(To summarize)
15) the (general) Relativity or Unreality in all these points; and
16) the general subjacent ultimate Reality in all these points.

[V. 6. a. 3] If reduced to a system (this theory of Relativity-Reality must be represented in such a form of 16 items). Among them (the 1st) the Relativity of the internal Elements refers to the Relativity, (i. e. the not ultimate Reality) of the Enjoyer, (i. e. the Ego); (the second), the Relativity of the external Elements, refers to the Relativity of the enjoyed objects; (the 3d), the Relativity of the internal and external Elements of life, refers to the Relativity (i. e. non-ultimate Reality) of our body, since our carcas is the place where the internal as well as (some) external Elements of our life are residing; (the 4th) is called the Great Relativity, since its compass is very great; it is the receptacle-world where our body dwells; (hence) it is the residence of the residence of the Elements of our life.

[V. 6. a. 6] The question now arises by whom (or by what kind of knowledge) are these four varieties of Relativity perceived? They are perceived by our knowledge of Relativity. (However this knowledge is itself relative) and the Relativity of this knowledge of Relativity is called Relativity of Relativity.

How is the concept of the Highest Truth conceived? (It is also relative). The Relativity of this concept is called the Relativity of Highest Truth.

Sthiramati's comment

[43. 19] In that section (of this work), which is devoted to a (systematical) specification of the chief varieties (of the manifestations) of the Absolute, (completeness is the aim). Every division must be mentioned, therefore (Vasubandhu) declares „there also is another division; the Absolute is sixteenfold". It is sixteenfold (not by itself, but) according to a distinction of the (chief) objects (in which it is concealed). (There are sixteen main items of phenomenal Relative Reality of which it constitutes the background of Absolute Reality). There is no difference in the essence of the Absolute (which is always the same, viz.) absence of duality (or Monism). In the „Discourse on Supreme Intuition" there is a passage[79] on these sixteen aspects of the Absolute, it begins with that aspect of Absolute Reality which corresponds (to the Relativity) of all the subjective Elements of life and concludes with that aspect of it (the 16th) which represents the „reality (subjacent) of unreality", (i. e. that Absolute Reality which is hidden behind phenomenal unreality). „We (now) must consider, says Vasubandhu, that very Absolute as a (coherent) system (of sixteen items in which phenomenal Reality conceals Absolute Reality).

[Stanza 1. 17]

The subject who enjoys,
His enjoyed objects,
His body, his surrounding world,
Are Elements of Relativity
(Whose background is Absolute Reality).
That knowledge also which cognizes this,[80]
The manner in which it is cognized
The aim for which it is cognized,
(This knowledge) is also Relativity,
(Whose background is Absolute Reality).

[43. 25] Absolute Reality is a Universal.[81] Its essence is Monism. It appertains to all the separate Elements (of Relative Reality which in their ultimate essence are not divided in the two parts of subject and object).[82] Since it is impossible otherwise to demonstrate the varieties (of what is unique in itself), its division into varieties is made from the standpoint of those (phenomenal) objects (in which Reality is concealed).

[44. 2] First of all (the Ego) who experiences (and enjoys life) must be minutely examined[83] in order to clear out the inveterate habit of cherishing it. Indeed this inveterate habit of cherishing the Ego represents the main obstacle on the way of attaining Buddhahood and of reaching (the eight degrees) of Liberation from the bonds of materiality.[84]

[44. 4] After that his enjoyments and after them the body which supports both (the enjoyer and the enjoyments), after which[85] the residence of the body supporting them, the surrounding world, should be minutely examined. (The latter) since it is subservient to the enjoyer (must be examined critically) with the view of diverting from it the grips of egoistic passion (for enjoying them).[86]

[44. 7] These are the four categories of objects, (viz. the enjoyer, his enjoyments, their residence and the residence of their residence). Their Relativity[87] (and the subjacent Absolute Reality) are called Relativity of objects, (in contradistinction from the following categories of the Relativity of knowledge).

[44. 8] „The Relativity of the enjoyer, says Vasubandhu, refers[88] here (to the relativity) of the internal bases of cognition". They are (the five organs of outer sense), the eye etc. and include the mind, (the sixth, the internal sense-organ).

[44. 9] Simple people[89] ascribe to these faculties (and to the intellect) the high office[90] of being the enjoying agent, because they notice that they are engaged in experiencing the sensible objects and because they admit of no other enjoying subject than them. Therefore the relativity (or phenomenality) of these six subjective bases of cognition are said to represent the enjoying subject's Relativity (and its corresponding subjacent Absolute Reality).

[44. 12.] The Relativity of enjoyments is constituted[91] by the external (six bases of cognition). They are (the five categories of sense-data), the colours and shapes etc.[92] and the objects of reflection by the inner sense.[93] They are called the „food", because in them the external objects[94] are (quasi) savoured.[95] Therefore the Relative Reality of the objects of the external world (and the mode of Absolute Reality corresponding to them) are called External Relativity.

[44. 14] Since both the enjoyer and the enjoyment reside in inseparable mutual union in the body or in the carcas (therefore the latter also represents a variety of relative reality). „Therefore, (says Vasubandhu), its relativity is called Outer-and-Inner Relativity".[96]

[44. 16) The thing (serving as) a residence is the outer world, it is the receptacle-world, since in every respect[97] we recognize it (as representing nothing but) a supporting thing[98] for the living beings, (annexed to them as a support). „Therefore, says Vasubandhu, since it is overwhelmingly extended, this (aspect of Relativity) is called the Great Relativity".

[44. 18] The word „object" (or thing) must be connected separately with each of these four varieties. (They represent the Relativity of things as contrasted with the Relativity of knowledge).

§ 7. The Relativity of Relativity and the Relativity of the Highest Truth

(The stanza 1. 17 further says —)

The knowledge also which cognizes this,
The manner in which it is cognized —
The aim for which it is cognized.
All this is also Relativity
(Whose background is Absolute Reality).

[44. 19] The Bodhisattva absorbed in deepest meditation during a fit of transic enlightment intuits the Absolute Reality behind the veil of the phenomenal Relativity of the four categories of these cognizable objects (viz. the sense faculties, the sense objects, the body and the world); (he intuits directly the unique Reality concealed by the manifoldness of phenomena). But (when the trance is over and) he realizes the same Absolute by attentive discursive (conceptual) thought, a new form of the objectivizing habit manifests itself.[99]

[44. 21] Indeed that intuition of the Absolute through which he realizes the inanity of the internal and external Elements of existence (being then realized in a special variety of conceptual thought requires an object and thus) the subject-object habit of thought (reappears anew).

[44. 22] (On the other hand) we must consider the manner in which this renewed conception, attained again after it was lost in the direct intuition of the Absolute, presents itself as having the form of Ultimate Truth. Now, both these conceptions, the conception of the inanity of the Elements of phenomenal existence and the conception of this (knowledge) as being the Ultimate Truth, both are the consequence of a direct mystic experience, they prove after minute examination to be themselves also relative. They contain that objectivity which constitutes a variety of Transcendental Illusion, that variety which still persists after (some of the highest) degrees of transic enlightment have been attained. We thus have two further varieties of Relativity covering the subjacent Absolute Reality, they are called the Relativity of Relativity and the Relativity of Ultimate Truth. They mean 1) the Relativity of the conceptual „knowledge" of Relativity and 2) the Relativity of the „form" (or of the concept) of Ultimate Truth. They represent the manner in which the Absolute is conceived in the moments following on the moment of mystic vision. The word „knowledge" in the first case and the word „form" (concept) in the second case are omitted and they are simply designated as the Relativity of Relativity and the Relativity of Ultimate Truth.[100]

[44. 26] (These last two modes of Relativity-Reality can also be explained thus). It has been mentioned that the knowledge of Relativity is itself also called Relativity because Relativity is its object. The „devoidness" in this notion of its object-subject relation[102] is called the Relativity of Relativity.[103] (It also has subjacent Ultimate Reality).

[45. 1] (As to the expression Relativity of the Highest Truth, it has also the following meaning). When all the Elements of Existence, internal and other, have been intuited (as inane) owing to a knowledge of the Absolute, this is the Highest Truth. The subjacent Absolute Reality corresponding to this form of knowledge is called the Relativity (and the subjacent Absolute Reality) of the Highest Truth.[104] Why? Because the Highest Truth is an intuition, it is devoid of every feature constructed by abstract thought.

(These are the first four aspects of object-Relativity and the two first aspects of knowledge-Relativity which conceal the subjacent unique Absolute Reality).

§ 8. The seventh and eighth modes of Relativity-Reality

[45. 8] Now what indeed is the aim for which (the Bodhisattva) realizes the Absolute?
The stanza 1. 18 says —

For the attainment of the double weal.
For everlasting help to living creatures,
For not-forsaking the phenomenal world,
And for attaining Bliss Eternal.

Vasubandhu's comment

[V. 6. b. 1] Now the aim for which the Bodhisattva realizes the Absolute is also relative. Indeed whatfore does he realize it? For a double weal. The double weal is the conditioned (preliminary) one and the unconditioned (final) one, (they are relative). They constitute the seventh and the eighth mode of Relativity (and subjacent Reality).

Sthiramati's comment

[45. 5] There is however a further objectivity-prejudice which is a calamity on (the Path) of realizing the Absolute, (viz.) the aim for which the Bodhisattva realizes[105] the Absolute is imagined as an objective reality.[106] In order minutely to examine and repudiate[107] that prejudice (the following eight modes) of Relativity which conceal Absolute Reality have been established, (viz.) beginning with (the 7th mode), the Relativity of the causally-interconnected Elements of Existence, and concluding with (the 14th mode), the Relativity of all Elements (without exception).

[45. 10] The Bodhisattva realizes the Absolute, i. e. actualizes [108] it in order to attain the „double weal" (and further results) up to the attainment of the pure,[109] (transcendent, miraculous) powers of a Buddha. „Weal" is the Path towards Nirvāṇa and Nirvāṇa itself. They correspond to the causally interconnected (non-eternal) Elements of existence and to the uncaused (eternal) one's. In connection with both (these classes) respectively we have the (7th mode) the Relativity (and subjacent Reality) of the caused Elements and the (8th mode) the Relativity (and subjacent Reality) of the uncaused Element (or Nirvāṇa).[110]

§ 9. The ninth mode of Relativity-Reality

Vasubandhu's comment

[V. 6. b. 2] (The stanza says) „For everlasting help to living beings" (does the Bodhisattva realize Salvation). This means that the Bodhisattva devotes his life to the eternal help to living beings (on their path towards Salvation). (Since this is also relative it constitutes the ninth mode of Relativity and subjacent Reality).

Sthiramati's comment

[45. 13] (The stanza says) „For everlasting help to living beings". (This means that the Bodhisattva takes the great vow in the form of) „in everyway and at any time will I work at the general welfare of all living creatures". [111] (This great vow of the Bodhisattva, since it implies the subject-to-object relation, represents also a mode of Absolute Reality which is concealed behind a cover of phenomenal Relativity). It is called the Endless Relativity (which conceals the monistic all-embracing Reality).

§ 10. The tenth mode of Relativity-Reality

Vasubandhu's comment

[V. 6. b. 3] (The stanza says) „For never forsaking the phenomenal world" (does the Bodhisattva realize the Absolute). Indeed not perceiving that the phenomenal world has neither beginning nor end the Bodhisattva gets desperate and is (willing) completely to forsake it. This his desire is also a mode of Relativity (concealing the subjacent Absolute Reality). (It is entered into the system of the modes of Relativity-Reality as its tenth mode).

Sthiramati's comment

[45. 16] (The stanza says) „For not forsaking the phenomenal world". (This means that the Bodhisattva takes the great vow in the form of) „for the benefit of all living creatures I will not forsake the phenomenal world". If the Bodhisattva will really forsake the phenomenal world, (he for ever will disappear in Hīnayānist Nirvāṇa), he never will attain (real) Enlightment and will (for ever) remain (extinct) in a Deliverance (according to the ideal) of the Hīnāyanists.[112] This mode of Relativity-Reality is called Relativity without Beginning and End.[113]

[45. 19] Whatfore is this mode of Relativity-Reality mentioned? (Vasubandhu answers) — „the Bodhisattva not perceiving the inanity of the phenomenal world which has neither a beginning nor an end (if he does not intuit its subjacent monistic Absolute Reality) becomes desperate and is willing to forsake it completely (in a Hīnāyanistic Nirvāṇa)".

§ 11. The eleventh mode of Relativity-Reality

Vasubandhu's comment

[V. 6. b. 3] (The stanza says) „And for attaining Bliss Eternal" (does the Bodhisattva realize Salvation). This means that even in that Nirvāṇa where no rest of the Elements of phenomenal life are at all left, even then he will not forsake, not throw away (the root-Elements of virtue, they will remain immanent in his Nirvāṇa. But this is Relativity. This is the eleventh mode of Relativity-Reality).

Sthiramati's comment

[45. 22] (The stanza says) „And for attaining Bliss Eternal". (These words refer, Vasubandhu explains, to the fact) that even (in Final Nirvāṇa), in Nirvāṇa without any rest (of phenomenal Elements) (there nevertheless remains something which the Bodhisattva does not throw away, does not forsake). (He takes the great vow) „even in Final Nirvāṇa I will not reject the roots of good".[114] (The words) „does not throw away" express just the same as „does not forsake". (And in realization of this great vow some of the phenomenal Elements of his personality remain immanent in the Absolute Reality of his Final Nirvāṇa).

[46. 1] Objection of the Hinayānist. But if that be so, how can then the Absolute Reality of Final Nirvāṇa be realized, since it (is supposed) that no Elements of phenomenal life are at all left living in it?[115]

Answer of the Yogācāra. It is our established dogma (in this matter) that the Cosmical Body of our Lords the Buddhas continues to exist even in that Nirvāṇa in which there is at all no rest of the Elements of phenomenal existence.[116] Therefore this mode of the (forsaken) phenomenal Relativity (with its subjacent Absolute Reality) is called the Relativity-Reality of Non-rejection.

§ 12. The twelfth mode of Relativity-Reality

(The stanza 1. 19 says) —

For the Purification of his Lineage,
(For Transsubstantiation)
The Saint does realize Salvation.

Vasubandhu's comment

[V. 6. b. 4] The Lineage is the Nature, (the family of the Buddhas). Its purification is a change) of essence (or Transsubstantiation). (But inasmuch as it is objective, it is also partly relative, it constitutes the twelfth mode of Relativity-Reality).

Sthiramati's comment

[46. 6] (The stanza says) „And for the Purity of the Lineage" (i. e. the Absolute Reality is realized under the cover of phenomenal Relativity).

[46. 7] This mode of Relativity-Reality is termed the Absolute of Nature. (Vasubandhu states the reason for this). „Lineage, says he, is Nature". Why is that? (He says) — „it is essential". Essential means (primordial), existing from beginningless time, not accidental. How is that? In the beginningless run of phenomenal existence there are animate beings and inanimate things. Just so here, (on another plane), there are among the sentient beings those who belong by their lineage to the family of Buddhas and there are those who belong to the family of Hīnayāna-Saints, etc. This family descent is not accidental, it comes from a beginningless, eternal sequence (of births). (The difference is as fundamental as that) between the animate and inanimate world.

[46. 12] However there are some philosophers who maintain that all living beings belong to the family of Buddhas. The term „lineage" must be then accordingly interpreted.

§ 13. The thirteenth mode of Relativity-Reality

(The stanza 1. 20 says)

For the attaining (on his body)
Of attributes and tokens
The Bodhisattva then proceeds.

Vasubandhu's comment

[V. 6. b. 5]. (This means) „for obtaining the great and minor marks of the body of a Superman (does the Bodhisattva realize Salvation). Indeed a Superman possesses beautiful marks, great and minor, on his body. (This however is also relative, it constitutes in the system the thirteenth mode of Relativity-Reality).

Sthiramati's comment

[46. 14] (The stanza says) „In order to attain the attributes and tokens" (sc. in order to attain this manifestation of the Absolute, this mode of manifested Relativity and its subjacent Reality are established in the system).

[46. 15] The Superman (i. e. the Buddha in his manifestation of the Body of Supreme Bliss) possesses a body marked by 30 great and 80 minor attributes of beauty. Their Relativity (and the subjacent Absolute Reality) are called the Relativity(-Reality) of the Attributes.[117]

[46. 16] And further —

§ 14. The fourteenth mode of Relativity-Reality

The stanza 1.19 says —

For (the absolute) Purity
Of Buddha's (mystic) powers,
(For Transsubstantiation)
The Bodhisattva then proceeds.

Vasubandhu's Comment

[V. 6. b. 5] (The stanza says) „For (Transsubstantiation), for the absolute purification of the Buddha's miraculous powers, the Bodhisattva then proceeds". This refers to the (ten) miraculous powers of the Buddha, to the modes of Buddha's intrepidity and his other exceptional endowments. (They also, inasmuch astheyimply the subject-to-object relation, are relative, and this constitutes the fourteenth mode of Relativity-Reality).

Sthiramati's comment

[46. 18] The word „proceeds"[118] placed at the end (of the stanza) should be referred to all (the preceeding aims of the cognition of the Absolute) likewise, e. g. the Bodhisattva proceeds towards „the realization of the double weal" (stanza 1. 18a), he proceeds towards „the everlasting help to all the living beings" (stanza 1. 18b), etc. etc.

[46. 20] What are the pure transcendent powers of the Buddha aimed at by the Bodhisattva? (Vasubandhu answers) — „his ten great powers, his intrepidity and other exceptional attributes". In short he makes the following resolution — „To attain all the attributes of a Buddha I must make a (creative) effort (of the mind)", therefore he „realizes", (i. e. creates by thought).[118]

[46. 23] This mode of the Absolute is termed the Absolute (subjacent to) the Relativity of the totality of all the Elements (of phenomenal existence).[119]

What is here meant by „thought creation"? It means (a mystic vision), a direct procedure of (mystic) knowledge[120] towards the cognized thing.

§ 15. The last two modes of Relativity-Reality

Vasubandhu's comment

[V. 6. b. 5] This is the manner in which we first of all must envisage the system of the first fourteen varieties of phenomenal Relativity (concealing the subjacent Absolute Reality). (We again must ask) what is here that Relativity (behind which lurks Absolute Reality)?

[Stanza 1. 20] (declares —)

This Relativity (is double):
Of Individual and of its Elements.
Here Relativity means unreality.
But to this unreality (subjacent)
There is an Absolute Reality
It is the Counterpart of Relativity.[121]

[V. 6. b. 6] The term śūnyatā „voidness" refers to the fact that both the living Individual (of the realists and its 75 ultimate) Elements (as established by the Sarvāstivādins)[122] (are only relative Reality), they are not real ultimate Reality in itself.[123] However there is another, a real Ultimate Reality subjacent to the phenomenal Relative Reality of the Elements assumed by the Sarvāstivādins. This we have already stated above when giving the definition of (our term) Relativity-Reality, on the occasion of dealing with „Internal Relativity" and other modes of it.

[V. 7. a. 1] Now in order to repudiate the imputed reality of the Individual (by the Vātsiputrīyas) and of its Elements (by the Sarvāstivādins), (on the one hand) and in order to repudiate the debasement[124] of their Relativity (into absolute unreality by the Mādhyamikas, on the other hand); we now at the conclusion (of this section on the various modes of the Absolute) will (supplement our system) by establishing two further (general) varieties, (the 15th and 16th variety, viz. the 15th), the Unreality (of the object-subject relation) and the (16th), the Reality (subjacent) of this unreality, (i. e. the ultimate pure Reality subjacent to the object-subject Relativity).

Sthiramati's comment

[46. 24] „This is the manner, says Vasubandhu, in which we first of all must envisage the system of the first fourteen varieties of the Absolute", i. e., the varieties beginning with the Relativity of the internal Elements and ending with the Relativity (and subjacent absolute Reality) of all the Elements of life.

[17. 2] (Vasubandhu asks) „What is here that Relativity (behind which lurks Absolute Reality)?" „Here" namely (in the section devoted to) the Relativity (and subjacent Absolute Reality) of the enjoying Individual and all its other modes?

To this (the stanza) answers —

This Relativity (is double):
Of Individual and of its Elements.
Here Relativity means Unreality.
But to this unreality (subjacent)
There is an Absolute Reality.
It is the counterpart of Relativity.

[47. 5] The word „here" (in the phrase „here Relativity") refers (to the section about the 14 modes of Relativity-Reality), viz. the Relativity of the

Enjoyer, (the Individual) etc. The term ś ū n y a t ā (which literally means „voidness") refers to the unreality of the Individual and of its Elements and also means that Absolute Reality (which is subjacent) to this unreality, (i. e. the denial of ultimate reality of the Individual in Hīnayāna, the denial of ultimate reality of all Elements in the Mādhyamika system, and the assertion of a subjacent ultimate reality in the Yogācāra system are the three meanings of the term ś ū n y a t ā).[125]

[47. 6] Here (says Vasubandhu) „the unreality of the Individual and (the unreality) of the Elements of life constitute (the 15th mode of the Absolute, it is called) Relativity of Unreality. The ultimate Reality (subjacent) to this nonexistence (constitutes the last, 16th mode) of the Absolute and is called Reality of Unreality.

[47. 7] Whatfore are these two last modes of the Absolute added (to the list of the fourteen modes, whereas they represent only its general definition)?[126] This (Vasubandhu) explains — „because they put a stress[127] on (our) definition of the Absolute".[128]

[47. 9] Whatfore has it been found necessary to put a stress on the definition of the Absolute? (It has been found necessary to establish two additional modes) in order respectively to repudiate 1) the imagined (ultimate) reality of the Individual as well as of the Elements (on the one hand), and 2) the denial of their (subjacent) Absolute Reality (on the other).

[47. 11] In order to repudiate the imagined ultimate reality of the Individual and of all its Elements, the Unreality-Relativity, (the 15th mode), has been established and in order to repudiate the denial of their (subjacent) Absolute Reality (the 16th mode or) the Reality (subjacent to this Unreality) has been established.

[47. 13] If the unreality-aspect of Relativity would not have been emphasized,[129] we would be obliged (to face) the consequence of assuming the ultimate reality of the Individual and of all the Elements (of his life), whereas they really are nothing but constructions of our productive imagination. If, on the other hand, the „reality of unreality" (i. e. the ultimate reality of the subjacent) Absolute would not have been emphasized,[129] we would be obliged to face the consequence of assuming that our subjacent Absolute Reality[130] does not exist at all, and then, since there would be no (Absolute with which the relativity of all the Elements of phenomenal life could be contrasted), the final reality of the Individual and of all his Elements would be again established as before.

§ 16. Review of the 16 modes

[47. 16] Here (among the 16 modes of the unique Absolute Reality subjacent to the 16 aspects of Relative Reality) the first item corresponds to the unreality of the subject. It is constituted by the five sense organs and the intellect as the internal sense-organ. (According to our system these organs) are nothing but ideas, appearing as a mature result of the processes going on in the subliminal) sphere of the Psyche. Simple humanity is agreed to ascribe to these ideas the rôle of an „Enjoyer", i. e. of a concrete Individual (*pudgala*) and to designate them as his eyes and other (sense-organs), although in their essence (according to our system) they are nothing but constructions of our imagination. Their unreality, and the (mental) reality subjacent to this unreality, constitutes the first mode of the Absolute, (it is the Absolute hidden behind) the unreality of the subject.[131]

[47. 19] (The second mode of the subjacent Absolute is characterized by objective unreality). It is constituted by the five categories of sense-data (corresponding to the five sense-organs and by those mental objects which are reflections of our mind). (According to our system these six categories of objects are) nothing but ideas appearing as sensations intimating (the presence in the ken) of colours and other sense-data (inclusive of the mental objects of the inner sense).[132] Simple humanity is convinced that in these sensations they have real enjoyed external objects. The non-existence of these personally enjoyed objects and the non-existence of coloured surfaces or of all other sensible external objects which, in our opinion, are but constructions of imagination, (their non-existence) as well as the Ultimate Reality subjacent to this non-existence constitute our second mode of the Absolute called external Absolute, (it is the Absolute hidden behind the phenomenality of the external sense-data).[133]

[47. 22] (The third mode of the subjacent ultimate Absolute is termed the subjacent Absolute of outer and inner unreality). Both the Enjoyer, the Individual (or the Ego) and objective sense-data, pieces of coloured matter etc., are imagined by simple people to have a common residence in the body, i. e. in the carcas of a living being.[134] The non-existence, (i. e. the not ultimate reality) of them as well as of the body itself, and that Ultimate Reality which underlies this unreality is termed the Absolute (subjacent to) outer and inner Elements.[135]

[47. 24] (The fourth mode of manifestation of ultimate Absolute Reality is termed the Great Absolute, it embraces the external world). It is constituted by the unreality (of the imagined fact) that all the living beings reside in an inanimate material world which is their receptacle. The unreality of the imagined reality (of such a receptacle) and the Ultimate Reality (which is subjacent) to this unreality are called the Great Absolute.

[47. 25] (The fifth and sixth mode of the Absolute as manifested in phenomenal Relativity, according to our system), are respectively called the Relativity of the knowledge of Relativity itself and the Relativity of the Absolute itself.[136] (This means that when the Bodhisattva has had, in a moment of mystic ecstasy, a direct vision of the Absolute and when after that he, in digesting such an ecstatic experience, meditates on the Absolute in concepts, then the object-subject relation reappears to him). Such a cognition of the Absolute and such an idea itself of the Absolute are relative, because they are constructed by the productive imagination of the cognizer and of that individual who has given to this idea its form. (However subjacent to this unreality there is an Ultimate Reality). The two modes are called respectively 1) Relativity (of the cognition) of Relativity and 2) Relativity of the Highest Truth itself. (They constitute in our system the fifth and sixth modes of the Absolute as hidden behind phenomenal Appearance).[137]

[48. 4] (These are the fundamental six modes of phenomenal relative Reality behind which lurks the non-relative, unique Absolute Reality). Now (after them the further eight modes) beginning with the Relativity of all those Elements of phenomenal existence which are dependent on causes[138] (the 7th mode) up to the possession of all the miraculous powers of a Buddha (the 14th mode) are described[139] in order to elucidate the aim for which the Bodhisattva exerts himself, since their raison d'être is to represent those expedients[140] through which the condition of a Bodhisattva is being realized. The Relativity of all the Dependent Elements (the 7th mode and all the other modes) up to the Relativity of all the miraculous powers of the Buddha (the 14th mode), gradually elucidate the fact that the Individual and all its Elements, inasmuch as constructed by our productive imagination, have no ultimate reality, but that behind this phenomenal unreality there is the Ultimate Reality of the Absolute.

[48. 7] Indeed the dependent Elements of existence (are dependent on their causes), they have no proprietor, no real Individual disposing of them. Neither is there in every such a dependent Element[141] itself any ultimate reality[142] as assumed by the simpleminded (Sarvāstivādins).

[48. 9] The sixteen modes of Relativity (which overlay the unique ultimate reality of the Absolute) have been taught (by the Buddha) in order tersely to counteract all habit of discursive thought-construction and to indicate in a concise manner the concealed deep meaning of all Buddhist Scripture. They are a special Bodhisattva doctrine (of the Mahāyāna); they do not equally belong to the Hinayāna.[143]

[48. 11] By this (doctrine) our Lord has established[144] (three things), 1) the scope of the Absolute, 2) its essence and 3) the aim of its realization. Its scope embraces (the totality of all things) beginning with (the internal Elements of a personality), the Enjoyer (of the fruits of his former deeds) and so on up to the (special, miraculous, transcendent) powers of the Buddha. This indeed is taught in order to intimate that the Absolute embraces the totality of all the Elements of existence.

[48. 14] The essence of the Absolute consists in the unreality (of the object-to-subject relation) and in the ultimate Reality (which is subjacent) to that unreality. This is taught for (the double aim) of repudiating the exaggerated realism and the exaggerated scepticism, and in order thus to promote (the intuitive direct) cognition (of the Absolute), (that mystic vision) whose essence it is to dislodge all theoretic constructions.[145]

[48. 16] The aim for the attaining of which the Absolute must be realized (by purifying it from all phenomenal impurity) is indicated beginning from stanza 1. 18—viz. „for attaining the double weal", (i. e. of Nirvāṇa and of the Path towards it), including the stanza 1. 19—viz. „for attaining the transcendent Purity of Buddha-powers".

[48. 18] It is also suggested by these words that the realization of the Absolute in profound meditation is the only direct expedient of attaining transsubstantiation into a Budda's Body of Supreme Bliss for one's own Final Deliverance and into the Buddha's Cosmical Body for Final Deliverance of all living beings. (This double result represents) the highest reachable point of personal and altruistic perfection.[146]

[48. 20] „Thus, (says Vasubandhu), should we envisage the system (of the sixteen varieties of the manifestation) of the Absolute". This means that the Absolute which is impure in the phenomenal condition and pure in the (transcendent) purified form, this unique Absolute, can be recognized (in another form, viz.) a form divided into sixteen varieties called the Absolute (subjacent to the Relativity) of the subjective Elements of existence and to all other varieties (of relative reality).[147]

§ 17. The proof establishing the existence of the Absolute

Vasubandhu's comment

[V. 7. a. 2] How is the argument (in favour of the existence of an Absolute Reality behind the veil of the phenomenal world) to be determined? (The stanza 1. 21 says) —

If there were no phenomenal impurity
All living beings would be Saints,
But if the Pure Transcendent Absolute did not exist,
The effort for Salvation would be vain.

[V. 7. a. 3] If the Absolute Reality underlying all Elements of phenomenal life could remain uncovered by accidental, non-substantial, phenomenal impurity, then, in the absence of phenomenal impurity, all living beings would attain Final Deliverance (automatically), without any effort, even without having recourse to purifying remedies. But even if the purifying remedies would be applied, they (also) would not attain complete purity; in that case the work for reaching Salvation would remain fruitless.

[V. 7. a. 5] In that case (says the stanza 1. 21 the Absolute will be—)

Neither obscured nor non-obscured,
Neither pure nor non-pure.

[V. 7. a. 6] How can it be (both) not-obscured (by phenomenal impurity) and also not impure, (i. e. pure)? (This double negation is an emphatic assertion. Scripture declares) „consciousness is by its nature resplendently pure". How can it be (both) „not non-obscured" (by phenomenal impurity, i. e. obscured) and also „impure"? (This double characteristic emphasizes the fact) that phenomenality is accidental. By this argument the division of the Absolute (in impure and pure) is established.

But this general meaning of (the term) Absolute must moreover be considered from the standpoint of its (chief) characteristic features—a negative characteristic and a positive characteristic, (i. e. unreality and reality).

Sthiramati's comment

48. 23] (Stanza 1. 21 determines the topics to be discussed in connection with the problem of the Absolute). Following on the topic of division, the argument (establishing the existence of the Absolute is mentioned). Therefore after a discussion of its division (into different modes) the question is raised (by Vasubandhu), „how is this argument to be conceived?" Indeed what is here the thesis to be proved (by argument)? (It is double), the fact of the obscuration of the Absolute by accidental, non-substantial, phenomenal impurity and (the fact of) its natural condition of absolute purity.[148] Regarding (the first, i. e.) the proof establishing the existence of a phenomenal veil, (the first half of stanza 1. 21 says)—

If there were no phenomenal impurity,[149]
All living beings would be Saints.

[49. 2] (What is Salvation?) Salvation means annihilation of phenomenal oppression,[150] and this annihilation of phenomenal oppression can be attained by the creative effort[151] (of the Mind) on the Path of Purity. Now if that (unique) Absolute Reality[152] (which is subjacent) to all the Elements (of phenomenal existence) would not be concealed and oppressed by occasional non-substantial phenomenal impurity, then in that case, there being at all no phenomenality (in the world), all living beings would be saved without any effort on their part.

(Vasubandhu says) „Even without applying the remedies against phenomenal impurity" (all beings would be saved automatically). The word „even" suggests that the result would be the same if the remedies were applied, (since the remedies would be then applied against a non-existing phenomenality).

[49. 6] „Without any effort" means without the creation of the antidote. But without the creation of an antidote (on the Path of Saintliness) the living beings are never saved (from the bonds of phenomenality). It is therefore necessary to assume the existence of a Unique Reality which manifests itself in the condition of a worldling as oppressed and concealed[153] by adventitious impurity.

[49. 8.] Thus (by this argument) the existence of the phenomenalized variety of the Absolute is established.

[49. 9.] Now[154] in order te establish the other variety,[155] the Pure Absolute, the stanza says —

But if the Pure Transcendent Absolute did not exist
The effort (towards Salvation) would be vain.

We must understand (the effort) of the living beings.

[49. 12]. „Then (says Vasubandhu) even if the antidote (against phenomenal impurity) would be created" — the word „even" suggests that the same would happen if the antidote were not created — „if the Pure Absolute did not exist, then, in that case, the effort towards Salvation would be vain". In that case (sc. if the pure Absolute did not exist, the phenomenal) impurity (of our life) could never disappear, even when profound meditation would create an antidote against it.

[49. 15]. However the Salvation of a being (as long as it is enveloped in phenomenal) impurity is impossible. Neither can we a priori admit[156] that the (natural striving for Final Deliverence[157] is senseless and) can remain fruitless. Therefore we necessarily must admit the existence of a Pure Absolute and the possibility of its realization through the creation of the antidote,[158] (i. e. by entering the Path towards Salvation) where the accidental, non-substantial phenomenal impurity must disappear.

[49. 18]. We have thus established the existence of the Pure Absolute as one of its varieties. However we cannot admit neither that this impurity nor that this purification belong directly to the Absolute itself. It is impure when its impure attributes are perceived and it is pure when its pure attributes are perceived. Indeed the Absolute depends on the attributes (with which it appears). It is just in this sense that the stanza says „all living beings would be saved" (automatically if there were no impure attributes in the Absolute). Under the expression „all living beings would be saved" we must understand that the Absolute Reality subjacent to them would be purified. Otherwise, if the Absolute itself could be (in its essence) impure or pure, the intervening function of the living beings would be useless. (The living being would have no *raison d'être*). But so (as the things stand) the purity of the Absolute produces the purity, (i. e. the transsubstantiation) of the living being; the impurity of the Absolute produces the phenomenal impurity of the living beings.[159]

[50. 1]. Now, if the Absolute is covered by phenomenal impurity for the simple man, and if it becomes pure when the condition of Saintliness is reached, it is then (in itself) —

(The stanza 1. 22 says)

Neither obscured nor non-obscured
Neither pure nor non-impure.

This is established.[160]

First explanation

[50. 4]. How can it be both „not obscured (by phenomenal impurity) and also not impure?" (asks Vasubandhu). (Whatfore this double characteristic „non-obscured" and „non-impure"?) The meaning which follows from the general trend of this section is purity simply, through the double characteristic it only is emphasized.[161] (Vasubandhu) quotes Scripture — „the intellect is by its nature resplendently pure". In this (scriptural passage) the term „intellect"[162] is to be taken just in the sense of the Absolute,[163] although the term intellect generally (in other contexts) means the phenomenal[164] Mind.

[50. 7]. How can it be both not non-obscured and not pure?, (i. e. twice impure). The double negative characteristic only means that it is just quite obscured (in phenomenal life). But it is obscured by occasional vices which do not affect its (pure) essence. This has been (sufficiently) indicated. This also is confirmed by Scripture which says „it is occasionally obscured by occasional vices".

Second explanation

[50. 10]. When this main division into two varieties, impure and pure, has been established, whatfore is it further divided into four varieties? According to some (authorities) it is done in order to make a distinction between (the Absolute, on one hand) and the mundane and the supra-mundane Paths of Purity (on the other). Indeed on the mundane Path of Purity (the Absolute) is obscured by those vices which still remain unextinguished on the respective stage of the progress, but not by the vices which have been eradicated on the preceding lower stages,[165] because for those vices an impediment has been (there) created.

[50. 13]. The supra-mundane Path (can be feeble, middle or intense. When) it is feeble or middle it is still impure. When it is intense and absolutely free from every trace of „influence" by the obscuring forces of phenomenal life, it becomes pure. The Absolute is not so (divided). (The Absolute is thus fourfold, 1) obscured and impure on the mundane, preparatory Path of the Saint, 2) non-obscured, but still partly impure on the lower stages of the supra-mundane Path, 3) non-obscured and pure on the highest „uninfluenced" stage of the supra-mundane Path and 4) the Absolute itself, i. e. the Buddha, which is to be distinguished from the Path, or from the Saint, when the final point is reached).

Third explanation

[50. 14—15]. According to another opinion (the text) after having said[166] „not obscured" (repeats) „not impure" in order to make a distinction between (the principle of the Absolute and a special category of Elements which also are non-obscured although for another reason). The (sense-organs), the organ of vision etc. belong to the category of those Elements of phenomenal life which are non-obscured, (i. e. not vicious) because they have by themselves no outspoken moral character at all, (they are neither virtue nor vice).[167] Hence they also are non-obscured (although in another sense of the term). But since they belong to the category of Elements „influenced" (by the forces producing phenomenal life) they are not „pure" by their nature; they are called „impure". (They are thus „non-obscured", not vicious, but nevertheless impure).

[50. 17]. (And vice versa along with Elements which are not-obscured, but nevertheless impure there are other Elements or events which are although obscured, but nevertheless pure). Therefore when it is stated (in the stanza) that this our Absolute is neither not obscured[168] nor pure, (i. e. it is both obscured and impure), it is thereby intimated that it is distinguished from (those Elements or events of phenomenal life which) are morally good, but phenomenal.[169] Indeed those morally good, but phenomenal Elements belong to phenomenal life, they cannot be said to be „unobscured" (by phenomenality). Nevertheless they are „pure", (in that sense namely that) they are the ripe retribution for former virtuous deeds and afford a happy and pleasant experience.[170] The Absolute is different. In its phenomenal condition it is obscured.[171]

[50. 20—21] Thus it is established that this (supposed) classification (of the sixteen varieties) of the Absolute represents nothing but a discrimination between the impure and the pure Absolute.[172]

§ 18. Summary

Vasubandhu's comment

[V. 7. a. 6] Summarizing the contents (of the chapter dealing with) the Absolute we can regard it (as divided in two sectors dealing respectively, the one) with the definition (of the Absolute, the other) with the establishment (of that definition). This definition contains two features, a negative one (negation of duality) and a positive one (subjacent reality). The positive feature is again double: 1) being „the reality of unreality", the Absolute is neither mere affirmation nor mere negation, 2) it is neither separate from nor identical with (the Thing-in-Itself).

[V. 7. b. 1] The establishment of this definition can be regarded as the establishment of the names of the Absolute and their (different shades of) meaning, its division into varieties and the proof (establishing its existence).

[V. 7. b. 2] By indicating here these four topics, (i. e. definition, names, division and proof, four other topics have indirectly been) suggested, viz. 1) the proper essence of the definition, 2) the essence of its results, 3) the essence of its (division) in a phenomenalized condition and purifying function and 4) the essence of the arguments (establishing its reality). Their importance is to react against the four minor vices of uncertainty, fear, want of energy and doubt (respectively).

End of the first book of Vasubandhu's comment upon the Discourse on Discrimination between Middle and Extremes, the book on the Essence of Reality.

Sthiramati's Comment continued

[50. 21] (Vasubandhu) says „in summarizing we can regard (the chapter on the Absolute as giving) its definition and as establishing it. The definition is negative and positive". The negative is indicated in the words „the absence of duality" (stanza 1. 13), the positive in the words „and the reality of that unreality" (ibid.).

[51. 1] This positive definition[178] however is very far removed from (our usual concepts) of affirmation and negation, (it is dialectical inasmuch as the Absolute is here characterized as the Reality of Unreality). It is accordingly stated in stanza 1. 13 c that it is —

Neither an affirmation
Nor a negation.

[51. 3] (It also must be regarded as a dialectical definition in that sense that it refers us to an irrational condition which) lies beyond (our concepts) of identity and difference.[171] It has indeed been stated above (p. 40. 3—6, trsl. p. 79) „This is the essence of the Absolute, (viz. Reality of Unreality, ... affirmation itself is nothing beyond a double negation, therefore in regard of the single) Constructor of phenomenal Unreality the Absolute (as the universal principle of all such constructions) is —

Neither a separate Ens
Nor is it essentially the same.

Such is the summary (of the chapter on the Absolute) as far as the definition is concerned.

[51. 5] And what is the summarized meaning in regard of the establishment of that definition? (Vasubandhu) says „its establishment is to be regarded as the establishment of its names etc.", i. e. its names, their special meanings, its division and its proof.

[51. 8] By the indication[175] of these four topics, (viz. definition, names, division and proof), (four other topics) having the aim of reacting against four (respective) minor vices are indirectly suggested, viz. 1) the proper essence of the Absolute (against uncertainty), 2) its results[176] (against fear), 3) its phenomenalized and purified aspects (against want of energy) and 4) the essence of the argument[177] by which it is established (against doubt).

[51. 10] Indeed in order to react against all uncertainty the proper essence (of the Absolute is definitely stated). (Four features have been clearly indicated), they consist in realizing that it has a positive essence, a negative one, a double one (which neither is pure affirmation nor pure negation), and the essence of being neither separate from nor identical[178] with (the Thing-in-Itself).

[51. 11] (In order to react against the feeling of alarm inspired by the definition of the Absolute, the result of that definition is explained). Indeed when uninitiated persons hear that definition, they become terrified (at the idea that neither the surrounding world nor they themselves really exist). Against such a state of mind that essence of the definition which explains its results is pointed to. The results are 1) the meaning of a never changing Selfsame Reality;[179] 2) the meaning of the (Highest Truth), never illusion;[180] 3) the meaning (of Reality unique), all differentiation extinguished;[181] 4) the meaning of the Ultimate Object intuited only by the transcendent supra-mundane Omniscience[182] of the Saint; 5) the meaning of the source[183] of the miraculous powers of the Buddha and the Bodhisattva.

[51. 14] (In order to react against the want of energy in the effort to attain the condition of a Buddha the graduation of that path is explained). There are indeed indolent persons who, having learnt the essence and the result of the definition of the Absolute, have enough[184] of it (despairing ever to attain the goal). In order to react against this state of mind the division of the Absolute (showing the gradual progress from phenomenality to sanctity is brought home to them).

[51. 16] In order to react against the feeling of doubt the essence of the argumentation (proving the reality of the Absolute is indicated). There are indeed persons who are in the grips of scepticism,[185] (they ask), how at all is phenomenalization possible? how is sanctity at all realizable? In answer to them the argumentation[186] (establishing the reality of the Saint and of the Buddha is indicated).[187]

End of the first part of Sthiramati's subcomment on the Discourse on Discrimination between Middle and Extremes.

NOTES

These notes were at first intended to contain, besides the original technical terms, 1) text corrections to the edition of V. Bhattacharya and G. Tucci, 2) elucidations of some difficult passages. In the mean while the edition of S. Yamaguchi contains already the emendation of many wrong readings and part of my notes are thus made superfluous. The other part contains chiefly literal renderings which it was unadvisable to leave in the translation because they often were by themselves quite unintelligible. The difficulty of translating the technical terms of a new system is well known. In the majority of cases I have followed Prof. L. de La Vallée Poussin's Vijñapti-mātratā-siddhi. The Collections of our Academy (Nova, n⁰ B 380) contain a commentary on the Madhyāntavibhanga by the Labrang lama Jamyang-tenpai-nyima (Hjam-dbyaṅs-bstan-pai-ñi-ma) which bears the title Mi-pham-dgoṅs-zab-gsal-bai-legs-bšad-sgron-me (here quoted Labrang). The kolophon is composed by lama Kalzan-thub-ten-wang-chug (bskal-bzaṅ-thub-bstan-bbaṅ-phyug) who was the fourth incarnation of Jamyang-žadpa, it contains 140 folios of the usual Tibetan size.

Part I, Chapter I

1 prāyeṇa-phal-cher.

2 śiṣṭa-krama-(anuvartin) = ya-rabs-kyi tshul. S. Y.—uttama-jana.

3 The Middle Path is a fundamental tennet of Buddhism, but in early Buddhism it means the middle between materialism and rationalism (uccheda-vāda and śāsvata-vāda); in the Mādhyamika system it means radical relativism or scepticism, nothing to be asserted as ultimate reality; in the Yogācāra system it means the middle way between the Hīnayāna pluralism for which whatsoever is a dharma is eo ipso real (sarvam asti = samāropa) and the scepticism of the Mādhyamikas for whom not a single dharma is ultimately real, all are only relatively real (sarvam śūnyam-paraspara-āpekṣikam-apavāda).

4 praṇetṛ-mdzad-pa.

5 vaktṛ-bśad-pa.

6 Read 3.4 with S.Y. vibhāgāya-rnam-par-dbye-bar, instead of viniścaye.

7 abhy-arcya-aty-arcya, cf. 5.5, perhaps abhy-arhya.

8 su-gata-suṣṭhu-gata 'having succesfully reached (Nirvāna)'.

9 The work is called both śāstra and sūtra, cf. 3.10, it pretends to be a revealed śāstra; it is āgama = śāsanam, corresponding to a brahmanic śruti.

10 Read 3.7 pūjāyām = mchod-na, instead of pūjayaiṣām; there is in Tib. nothing corresponding to either yeṣām or eṣām.

11 guṇavat = yon-tan-daṅ-ldan-pa.

[12] upakāraka-phan-ḥdogs-ḥdogs-pa, S. Y. has hita-kāribhyas.

[13] sam-ārambha analysed as samyag-ārambha-yaṅ-dag-par-brtsom-pa.

[14] vighna-vināyakaiḥ-vighnair vināyakaiś ca=bar-chad daṅ bgegs-kyis; vināyaka 'obstacle, impediment'=bgegs; bar-chad corresponds to vighna.

[15] alpena prayāsena-tshegs-chuṅ-ṅus.

[16] Read 3.9 praṇetroktasya vaktrā ca vivṛtasya samyak-pratipādana-kathanena-mzad-pas gsuṅs-pa daṅ ḥchad-pas bśad-pa yaṅ-dag-par-byin-par bsñad-pas.

[17] sarvam uktam-thams-cad smos-so. S. Y. 2.2 omits uktam altogether(?).

[18] sūtre-mdo.

[19] The Tib. translation suggests in 3.12 a reading praṇetrokta-pradarśanāt=mdzad-pas bśad-par bstan-pas, instead of praṇetr-praṇeya-pravacanāt.

[20] These characteristics clearly show that Sthiramati did not believe that Maitreya was an historical personage on earth, cf. E. Obermiller, IHQ, v. IX, p. 1024.

[21] kleśa-āvaraṇa and jñeyāvaraṇa are meant. Cp. Haribhadra's Ālokā, p. 14.4–19.

[22] abhijñā, cf. M. Vyut. § 14, Obermiller, Abhis., p. 44, H. Dayal, p. 140. According to the Daśabhūmika a Bodhisattva acquires the abhijñā's on the eighth bhūmi, but they are also sometimes represented as possessed even by an arhat, cf. pāli chaḷabhiññā, Vin. III. 88; bibliogr. in LVP, AK, VII, p. 97.

[23] Every Bodhisattva possesses his own dhāraṇī or glottolalic formula; a bhūmi, or stage of his perfection, is defined by Haribhadra, op. cit., p. 93.17, thus — prāpta-dhāraṇīkasya uttarottara-adhigama-pratiṣṭhā-yogena tajja-guṇa-ādhāra-yogena ça adhigama-avasthāviśeṣā bhūmaya iti.—The dhāraṇī is of three kinds, viz. kṣānti-dhāraṇī, guhya-mantra-dhāraṇī and padārtha-dhāraṇī. All three varieties are characterized as samāhita-prajñā, the first is gnas-lugs-stoṅ-ñid-kyi don-la mi-skrag-pai tiṅ-ṅe-ḥdzin daṅ šes-rab-bo; the second as—sdig-pa-sogs ži-bar-byed nus-pai gsaṅ-sṅags rtsom-nus-pai tiṅ-ṅe-dzin daṅ šes-rab-bo; the third as—tshig-don bskal-par mi-brjed-par ḥdzin-nus-pai tiṅ-ṅe-ḥdzin daṅ šes-rab-bo, cf. the work Yum-gyi mdoi ḥgres-rkañ brgya-rtsa-brgyad gsal-bar-byed-pa by lama Bšad-Sgrub of the Coni monastery in Kan-su (born 1675). For the simple man the mantradhāraṇī is a magic spell, for the educated man it is a formula (it can be long, middle or short) reminding of the unlimited firmness and never failing, extending over infinite aeons, memory of the Boddhisattva. The fundamental meaning seems to indicate firmness and absolute memory as charasteristics of the Superman. The dhāraṇā of the Yogasystem seems to be only indirectly connected with the dhāraṇīs of the Buddhists. The M. Vyut. § 25 mentions twelve varieties of Bodhisattva-dhāraṇī; cf. H. Dayal, p. 267 ff., Bodhisattva-bhūmi mentions four varieties, cp. LVP, p. 613—615.

[24] pratisaṃvid, pāli paṭisaṃbhidā, cf. M. Vyut. § 13, H. Dayal, p. 259 ff., cf. Saṃdhi-nirmocana-sūtra (ed. E. Lamotte), ch. VIII, § 19 ff.

[25] Read 3.15 with S. Y. samādhi-tiṅ-ṅe-ḥdzin, instead of samāpatti which always is sñoms-par-ḥjug-pa.

[26] vaśitā, cp. H. Dayal, p. 140. S. Y. reads indriya, cp. ibid., p. 141.

[27] kṣānti, cf. its sense in anutpatti-dharma-kṣānti, cf. MSA, XI.52 and the note of Sylvain Lévi, p. 123 of his translation; LVP, AK, VI.174. kṣānti in this context does not mean forbearance, but, as S. Lévi puts it, „la kṣānti est de l'ordre intellectuel, elle ne procède pas du sentiment". It is that stage in the progress of the Bodhisattva's meditation when he realizes that the external world does not exist, that all objects are Mind-only, but he still is conscious of his perceptive faculty. This stage kṣānty-avasthā precedes the final, but still phenomenal, stage of laukikāgra-dharma, cf. MSA bhāṣya ad XIV.26. kṣānti is a pṛṣṭha-labdha condition, the afterthought of trance, cf. E. Obermiller, Analysis, p. 229; it is śūnyatā-ruci, cf. Lankāv., p. 125, i. e. the Saint realizes that śūnyatā is not Nihilism, but paramārtha.

[28] Read with S. Y. 3.15 vimokṣāṇām-rnam-par-thar-pa; the eight degrees of liberation from the bonds of materiality, mentioned Dīgha III, 62 and M. Vyut. § 70. Cp. Rhys Davids, Sacred Books, II, p. 47—48. They are usually translated rnam-par-thar-pa-brgyad, whereas vimukti-mokṣa is rendered by rnam-par-ḥgrol-ba.

[29] mukhena-sgo-nar. Lit. 3.17 „Reverence to the commentary of the expositor is produced through the medium (of assuming) that it gives the right teaching". Acc. to S. Y. the four first words of 3.17 are missing in the MS.

[30] Read (with S. Y.) 3.18 bhadanta-Vasubandhu-brtsun-pa-dbyig-gñen.

[31] prajñā „analytical understanding", prajñā amalā-dharma-pravicaya, cf. AK, I.2.

[32] Read 4.1 ye pudgala-prāmāṇikās teṣām, as contrasted with the following dharma-pratisāriṇas, Tib. gaṅ-dag gaṅ-zag tshad-mar-byed-pa-de-dag...

[33] Read 4.3 ye'pi dharma-pratisāriṇas, Tib. gaṅ yaṅ chos-la brton-pa-de-dag. On pudgala-pratisārin and dharma-pratisārin, cp M. Vyut. § 74.

[34] Read 4.4 niścayaś ced utpadyate sa praṇetṛ-vaktr-avabodhād api prabhāvito bhavati, na kevalam āgama-mātreṇa tārkikaiḥ prabhāvito bhavatīti...-ṅes-pa skyes-na ḥdi mdzad-pa-daṅ-ḥchad-pa-yaṅ rtogs-pas rab-tu-phye-ba-yin-gyi, rtog-ge-pa luṅ-tsam-gyis rab-tu-phye-bar-ni ma-zad-do źes...; The Tib. ma-zad is usually a rendering of na kevalam; tārkikair āgamena in the sense of „by reasoners on scripture". rtog-ge-pa points to tārkika=mīmāṃsaka, «theologian», cp. MAV, p. 128, 11. The Peking T. reads rtog-ge-dañ-luñ=tarkeṇa āgamena ca where tarka could be „hypothetical judgment", „a guess" of the kind — yadi ghaṭa iha abhaviṣyad bhūtala iva adrakṣyata.

[35] Read 4.7 (probably) kīdṛśam for kim (svarūpam), Tib. ci-ḥdra-ba daṅ.

[36] Read 4.8 (with S. Y.) nāma-pada-vyañjana-kāya (instead of akṣara-samūha), Tib. miṅ-daṅ-tshig-daṅ-yi-ge-tshogs, cf. M. Vyut. § 104, where these viprayukta-saṃskāra's are found wrongly classified as caitasika dharma's.

[37] athavā.

[38] śabda-viśeṣa.

[39] jñāna-ye-śes.

[40] Read 4.10—11 praṇetṛ-vaktṛ-vijñapti-prabhavatvāc chravaṇa-vijñaptīnām nātra doṣaḥ, Tib. mdzad-pa daṅ ḥchad-pa-rnam-par-rig-pa-las ñan-pai rnam-par-rig-pa-rnams skye-bas ḥdi-la ñes-pa med-do.

[41] Lit. 4.7—13. „Now, what is this nature of šāstra? What is šāstra? We answer: šāstra are „pure intimations" appearing in the form of word-, phrase- and articulate-sound-complexes; or šāstra are „pure intimations" appearing in the form of special words conducive to supra-mundane knowledge. How are „pure intimations" revealed and explained? Because auditive intimations are produced from „intimations" of a revealer and of an expositor, there is no fault. Indeed a man being trained, since he produces special morality, exstasy and intuition, turns away from deeds—corporeal, vocal, mental—which do not produce puṇya-sambhāra and turns towards such deeds which produce sambhāra". — In order to understand this literal translation we must consider the following points. First of all šāstra is here not contrasted with sūtra, it is its synonym, it means Revelation or Holy Scripture, Tripiṭaka. This is also the original meaning of the term in brahmanical literature where it is used as a synonym of vidhi or niyoga, a vedic injunction to perform sacrifice leading to rebirth in heaven, just as a Buddhist šāstra leads to lokottara-jñāna, i. e. to Buddhahood. Cp. Mandanamišra's Vidhiviveka and Vācaspatimišra's Nyāyakaṇikā, p. 20 (Reprint from the Paṇḍit). šāstra, Revelation, is here said to be vijñapti, i. e. pure, unutterable sensation underlying a superinduced form of words and sentences. The meaning of this is the following one. vijñāna-skandha is defined in early Buddhism (cp. my CC, p. 12.16) as prativiṣaya-vijñaptiḥ and contrasted with saṃjñā-skandha which is defined as nimitta-udgrahaṇa, i.e. abstraction of the marks of the object. The first is thus unutterable pure sensation, the second is utterable definite representation. In the vijñapti-mātratā system the vijñapti which in the Sarvāstivāda was, so to speak, primus inter pares among the Elements of existence, became the unique monistic reality, all other Elements (dharma's) became borrowed realities or transcendental illusions. vijñapti etymologically means „announcement", especially announcement to a person of a higher rank. In philosophy it means announcement to our senses of the presence of something in the ken. vijñaptimātra means pure sensation, unutterable and unrepresentable, the bare fact of the existence of something (vastu-mātram-svalakṣaṇam). In early Buddhism vijñāna is therefore nirākāra. It becomes sākāra in the vijñapti-mātra system, but the ākāra is bhrānta, ultimate reality belongs to mere pure vijñapti and ākāra is then simply vijñaptikriyā. Cp. LVP, p. 196; MAV, 16.16. The problem of the reality of the external world thus loses all its importance, because when the extreme point of pure sensation is reached there is absolutely nothing beyond it which would not be an illusion. Applying these principles to the definition of Revelation Sthiramati here says that the Holy Scriptures are no exception to the rule, the words and phrase-complexes are external objects, hence mere illusions, absolutely real are only the pure sensations subjacent to them. However the auditive sensations subjacent to the Buddha's preaching have the force (šruta-vāsanā) to produce the lokottara-višuddhi, what we can call Transsubstantiation (āšraya-parāvṛtti). The corresponding doctrine is developed in detail by Asanga in his Mahāyānasaṃgraha (at the close of the first chapter). The vijñapti's and all their illusive superstructure are produced from germs (bīja) lying

dormant in one's own Psyche (ā l a y a - v i j ñ ā n a). These germs can be pure (a n ā s r a v a), they then lead to Transsubstantiation, cp. LVP, pp. 100—101 and 113—114. The revealer and the expositor are thus nothing but illusion. When an objector asks, how is it that unutterable pure intimations are revealed and explained by another person, the answer of S t h i r a m a t i is the same as the one always given by all solipsists, namely „the revealer and the expositor are themselves nothing above our ideas of them", nothing beyond pure v i j ñ a p t i's, there is no exception to the rule that ultimately nothing exists beyond our v i j ñ a p t i's, cp. LVP, pp. 18 and 83; the ideas of one man can never grasp directly the ideas of another man. A quite free paraphrase of the passage 4.7—13 would have been the following one—„Revelation is for the consequent Idealist nothing but his own ideas, the outcome of their germs lying concealed in the subliminal consciousness of his own Psyche (ā l a y a). The words and phrases are mere illusions. However these germs (š r a v a ṇ a - v ā s a n ā) are germs of purity (a n ā s r a v a b ī j a) leading to Transsubstantiation and omniscience in the eternal Body of a Buddha. If it is asked how can my own germs of Transsubstantiation be revealed and explained to me by another person, the question is futile, since these revealer and explainer are themselves nothing beyond my ideas of them and beyond the respective subjacent „intimations" or germs. However that does not interfere with the fact that a Bodhisattva through his training in morality and knowledge attains transcendental powers leading to Transsubstantiation into a Buddha; by his training he clears away the impurity of phenomenality and attains the purity of the Absolute". — The implications of this passage seem to be the following ones. S t h i r a m a t i is perfectly aware that in a monistic Universe the Bodhisattva cannot be an ultimate reality, since there is only one ultimate reality— e k a m d r a v y a m (= substantia sive Deus), all the rest is phenomenal and illusion. He is also aware that consequent Idealism leads to Solipsism and consequent phenomenalism undermines all moral teaching. He e x p r e s s i s v e r b i s says p. 25.11: this would be an enormous calamity for our religion = m a h ā ñ c h ā s a n a - u p a p l a v a ḥ p r a s a j y a t e. Therefore an escape forcibly must be found. Buddhists must q u a n d m ê m e, in spite of logic, assert the efficiency of their system of morality, in order to save religion. Logic must be condemned, not religion. This condemnation of logic is conditional in the Yogācāra system, absolute with the Mādhyamikas.

Among all Buddhist schools the Vaibhāṣikas are known to refer the Tripiṭaka to s a ṃ s k ā r a - s k a n d h a as consisting of n ā m a - p a d a - v y a ñ - j a n a - c i t t a - v i p r a y u k t a - s a ṃ s k ā r a's. The Vijñānavādins, as is seen from this passage of S t h i r a m a t i, refer it to s a ṃ s k ā r a - s k a n d h a in first line and ultimately to v i j ñ ā n a - s k a n d h a, however to a monistic v i j ñ ā n a - s k a n d h a; the Sautrāntikas and all other schools which do not admit the n ā m a - p a d a - v y a ñ j a n a - s a ṃ s k ā r a's refer it to r ū p a - s k a n d h a as being š a b d a, thus siding partly with the M ī m ā ṃ s a k a s for whom the veda is abso š a b d a. Cp. V i n ī t a d e v a's Comment on S a ṃ - t ā n ā n t a r a s i d d h i (in the Introd.)

[42] Read 4.11 — š a i k ṣ a - d h a r m ā n ā m; s l o b - m a c h o s - p a - n i „a religious student"; s l o b - m a is usually a rendering of š i ṣ y a, not of š i k ṣ ā or š a i k ṣ a which are rendered by s l o b - p a, but here the meaning remains the same, it includes every individual practising the Path up to the degree of the a r h a t who is a š a i k ṣ a. Cp. LVP, p. 279 and 507 š i ṣ y a - d h a r m a n or š a i k ṣ a - d h a r m a n is a formation like v i d i t a - d h a r m a n. Y.'s retranslation of the following phrase seems to be quite all right, the term s a ṃ - b h ā r a - u t p a t t i - k a r m a n and s a m b h ā r ā n u t p a t t i - k a r m a n must then

be taken as technical terms where sambhāra is pars pro toto and embraces sambhāra-, prayoga-, darśana- and bhāvanā-mārga, not saṃbhāra-mārga alone.

[43] athavā-yaṅ-na.

[44] Read 4.14 — śāstra-lakṣaṇa-yogāc chāsanāc chāstram, the Tib. has bstan-bcos-kyi mtshan-ñid-du ḥthad-pai-phyir bstan-bcos-te, it omits the equivalent for śāsanāt, the sanscrit omits yogāt, which hardly is an invention of the translators. The original probably had both words.

[45] In place of yad-upadeśena the Tib. has — luṅ-mnos-pa-gomspar-byed-pas-upadeśa-abhyāsena.

[46] Read 4.16 — vividha-tīvra-duḥkha-bhayānaka-durgatibhyo bhavāc ca trāṇam; Tib. sdug-bsṅal-drag-po-sna-tshogskyis ḥjigs-pai ṅan-soṅ-rnams daṅ srid-pa-las skyob-pa (skyob is usually trā, neither rakṣaṇa nor saṃsāra).

[47] Read 4.17 — kleśa-śatru-śāsanād durgati-bhavāc ca trāṇāc (chāstram iti) śāstra-lakṣaṇam; Tib. ñon-moṅs-pai dgraḥchos-pa daṅ ṅan-ḥgroi sridpa-las skyobs-pas bstan-bcoskyi mtshan-ñid-de. This is an etymological explanation, therefore the roots śās and trā are here rendered by their usual Tib. equivalents ḥchos-pa and skyob-pa.

[48] An often quoted verse from the Vyākhyāyukti of Vasubandhu, cp. MV, p. 3.

[49] pratyakṣa.

[50] saṅgraha.

[51] Lit. 4.24—25 „Through the medium (mukhena) of the three yānas a summary of seven topics"; but the meaning is, on the contrary, that the seven topics are examined directly and the three yānas through them, indirectly.

[52] tri-yāna, śrāvaka-, pratyeka- and bodhisattva-yāna.

[53] kleśa-jñeya-āvaraṇa.

[54] Read 5.2 — pra-śabda-saṃvyāhṛtaḥ, Tib. rab-kyi sgra=daṅ sgrogs-na. The editors read in the MS karaṇe where S. Y. reads viśesārthako (?!).

[55] Cf. MV, p. 5.

[56] This phrase is translated in Tib. after the explanation of ca in 5.23 where we read mṅon-mchod źes-bya-ba rjed-pao (xyl. rjes-pao), mṅon-par žes-bya-ba-ni mdun-nas...

[57] su-gata-śintu gśegs-pa „successfully gone (sc. to Nirvāṇa). ātmaja does not here mean „a son", but „produced (-ja) out of the essence (ātma) of a Buddha", i. e. out of tathatā, śūnyatā.

[58] Read 5.7— kleśa-āvaraṇa-jñeya-āvaranād apratiṣṭhitam nirvāṇam gata iti sugataḥ, Tib. ñons-moṅs-pai-sgribs-padaṅ śes-byai sgribs-pa-las mi-gnas-pai mya-ṅan-las-ḥdaspar śin-tu gśegs-pas bde-bar gśegs-pao; kleśa-jñeya-āvaraṇa can be rendered as emotional and intellectual obscurations or limitations; vāsanā-bīja.

[59] apratiṣṭhita-nirvāṇa can be rendered as „illimited" or absolute Nirvāṇa, because it is not limited by the Hīnayānistic idea of complete annihilation in Nirvāṇa. It also can be called „Mahāyānistic Nirvāṇa". For the Mahāyānists it is the only real Nirvāṇa, its synonym is dharmakāya. It is difficult for me to admit that this term means residence somewhere between saṃsāra and nirvāṇa, LVP, p. 672. But it means

that owing to mahā-karuṇā (the mahayanistic thugs-rje-chen-po) the Buddha makes the sacrifice of his personal (Hīnayānistic) Nirvāṇa and this sacrifice constitutes his real Salvation, cp. MAV, p. 68.15. (S. Y.).

[60] sarva-vāsanā-āvaraṇa-prahīnaḥ „completely liberated from all obscuration habits"; vāsanā here means the habitual properties of a thing, its potential causality, cp. LVP, p. 80. The Bodhisattva has eradicated the habitual properties of a human being and has become a being of another kind, a superman, a divine being.

[61] i. e. he has attained the sarvākāra-jñatā or the Mahāyānistic Omniscience which is the property only of the Buddhas. There are two kinds of omniscience, sarvākāra-jñatā and sarvajñatā simply or sarva-vastu-jñatā, Tib. rnam-śes and gźi-śes. The first is attained only in the mahāyānistic apratiṣṭhita-nirvāṇa. The second is attained in Hīnayānist Nirvāṇa. The latter, speaking generally, supposes a knowledge of all elements (dharmas) as realities, the first is the knowledge of all dharmas as un-realities, of their Relativity or of their śūnyatā. Cp. Obermiller, Analysis.

[62] Read 5.9 — āśraya-bhūta- instead of bhūtaś, since it must be referred to vigraha as a part of the bahuvrīhi. The Tib. drops the word for vigraha „body"; the body for the Vijñānavādin is spiritual, ālaya-vijñāna-svabhāvaḥ kāyaḥ, cf. Kamalaśīla, TSP, p. 537.8.

[63] jñāna-ye-śes.

[64] Cf. Dignāga's verse quoted in my introduction to the ed. of Abhisamayālaṃkāra in Bib. Buddh. XXVI, where the Buddha is identified with prajñā-pāramitā.

[65] tathatā, synonym of śūnyatā, cf. MAV, 41.2.

[66] viśuddhi, synonym of śūnyatā. Read either viśuddhis tathatā, or viśuddha-tathatā, Tib. rnam-par-dag-pai de-bźin-ñid.

[67] nirvikalpaka-rnam-par-mi-rtog-pa.

[68] jñāna-ye-śes is not a mere noetic phenomenon, but Gnosis, a transic condition, the experience of a union with the Absolute, the experience of enjoying the flavour and rapture of such meditation. On the eighth stage of the Bodhisattvas progress his ālaya-vijñāna is no more a vijñāna, but a jñāna, it is ādarśavat; the Tib. translators very judiciously always mark the difference by using the term ye-śes.

[69] i. e. he possesses the sarvākāra-jñatā, omniscience in the Mahāyānistic sense.

[70] Read 5.17—20 (according to the Tib.) — atra sugatātmaja iti śāstra-praṇetus tattvāvabodha-sampan nirdiṣṭā, lābha-satkāra-nirapekṣa-praṇetṛtvena karuṇā-sampat prajñā-sampac ca nirdiṣṭā, Tib. ḥdir-ni bde-bār-gśegs-pai bdag-ñid-las skyes-pas bstan-bcos-mdzad-pa de-kho-na-thugs-su-chud-pa-phun-sum-tshogs-par bstan-pa daṅ, rñed-pa daṅ bkur-sti-la mi-blta-bar bstan-bcos mdzad-pas thugs-rje phun-sum-tshogs-pa-daṅ śes-rab-phun-sum-tshogs-par bstan-pao.

[71] Read 5.22 — dharma-srotasā śāstram idam āvir-bhūyoktam, Tib. chos-kyi rgyun-gyis bstan-bcos-ḥdi mṅon-du gyur-ciṅ bśad-do. The dharma-srotas-samādhi is practiced by the Bodhisattva beginning from his prayoga-mārga. Cf. E. Obermiller, Analysis.

[72] These words sound like a confession that the real author of MAV was Asaṅga.

[73] In Tib. the explanation of the words asmad ādibhya iti precedes the explanation of ca (yaṅ) and the latter is followed by the explanation of the words abhyarhya which in the sanscrit text is attached to the mention of this word on p. 5.5.

[74] The Tib. adds the words gaṅ-yaṅ ruṅ-ba-dag-la. The interpretation of „and" (ca) as „etc." is usual, especially in sūtras, cp. LVP, p. 377.

[75] After the words asmad-ādibhya p. 5.26 the Tib. adds — ḥdi-ni bdag-ñid-kyi mi-slu-ba-las luṅ-mnos-par ston-to-sa hi svayam eva avisaṃvāditvād upadeśam nirdiśati. — I cannot understand the retranslation of this passage by S.Y. p. 5.2—3.

[76] The Tib. renders iyam ca nimittārthā samptamī by bsgrim-par-bya-pai-phyir (before which a cheda must be inserted) źes-bya-ba ḥdi-ni rgyui don-te. The regular translation of nimitta is rgyu-mtshan, saptamī is not translated at all and bsgrim-par-bya-bai-phyir is added.

[77] Drop the word sambandhe in 6.5.

[78] dharma-nairātmya.

[79] abhyāsa repetition, intensification, production of karma.

[80] niḥšeṣa-savāsana-kleša-jñeya-āvaraṇa-prahāṇa, 6.7 lit. „absolute annihilation of the obscuration of vices and (of the obscuration of) the cognizable, with their germs, without any residue".

[81] Read 6.8—10 — dharme nairātmyam api sarva-dharma-nāstitva-dharma-nairātmyam, antar-vyāpāra-puruṣa-nāstitvam ca dharmeṣu nairātmyam ity etayor viṣama-vādayor nirāsena yathā-bhūta-dharma-nairātmya-pratipādanārtham śāstrārambhaḥ. Tib. chos-la bdag-med-pa-yaṅ chos-thams-cad-med-pa-ñid chos-la bdag-med-pa daṅ, naṅ-na-byed-pai skyes-bu med-pa-ñid chos-rnams-la bdag-med-pao źes mi-mthun-par smra-ba-de-dag bkag-pas, chos-bdag-med-pa yaṅ-dag-pa ji-lta-ba bźin-du bstan-par-bya-bai-phyir bstan-bcos brtsam-mo. Lit. „In every (single) dharma there is nairātmya, this is nairātmya of dharma, meaning non-existence of all dharmas; and the absence of an internal active soul meaning nairātmya in the dharmas (collectively); by the repudiation of these two wrong theories, in order to establish the really right doctrine of dharma-nairātmya this śāstra has been undertaken".

Thus the two competing theories of the mahāyānistic sarva-dharma-śūnyatā and hinayānistic pudgala-śūnyatā are here interpreted as dharme šūnyatā and dharmeṣu šūnyatā respectively. Cp. LVP, p. 568. According to the Yogācāras these theories do not exclude the ultimate reality neither of the paratantra-Element in every dharma singly taken, nor the pariniṣpanna-Element in all dharmas taken collectively. But according to the Mādhyamika school these Elements are likewise relative and ultimately unreal. S.Y.'s retransltion. 5.14 ff. is quite incomprehensible.

[82] According to the Tib. the five categories of the cognizable here quoted are loka-dhātu, sattva, dharma, vinaya and upāya. Y. 5.21 reads upāya-dhātu in the place of upāyatva, but this seemingly does not agree with the division being fivefold. In 6.14 read citta-saṅkocas with S.Y., p. 5.23.

[83] Cp. above, text p. 4.7 ff.

[84] āyatana, here the same as dharma.

[85] Read 6.26 (instead of vistareṇa etc.)—dṛṣṭa-bhūmi-niḥśaṅka-aśva-dhāvanam iva, Tib. dkyu-sa-bstan-pai rta thags-thogs-

med-par rgyug-pa bźin-te. Xyl. reads dkyus-kyis, evidently a very early confusion, if not to be read dkyus-kyi-sa; dkyu-sa „race ground"; thags-thogs-med-par-niḥśankam. The Labrang Commentary reads f. 9.b.3—dkyus-bstan-pai rta bžin without explaining. This can only mean „like a horse which has been trained to run (a certain length on the race-course).

[86] Read 6.26—nānyathā, Tib. gźan-du ma-yin-no; drop the following santi with Y.

[87] After the words sampūrṇam ity arthaḥ, 7.2, (S. Y. 6.12 samāptam) Tib. has śes-par-bya-ba-yin-pas don-de khon-du-chud-par-bya-ba źes-bya-bai tha-tshig-go, this seems to correspond to arthyanta iti arthā adhigamyanta iti yāvat.

[88] saṃkleśa-lakṣaṇam-samalam, cf. below MAV, p. 42.21. The saṃkleśas are the 12 nidānas, the ever reverting stages of phenomenal life, regarded as „phenomenalizers" or agencies which convert absolute pure reality into a phenomenal or impure (samala) one. Cp. LVP, p. 215.

[89] Read 7.8 (with S. Y.)—saptadhābhūta, i. e. abhūta for bhūta, cf. MAV, p. 34.7. Tib. rnam-bdun yaṅ-dag-mi-rtog-las, evidently for yaṅ-dag-min-rtog-las. The nine lakṣaṇa's are rehearsed p. 37.13—25.

[90] saṃkleśa-vyavadānābyām bhinnam.

[91] Read 7.11 iti cet, naitad evam, Tib. źe na, de-ni de-lta ma-yin-te.

[92] svabhāva eva hi bhāvānām lakṣaṇam, Tib. dṅos-po-rnams raṅ-bźin-ñid-de, lit. „of the Ens-es the essence (or the definition) is the own-Ens (itself)", i. e. the essence of a reality is the real itself, not something extraneous to it, i. e. the essence of a thing is the Thing-in-Itself.

[93] khakkhaṭatva, Tib. sra-ba-ñid. (S. Y.—kharatva).

[94] pṛthivī-dhātuḥ, Tib. sai-khams. Cp. LVP, p. 65—„la solidité n'est pas distincte de la terre".

[95] i. e. lakṣaṇa can be analysed as a karaṇa-sādhana, it then means lakṣyate anena iti lakṣaṇam, or as a bhāva-sādhana, it then means lakṣyate etad iti laksaṇam.

[96] saṃkleśa-vyavadānābhyām (Instr.).

[97] Thus the two main principles, the two central conceptions of the system are here brought in connection with the division of reality into phenomenal and absolute. The Particular (svalakṣaṇa) in the sense of the extreme concrete and particular, the absolute particular, the Thing-in-Itself, is nothing but that Constructor of phenomena which will be described in the next stanza. In the idealistic system of the Yogācāras it of course cannot represent an efficient point-instant of external reality which the svalakṣaṇa represents in the Sautrāntika system, but the meaning of a pure sensation, of an extreme concrete and particular Ens remains. The Thing-in-Itself becomes spiritual, its other names are paratantra, saṃskṛta or abhūta-parikalpa. It is transcendental, still phenomenal although the extreme limit of phenomenality, it is śuddha-laukika, cp. MAV, p. 19.19. The other central conception is śūnyatā-tathatā=pariniṣpanna etc. etc. It represents the vyavadāna-part, the transcendent (lokottara), pure (viśuddha) aspect of Reality; the stanzas of MAV beginning with I. 12 describe it.

[98] sa bhāvyata iti bhāvanā, Tib. de goms-par-bya-ba-ni bsgom-pao, the term bhāvanā implies the meaning of meditation and

mental creation, in an idealistic system creation in general, it is originally a term of the Mīmāṃsakas, cp. Maṇḍanamiśra's work Bhāvanāviveka.

[99] gotra-avasthā-gotra-bhūmi, Tib. rigs-kyi gnas, the Element of Buddha's lineage is eternal according to the Mādhyamikas, non-eternal according to the Yogācāras, cf. E. Obermiller, Pr. P., p. 49.

[100] 7.25 pratipatti, Tib. sgrub-pa.

[101] adhimukti-caryā-prayoga-mārga, Tib. mos-pas spyod-pa, cf. E. Obermiller, Pr. P., ibid.

[102] Read 8.7—tat tattvam ity avagantavyam, Tib. de-ni (de-) kho-na-ñid yin-par khoṅ-du chud-par byao (xyl. de-ni kho-na yin-par).

[103] Read 8.8—tad-ālambanena. Tib. dmigs-pa-des.

[104] gotra-avasthā, cf. above, note 99.

[105] Read 8.11—srota-āpatti-phalādi-jñeyam, Tib. rgyun-du ḥjug-pai ḥbras-bu-la-sogs-par śes-par-byao (instead of phalādi saṃtāna-gatam).

[106] Read 8.12 (according to E. O.)—saśiṣya-śrāvakādīnām, Tib. slob-ma-daṅ-bcas-pas. The Tib. context points to a reading—etac ca sarvam saśiṣya-bodhisattvānām śrāvakādīnam ca sādhāraṇam-de-dag thams-cad kyaṅ slob-ma-daṅ-bcas-pai (xyl. pas) byaṅ-chub-sems-dpaḥ daṅ ñan-thos-la-sogs-pa daṅ thun-moṅ ste. The Peking T. reads bla-ma instead of slob-ma whence S. Y., 8.5 has probablly derived his sottarāc (?).

[107] kauśala, Tib. mkhas-par-bya-ba „cleverness", „deeper insight", „learning". Drop the cheda before tataḥ in 8.20.

[108] Read 8.23. (with the MS)—bodhisattvasya.

[109] Read 9.5—apare'pimanyante sad-asad-dharma mohāt, Tib. gźan-yaṅ sems-pa yod-pa daṅ med-pai chos-la rmoṅs-nas. The sentence is continued up to atra nirdiṣṭam in 9.11, where, in accordance with the Tib., ante nirdiṣṭam must be read. Tib. thamar bśad-do sñam-mo. Just as on p. 29.7 and 29.11 the editors have mistaken sems-pa=cetanā for citta=sems, so they have here mistaken sems-pa=manyate for citta, since they identify sñam-mo with manyante, sems-pa with cittasya, whereas sñam-mo is „iti" sems-pa corresponds to manyante and cittasya is altogether superfluous. sems-pa is never citta, but either cetanā, or cintayati.

[110] kauśala, kuśala=mkhas-pa=paṇḍita. Asaṅga's theory of the bhūmi's is here alluded to.

[111] Read 9.9—avasthayā phalam prabhāvitam iti, Tib. gnas-skabs-kyis ḥbras-bu rab-tu phye-bas.

[112] Read 9.10—11—sarvam etan mahāyānam āgamayatīti (or āgamayyeti), Tib. de-dag thams-cad-kyaṅ theg-pa-chen po-la brten-pas; lit. „all this serves as an introduction (to Mahāyāna)". The Tib. means that the preceding topics are founded on Mahāyāna, but this stands in contradiction to the preceding three explanations according to which the preceding six topics are not the real Mahāyāna, they also are found in Hīnayāna, but the last topic alone shows the difference of Mahāyāna.

[113] Read 9.11 with V., 9.8—ante nirdiṣṭam iti, cf. above, note 109.

Part I, Chapter II

[1] The whole first part of MAV is devoted to the definition and detailed desoription of two items, abhūta-parikalpa and śūnyatā. Their meaning, I hope, and all their fargoing implications will clearly emerge at the end of this translation.

The term abhūta means „unreal", but not unexistent; the Tib. translators accordingly do not render it by „not-existent" (med-pa or dños-po-med-pa-abhāva), but by „not quite real", „not ultimately real" (yan-dag-pa-ma-yin-pa), which can be rendered as „relatively real", „phenomenal", „not absolute", its synonym is vitatha, i. e. non-tathatā. Indeed it will be seen that it must be distinguished, on one side, from an absolute non-Ens (abhāva or atyanta-abhāva), on the other side, from an absolute Ens (bhūtārtha-tattva-tathatā-parinişpnana-śūnyatā). We thus have the full right to call it phenomenal appearance, Appearance simply, illusive appearance, world-illusion, transcendental illusion, phenomenal world or worlds, since all single phenomena, as well as all the worlds, everything except the transcendent Absolute, are embraced by it. „pari-kalpa" is rendered in Tib. as kun-nas-rtog-pa „universal constructor", but the characteristic of „universal" can be dropped, the term can be replaced by vikalpa and even simple kalpa, cf. MSA, XI. 31 and MAV passim. In logic we have rendered vikalpa by „imagination", „productive imagination" (in the Kantian sense). In the early Vijñāna-vāda (āgama- anusārin) it would be a grave mistake to retain this interpretation, because parikalpa is here contrasted with parikalpita „the thing imagined". We must distinguish and even oppose „creative imagination" to „created by imagination". Therefore „Imaginator", „Constructor of phenomena", „Creator of Appearance", „Creator of the phenomenal worlds", „Creator of the world-illusion", „Creator of a transcendental illusion" will be adequate renderings for abhūta-parikalpa with the proviso that it is by no means a personal Creator, but simply the human Mind as the faculty of Imagination. This is the „real creator of the unreal", i. e. of all phenomena; it is that Reality which creates Appearance. On the difference between parikalpita and vikalpita cp. MAV, kārikā III. 17 and LVP, p. 516.

[2] dvaya „division" or „duality". The division of concrete reality in two parts, the one grasping the other, the object and subject, is the first step of the constructive Mind, when consciousness just arises in the subconscious Mind-store. Cf. Kamalaśīla's remark, Tattva sp. 369.8, that in the logical Yogācāra school vikalpa means „construction of an image capable to coalesce with a name (cp. N. bindu, p. 7.20 ablilāpa-saṃsarga-yogya-pratibhāsa-pratīti), whereas in the early Yogācāra it means first of all grāhya-grāhaka-kalpanā, construction of subject and object, or division into subject and object. The construction manifests itself in a division, vikalpa means both division, construction and constructor (parikalpayitṛ).

[3] śūnyatā, the meaning of this term will be clearly established later on, it has in the Vijñānavāda system the meaning of an Absolute Ens as a positive all-embracing reality in itself, whereas in the Mādhyamika system which denies the existence of all reality-in-itself, the same term means just the opposite, i. e. Relativity, the absence of an Absolute. Cf. below MAV, p. 38 ff.

[4] vikalpa-rtog-pa-ni. Xyl. corresponds to — tatra abhūta-parikalpo grāhya-grāhaka-vikalpaḥ. Read kun-tu-rtog-pa-ni instead of kun-tu-rtog-pai-ni.

[5] Read — gñis-po-ni gzuṅ-ba-daṅ-ḥdzin-pai dṅos-po-o, de daṅ bral-ba-o. grāhya-grāhaka-bhāva, cp. kārya-kāraṇa-bhāva, dṅos-po-bhāva, relation.

[6] sarve dharmāḥ.

[7] The Mādhyamikas have never maintained that they do not exist at all, that they are abhāva. They maintained that they are svabhāva-śūnya (or simply śūnya), dīrgha-hrasva-vat, real only relatively as „the long and the short", cp. MV, pp. 10, 252, 264, 458. 529; cp. the emphatic protest against abhāva-ābhiniveša, ibid., p. 248.

[8] According to the Mādhyamikas there is absolutely nothing real in itself, every thing is relative; they deny the Thing-in-Itself, because it is dependent; the Yogācāras, on the contrary, maintain the reality of everything causally dependent, cp. Triṃš., p. 16.16 — vijñānam punaḥ pratītya-samutpannatvād dravyato'stīti.

[9] The parikalpa is dvayarahita but šūnyatā is dvayarahitatā and that is all the difference, cp. below, p. 19.20; the passage **10.2-3** (and S. Y. 11.2) must be sublined.

[10] Lit. „not saved".

[11] Read 10.9 — athavā citta-caittasikavad rūpam api dravyato'stīti... - Tib. yaṅ-na sems daṅ sems-las-ḥbyuṅ-ba-rnams-ltar (Xyl. rnams-so) gzugs daṅ rdzas-ñid-du yod-par... Cf. Trimś., p. 16.9 — vijñānavad vijñeyam api dravyato, sti (cf. H. Jacobi's translation). Cp. S. Y., p. 11. 10, onyatra (?).

[12] Read 10.11 — sa eva asti dravyataḥ (cp. S.Y. 11.13).

[13] Lit. 10.14 — „the bare thing deprived of apprehended and apprehender".

[14] Lit. 10.16 — „and what is the cause of what (yad yasya), its production in the absence of that, (i. e. of its cause) is impossible".

[15] Read 10. 18-19 — grāhakasyābhāvād asatigrāhye grāhakabhāvo na yujyate. Cf. Abhisamayāl., v. 7. This of course does not interfere with the existence of the Absolute. But the Mādhyamikas on this score, viz. on the score that subject and object are relative, deny the absolute reality of consciousness, they thus deny the reality of the cogito-manas, cf. Madhy. avatāra, VI, 48 and VI, 51.

[16] Lit. 10.20 — „apart from the universal arranger of the not-ultimately-real".

[17] rūpam.

[18] Salvation consists in this that the Saint reaches absolute knowledge and perceives Nirvāṇa. This is called the Pure Object (pariśuddha-ālambana). It transcends the boundaries of the phenomenal world, it is lokottara, it is transcendent; whereas abhūta-parikalpa is śuddha-laukika-gocara (cf. below 19.22); i. e. it is still in the phenomenal world (as its condition), it is not transcendent (lokottara), but transcendental, to use Kantian terminology.

[19] Read 10.22—23 — viśuddhyālambanam - Tib. rnam-par-dag-pai dmigs-pa-ste (not dmigs-pa-can).

[20] Lit. 10.23 „And it is the universal (-tā) deficiency of apprehended and apprehender". Indeed the definition or essence (lakṣaṇa-mtshan-ñid) of the Absolute (śūnyatā) consists in the concerted universal absence of both the object and the subject and the presence of their subjacent substratum, i. e. in Monism.

[21] Lit. 11.6 „But those who think that just as the material (Elements) etc. appear, just so, separately from the Constructor of the unreal, they exist in their own reality, against them it is said in order to repudiate imputation (of reality) upon the non-real «there is here no duality»".

[22] Read 11.7 — parikalpat-kun-tu-rtog-pa-las (with S. Y., p. 12.12).

[23] uccheda-rūpa-uccheda-svarūpa, materialism, denial of the law of karma. S. Y. — cheda-rūpo (?).

[24] dharmāṇām śūnyatā; thus it is clear from this passage that śūnyatā means for the Sautrāntikas no other ultimate reality than the dharmas, for the Mādhyamikas no absolute Ens altogether, every thing relative, and for the Yogācāras every thing relative save one, the Absolute Ens. The latter unfairly accuse the Mādhyamikas of Nihilism, whereas they are Relativists, they only deny the Thing-in-Itself. Although śūnyatā, svabhāva-śūnyatā and nairātmya or bhūta-nairātmya are synonyms, Sthiramati uses here śūnyatā in the Yogācāra implication as a repudiation of the denial of every ultimate reality, and nairātmya in the Sautrāntika-Vaibhāṣika sense as pudgala-nairātmya, or puruṣa-rahitatā.

[25] antar-vyāpāra-puruṣa.

[26] bhūta-nairātmya, i. e. real non-substantiality or the phenomenal non-substantiality regarding the (absolute) reality.

[27] 11.15 — saṃkliṣṭā-samalā, cf. below, p. 42. What the saṃkleśas are will be ecxplained below, p. 29 ff.

[28] Read 11.15 — viśodhayitavyā - Tib. rnam-par-sbyaṅs-dgos-pas.

[29] Cf. above, p. 8.17 ff.

[30] parīkṣārtham (11.18).

[31] saṃkleśa (11.19) is the phenomenal life (saṃvṛti) or the 12 stages of that ever reverting process, cf. below, p. 29 ff. abhūta-parikalpa belongs also to the phenomenal world, it is śuddha-laukika-gocaraḥ (19.14). Therefore there is an existential identity between them. abhūta-parikalpa, alias paratantra, is according to the definition of the Tibetans (grub-mthaḥ-chen-mo) ḥkhrul-pa daṅ ḥkhrul-gźi-brhāntir bhrānteś ca āśrayaḥ, it is the Thing-in-Itself (svalakṣaṇam) which is the foundation of the construction of the corresponding illusive phenomenon, and also this phenomenon itself. abhūta-parikalpa-svabhāvaḥ has here the sense of abhūta-parikalpita-svabhāvaḥ.

[32] Lit. 11.22 „The illusion-essence is clear through the imputed (prakhyātena-pratibhāsitena) object-subject form".

[33] Lit. (11.17 12.2) „Or essence is not different from the above-mentioned essence of great oppression and purification. Therefore in order to consider the essence of great oppression and purification, he says „the construction of unreality exists, etc". Great oppression has the essence of a general construction of unreality, because it has the essence of illusion. How is it known that it has the essence of illusion? Because „duality is not found here". The essence of illusion is evident through the form of apprehended and apprehender which does not exist in itself, (but) appears. Now in order to consider the purification-essence he says „the Absolute is found here". Purification has the essence of the Absolute, because it has the essence of non-duality. And we must know that here extinction and the path are both taken, since they are made powerfull (prabhāvita) through the Absolute. Only from the part of great oppression (saṃkleśa) the part of purification

can be path-converted (mārgayitavya), but it has no separate existence; in order to indicate this he says «here»".— The Tib. points to a reading na svasantānāt pṛthak sattvam asya asti instead of na punaḥ pṛthak sattvam asya asti. This would mean that the Absolute must be found introspectivly by deep meditation in the depths of one's own consciousness, it is pratyāma-vedanīya, every one can find it in himself, an idea very much in vogue in the schools of Mahāyāna. Probably both readings go back to some discrepancy in early Mss. Tib.—raṅ-gi rgyud gud-na med-par rab-tu-bstan-pai-phyir ḥdi-la źes-bya-ba gsuṅs-so.

[34] vikalpaḥ (12.4)-abhūta-parikalpaḥ.

[35] Read 12.4—hastyādi-śūnya-māyāyām, Tib. sgyu-ma-ni glaṅ-po-che la-sogs-pas stoṅ-yaṅ, glaṅ-po-che-la-sogs-par snaṅ-ba-lta-buo. Drop ākāra after hastyādi in 12.4.

[36] vikalpaḥ (12.12) in the sense of both construction and division.

[37] Read 12.16 with S. Y.—viviktatā instead of the second rahitatā. (E. O.). The Tib. has here two different words or synonyms—bral-ba-ñid-de, dben-pa-ñid-ni, the sanscrit must probably also have had two different words.

[38] Lit. 12.15 „The fact (-tā) of devoidness from the relation (bhāva) of grasped and grasper, the fact of its non-existence, is the „devoidness", (the Absolute) which belongs to the constructor of the unreal".

[39] Thus the abhūta-parikalpa-Element which above, p. 11.20, was characterized as unreal (bhrānta) is here emphatically characterized as real. The reason is this, that it represents a reality covered by an unreality, the Thing-in-Itself under the cover of the phenomenon. śūnyatā the Absolute is thus the appurtenance, or the universal quality (dharma) of all things non-absolute, which become the possessors (dharmin) of this quality, they are na anya na ananya. Cf. below, p. 14.2. The same relation obtains between pariniṣpanna (-śūnyatā) and paratantra (-abhūta-parikalpa). Cf. below, p. 14.1—2.

[40] upakliṣṭa (12.20).

[41] This means that vijñāna is sākāra, but both parts (nimittabhāga and darśana-bhāga) are only one reality, the ākāra (or samijñā) is bhrānti-mātram, cp. below, MAV, p. 27.2

[42] Two things remain, viz. 1) the transcendental pure reality of the (idealistic) Thing-in-Itself remains, it is svalakṣaṇa, kṣaṇika and paramārthasat, but not paramārtha-satya, and 2) the transcendent pure reality of the (idealistic) Whole remains, it is sāmānya-lakṣaṇa, nitya, both paramārtha-sat and paramārtha-satya, but paramārtha-sat only for the yogī who perceives it directly; in other words two limits remain, viz. 1) the extreme concrete and particular, the point-instant, the Thing-in-Itself, and 2) the other limit, the extreme abstract and universal. Both these limits alone remain.

[43] Read 12.25—paśyan yathābhūtam prajānāti=Tib. mthoṅ-na yaṅ-dag-pa-ji-lta-pa-bźin-du rab-tu-śes-so (instead of samyag-yathāvat).

[44] The Voidness in the Yogācāra sense as the unique absolute, the absence of relativity, would not exist if we would share in the Sautrāntika view that all Elements (sarve dharmāḥ) are absolutely real, are pariniṣpanna (cf. below, p. 27.2). According to the Sautrāntikas all are pariniṣpanna, according to the Mādhyamikas not a single one is pariniṣpanna and, according to the Yogācāras there is one unique Element, Pure Awa-

reness (v i j ñ a p t i - m ā t r a t ā) that is really p a r i n i ṣ p a n n a. Naturally if we adhere either to the S a u t r ā n t i k a or to the M ā d h y a m i k a views we cannot share in the Y o g ā c ā r a view. The correct reading is probably the reading of the MS—s a r v a - b h ā v a - a b h ā v a u t u v i p a r ī t a m ś ū n y a t ā - l a k ṣ a ṇ a m (without the na). The Tibatans have rightly rendered it by t h a m s - c a d - m e d - p a - ḥ a m t h a m s - c a d - y o d - p a - n i since in the following explanation as everywhere else, the reputation of the M ā d h y a m i k a s precedes the reputation of the S a u t r ā n t i k a s. In sanscrit the author in accordance with the requirements of the śāstra-style must express himself in a compound wheresoever possible, but then he was obliged to invert the order of a b h ā v a and b h ā v a according to Pāṇini II. 2. 33—34.

[45] Read 13.5 — d h a r m a t ā y ā h i b h ā v ā y a t t a t a y ā a n i t y a t ā - d i v a t = Tib. c h o s - ñ i d - n i d ṅ o s - p o - l a r a g - l u s - p a i - p h y i r m i - r t a g - p a - ñ i d l a - s o g s - p a b ź i n - n o, cp. below, p. 39.25.

[46] Lit. 13.3—8. „Non-existence of everything and existence of everything are wrong definitions of ś ū n y a t ā, because of the consequence that ś ū n y a t ā itself will not exist. If there is deficiency of the „it is devoid", devoidness is not possible, because the fact of being a general quality depends on the existence of things, just as momentariness and other (general qualities). „Duality exists", if thus, then non-existence of voidness. If duality is similar to the horns of a hare, how through it the voidness of the Constructor of the unreal is possible. Indeed voidness is observed of the one through the other, as of the cloister through the monks".

[47] Read 13.10 — g r a h a ṇ a - n i r ā k a r a ṇ ā t = ḥ d z i n - p a b z l o g - p a i - p h y i r (instead of g r ā h y a - g r ā h a k a - n i r ā k a r a ṇ ā t).

[48] Lit. 13.8—13. „Just as a rope or a magical vision appears (p r a - k h y ā y a t e = p r a t i b h ā s a t e) as though in the form of a snake or of a man etc. which in themselves do not exist and this is said to be „void" of any serpent or man etc., because their perception has been dismissed, even so the constructor of the unreal also appearing in the form of grasped and grasper which does not exist in itself, in order that simpledons quit their habit of apprehending, this is said to be devoid of duality".

[49] The stanza in sanscrit runs thus —

> n a ś ū n y a m n ā p i c ā ś ū n y a m
> t a s m ā t s a r v a m v i d h ī y a t e,
> s a t t v ā d a s a t t v ā t s a t t v ā c c a
> m a d h y a m ā p r a t i p a t c a s ā.

It is quoted in the MV, cf. LVL's edition, p. 445, where in the third pāda s a t t v ā c c a must be supplemented.

[50] Read (V. 2. 6. 2) — s t o ṅ - p a - ñ i ḍ = ś u n y a t ā, instead of s t o ṅ - p a.

[51] Lit. (V. 2. 6. 4) „all are not exclusively void, nor exclusively non-void", — „void" in the sense of devoid of duality. There are, so to speak, two absolute or final Elements, the one is all-embracing, it is real Monism, the other represents the extreme limit of particularity, the „point-instant".

[52] s a ṃ s k ṛ t a m 13.22; it is clear from this passage that s a ṃ s k ṛ t a, a b h ū t a p a r i k a l p a and consequently also p a r a t a n t r a are synonyms. Drop the chedas before ś ū n y a t ā 13.22 and before v i d h ī y a t e 13.23.

[53] Lit. 13.21—14.1. „The Constructor of the unreal is established in the P r a j ñ ā p ā r a m i t ā etc. as causal (s a ṃ s k ṛ t a), since its realization is dependent on causes, but „voidness" as uncaused (a s a ṃ s k ṛ t a), since it is independent of them.„ Because of existence", namely of the Constructor of the unreal, that s a ṃ s k ṛ t a whose essence is a b h ū t a - p a r i k a l p a **is not ś ū n y a.**

„Because of non-existence, i. e. (non-existence) of duality; in its grasped-grasper essence it is śūnya". — It follows from this passage that saṃskṛta is a synonym of paratantra, i. e. those Elements of existence which in early Buddhism were called saṃskṛta (or also saṃskāra in its more general acceptance, saṃskṛtam anena iti saṃskāraḥ) receive another characteristic, they are unutterable extreme concrete and particular Entia, causally connected mental point-instans, idealistic Things-in-Themselves; they also are pratītya-samutpanna, but with the implication of the new sense of ālaya-pratītya-samutpāda. It is clear from this passage that the saṃskṛta Element of early Buddhism, although it was devised as an ultimate indivisible unity, a dharma-Element, is analyzed in the new school into two essences of which, the first is its causal essence which is but a point-instant, kṣaṇa=svalakṣaṇa. It represents consequently the idealistic Thing-in-Itself, the extreme concrete and particular, the limit and foundation of all mental construction. It is the causally interdependent core of every saṃskṛta-Element, its character quà saṃskṛta. It receives a special conventional name — paratantra, it is aśūnya, i. e. real. The other essence of every saṃskṛta-Element is the phenomenon, superimposed by our imagination on the causally dependent Thing-in-Itself, first of all its localization in time-space, its relations as either subject or object and all other relations, which are all constructed by imagination like a flower in the sky. They receive a special name parikalpita, they are śūnya, i. e. not real. For the Yogācāras, as mentioned above, causally depedent means real, for the Mādhyamikas unreal. The prajñāpāramitā-sūtra here mentioned refers probably to the Maitreya-paripṛcchā part of the Pancaviṃsati-sāhasrikā.

[54] Insert 14.1 — sattvād iti (or sattvāc ceti) before śūnyatāyās tu. The kārikā has sattvād asattvāt sattvāc ca, the first sattvāt has been explained in 13.23, asattvāt is explained in 13.25. The words śūnyatāyās tv... in 14.1 evidently contain the explanation of the second sattvāt (sattvāc ca) in strict accordance with Vasubandhu's commentary. The translation of this sattvāc ca is missing in the Tib. likewise. After kṛtvā sattvam with a cheda after it must be probably inserted.

[55] dharmatā (14.1).

[56] dharmin (14.2). Lit. 14.1—2. „And because of existence", (i. e.) of the Absolute in the Constructor, in the sense of being its universal dharma; but the Constructor is also present in śūnyatā in the shape of its dharmin."

[57] Thus it is clear that the dharma-theory is found in all the various forms of Buddhism. The Sarvāstivādins maintain that all their list of 75 dharmas are ultimate realites and interrelated by causal laws. The Mādhyamikas maintain that they are not ultimate realities because interrelated, i. e. relative, there is no ultimate reality altogether, we can neither ultimately assert nor ultimately deny anything. The Yogācāras again assert the reality of all dharmas (enlarging the number to 100). They again maintain that real are all Elements because related by causal laws (pratītya-samutpannatvāt), but they restrict their reality to their causal residue (paratantra), excluding from it their form (parikalpita). Thus only the Things-in-Themselves are ultimately real (paramārtha-sat), their pure causality layed bare of all phenomenal appearance, of the object-to-subject and all other logical relations except the only causal relation. When the Thing-in-Itself is layed bare even of this last causal relativity it becomes the Final Absolute, embracing in itself the absolute totality of all the Things-in-Themselves. Thus, as already stated, there are two Absolutes, the absolute particular and

the absolutely universal; the Thing-in-Itself as the extreme concrete and particular point-instant of reality, causally interrelated (paratantra) and the absolute totality of these points (parinişpanna); the „this" (kiṃcid idam=idaṃtā) and the „thisness" (tathatā-tattvam); the hicaliquid and the Quiddity or Haecceitas. The relation between these two Absolutes is the same as between every particular and the corresponding universal under which it stands, the particular is the dharmin the „possessor of the property", the Universal is the „dharma" or „property", they are nānya na ananya.

[58] Cf. Kāśyapa-parivarta (ed. Stael v. Holstein) § 60, p. 90, and MV, p. 270.

[59] Read (14.7) — pratipat; evam... Thus the Middle Path in the Yogācāra interpretation means the absolute reality of two Elements, and the relativity of all the others, but these two being related according to the principle na anya, na ananya, cf. Triṃs., p.p. 40, are reducible to one and the system is really monistic.

[60] It is not quite exact to say that „among" the 100 Elements there are two which are absolutely real. Absolutely real is only one item — parinişpanna=tathatā, the other represents only that core of reality which is hidden behind every one of the remaining Elements and is identical (na anya na ananya) with the universal unique Absolute Reality.

[61] aśūnyam, „non-relative", ultimately real.

[62] The xyl. f. 2. b. 5, has de-ni instead of da-ni.

[63] Lit. (V.3. a. 1) „The projections of things and bodies have no forms". The Aga block-print reads don daṅ sems-can-du snaṅ-ba-rnams med-pa-daṅ, this corresponds to artha-sattva-pratibhāsa-abhāvāt, but in the MAV, 16. 12—13 we find this passage quoted (it should be underlined up to the word iti since it represents a quotation from the bhāşya) and it has the form artha-sattva-pratibhāsasya anākāratvāt which is rendered in Tib. as don daṅ sems-can-du snaṅ-ba-rnam-pa-med-pa-daṅ. It therefore is probable that the rnams of the Aga block-print is a misreading for rnam-pa. Lit. „because the projections (pratibhāsa) of things and living bodies have no form (ākāra)". Since pratibhāsa and ākāra have nearly the same meaning and it is clear from the further context that anākāra is contrasted with vitatha-pratibhāsa, the latter means „wrong representation" and the former „no representation at all". The meaning will then be that „the representations of things and bodies are no representations at all" or that they are „representations of nothing". All representations, or ideas, refer to mental objects alone, there are no external objects altogether, cf. Trimş., p. 17.2 — vijñānam eva arthākāram utpadyate, i. e. the idea itself has the form of the object, it is not the representation of an external object. From this point of view the ideas of the two first categories of the fourfold division do not exist at all. They must be included in the fourth category. The ākāra is defined 16.17 as grahaṇa-prakāraḥ, hence if an idea is not grāhaka, or not vijñapti, it does not exist at all, it is then not, to speak with Leibnitz, phaenomenon bene fundatum, the foundation is abhūta-parikalpa, the mental Thing-in-Itsefl (dravya, cp. LVP, p. 128), and this is present only in the vijñapti class of ideas. Thus the difference between the idea of blue (first category) and the idea of the intimation of blue (fourth category) is this that the first is anākāra, the second sākāra.

[64] On the meaning of svalakşaṇa established in the Sautrāntika and the logical school cf. my Buddhist Logic, v. I, p. 183 ff.

[65] Sthiramati following his usual method to give several explanations of the same text begins here the first explanation by athavā (Tib. yaṅ-na) probably because the first explanation or the direct meaning is clear enough and needs no paraphrasing.

[66] The dhātu-classification of dharmas is here alluded to, cf. my CC, p. 9, it is the following one —

Six faculties (indriya)	Six objects (viṣaya)	Six Sensations (vijñāna)
1 Sense of vision	7 Colour and shape	13 Sensation visual
2 „ „ audition	8 Sound	14 „ auditory
3 „ „ smelling	9 Odour	15 „ olfactory
4 „ „ taste	10 Taste	16 „ gustatory
5 „ „ touch	11 Tangibles	17 „ tactile
6 Intellect	12 Ideas (dharmāḥ)	18 „ intellectual

[67] Read 15.4—6—tad-bhāva-mātram jñāpyate, na tu tat-svabhāvo, nāpi dvayābhave yad grāhy-grāhaka-abhiniveṣa-kāraṇam vijñāyate, dvayam ca nāsti yataḥ pratīyate tad api noktam...=Tib. de yod-pa-tsam-du śes-par-byed-kyi, dei-raṅ-bzin-ni ma-yin-pa daṅ, gñis-po med-par-yaṅ gzuṅ-ba-daṅ ḥdzin-pa-la mṅon-par źen-pai rgyu-gaṅ-yin-pa rnam-par-mi-śes-pa, gaṅ-gi-phyir gñis-po-med-par yid-ches-par-bya-ba-de-yaṅ ma-bśad-pas...

[68] Read 15.9—prādhānyena tu vijñānam gṛhyate.

[69] The mental phenomena which are present in the Mind-store, the so called sarvatraga, are indicated in Triṃś., p. 3.

[70] Cf. below, p. 23.3 ff. the explanation why the philosopher should begin by doubting the reality of the external world and then proceed to doubt the truth of the ideas representing it.

[71] This division differs from the forgoing fourfold division only in this that the two first items of the former division are here united and the fourth category is divided in six items according to the varietes of sensation-ideas. This division is virtually the same as the trividha-pariṇāma of Triṃś.,1.

[72] The ālaya-vijñāna is artha-sattva-pratibhāsa, i. e. corresponds to the two first categories of ideas in the fourfold division, virtually it corresponds to an external world, cf. MAV, p. 28.1—sattva-bhājana-loka (-artha)-vijñāpanāt tan-nirbhāsatayā vijñānam. It is also the first of the three vijñāna-pariṇāmas, cf. Triṃś., 1—2. The two other pariṇāmas are réspectively represented in this division by the third and fourth categories, i. e. by the phenomenal Ego and the sensation-ideas. Thus the sensation-ideas although they seemingly represent sensations of quasi external objects are radically distinguished from ideas of these external objects themselves. An idea of blue is thus referred to a quite different category than the idea of the visual sensation of blue. The sensation of blue has a real foundation, the blue itself has none. However ālayavijñāna is also described as sarva-bījaka, cf. Triṃś., 2 and MAV, p. 27.25—ālīyante sarve sāsrava-dharmāḥ. Sthiramati states, MAV, p. 15.16, that all the eight classes of vijñāna originate from ālayav. This he apparently contradicts by stating 27.16 that ālayav. is the cause of the remaining seven c'asses (śeṣāṇām saptānām hetuḥ). Triṃś., 15 mentions five sense-vijñānas as originating in mūla-vijñāna, and the sixth, mano-vijñāna, is added in 16, but the seventh, kliṣṭa-manaḥ is not mentioned in that context. Although arising from it the seven vijñānas have this same ālayav. as their object. According

to Trimś., p. 5 it is the object of kliṣṭa-manas. The ālayav. is thus separated in two parts the one grasping the other, the object-part (nimitta-bhāga) consists of artha-sattva-pratibhāsa and the subjective one (darśana-bhāga) consists of the remaining seven vijñāna-classes, i. e. of the kliṣṭa-manas and the six sense-perceptions (inclusive of one appercetion). However this division is asamviditaka, cf. Trimś., p. 19.10. Cf. Fan-yi-ming-yi, trans. by E. Chavannes (S. Levi, Matériaux, p. 126.13 ff. and 151.6—7). It is true that Sthiramati himself objects against the separation of vijñāna in two parts, cf. ibid., p. 153 and MAV, p. 17.11, but that only means that he considers one part (darśana-bhāga-svasaṃvitti) to be an ultimate reality, while the other (nimitta-bhāga) is an illusion.

[73] The ālayav. is a stream carrying the seeds of good and bad deeds, it is therefore itself neither good nor bad, indefinite, avyākṛta. If the seeds would be only good there could be no saṃsāra, if they would be only bad there could be no nirvāṇa. Cf. Triṃś., p. 21.16—vipākatvād vipākam prati kuśala-akuśalatvena avyākaraṇād avyākṛtam.

[74] Cf. nivṛta-avyākṛta, cp. Triṃś., 5—6 (pp. 22, 23).

[75] The satellites of sensation ideas are indicated in Triṃś., 9 ff.

[76] Lit. 15.16—18 „Therefore these eight vijñānas which are projections of things, beings, Ego and sensations with their inherent satellites arise respectively in the five destinies from the Mind-store, dependent on cooperating causes (and) included in the Truth of Origin".

[77] Read 15.18—19—-dharma-vāsanā-pariṇāma-viśeṣo'sti kaścit.

[78] Lit. 15.18—19 „There is some peculiarity in (every) ālayavijñāna consisting in the force (or capacity-vāsanā) of a good, bad or indifferent dharma, owing to whose influence a mutually discrepant vijñāna arises".

[79] Read 15.23—bālānām instead of kṛtavatām, in Tib. byis-pa-rnams instead of byas-pa-rnams.

[80] Read 15.25—artha-sattva-ābhāsam instead of arthābhāsam=Tib. don daṅ sems-can snaṅ-ba.

[81] Here the term paratantra appears as a synonym for abhūta-parikalpa and vijñāna as well of saṃskṛta or pratītya-samutpanna.

[82] aṣṭa-vijñāna-vastuka-rnam-par-śes-pa-brgyad-kyi dṅos-po-can.

[83] Remarkable is here sparśa instead of the spraṣṭavya of the Abhidharma, it is confirmed by the Tib. reg-pa (not reg-bya).

[84] i. e. dharmāḥ, corresponds to the dharmāyatana and dharmadhātu of the Abhidharma.

[85] A quite artificial derivation of the term sattva from sakta in order to limit its meaning to the living organized thing, the bodily frame supporting consciousness. Vasubandhu in Triṃś. uses for the living body the terms upādāna, āśraya, ātmabhāva, sādhiṣṭhānam indriyam.

86. The Tib. has (=16.2—4) sems-can-du snaṅ-bai dbaṅ-po-lṅar bdag-daṅ-gźan-gyi-rgyud-la gaṅ-yin-pao źes-bya-bani, snaṅ-ba źes-bya-ba daṅ sbyar-ro-sattva-pratibhāsam yat pancasv indriyeṣu sva-para-santānayor iti; pratibhāsa ity adhikṛtam. Lit. „«Appearing as a living being that which is in the five organs in one's own and in another one's continuity», i. e. that repre-

sentation, this (word must) be supplemented." The Aga-block-print reads sems-can-du snaṅ-ba-ni dbaṅ-po-lṅar bdag daṅ gźan-gyi rgyud-la snaṅ-ba-gaṅ-yin-paʼo, but that is probably an emendation, Vasubandhu evidently expressed himself omitting the second pratibhāsa-snaṅ-ba and Sthiramati adds it in the commentary. prātibhāsa in 163 should not be underlined, cf. S. Y.

[87] Read 16.7 — kliṣṭasya manasaḥ and drop the cheda after samprayuktatvāt in 16.8.

[88] This passage 16.12—13 must be underlined, it is a quotation from the bhāṣya.

[89] anākāratvam, cf. 16.16 ākāro hi grahaṇa-prakāraḥ, cf. LVP, p. 124.

[90] Real are only ideas, vijñāna-mātram. Vasubandhu and Sthiramati evidently think that it is not quite right to divide the ideas in four classes, and thus to put on the same level the ideas of an external material object and the idea of the sensation of that object, e. g. the idea of a blue surface (nīla-pratibhāsa) and the idea of the intimation of a blue surface (nīla-vijñapti-pratibhāsa). According to the principles of vijñana-vāda the latter alone exists, the first does not differ from it. As regards the partition of the idea in two parts, an objective one (nimitta-bhāga) and a subjective one (darśana-bhāga), admitted by many Vijñāna-vādins Sthiramati is in principle opposed to it, cf. MAV, p. 17.11 and below, note 102. — Lit. 16.12—16. „Since the projections (pratibhāsa) of things and living bodies (artha-sattva) have no form (anākāra, i. e. are no perceptive ideas) and the projections of an Ego and of intimations (ātma-vijñapti) are wrong projections, thus (says Vasubandhu) (it means that) both the projections of things and living bodies, since they appear in an apprehended form (and) cannot be wrong projections, just their formlessness (anākāratva-agrāhakatva) is the cause of the non-existence of objects. But by others it is maintained that since they appear in the form of apprehenders, it is not their formlessness, but their wrong-projectedness, which is the cause of the non-existence of (external) things".

[91] ākāra is prakāra „le mode de connaître", cp. LVP, p. 414; ākāra is predominantly a buddhist term, prakāra a Naiyāyika term, cf. tadvati tat-prakārakam jñānam. When Indian philosophy forsaking the nirākāra-vāda of the realistic schools and of early Buddhism admitted the sākāra-vāda it made an important step from realism towards idealism. Here Sthiramati intimates that the „manner" of apprehending the object and the form (or image, or idea) of the object are just the same thing, ākāra is always grāhaka, not grāhya, the „form" is always mental, it is savikalpaka-pratyakṣa, cp. NB, 15.9.

[92] That ākāra may also mean nirvikalpaka-pratyakṣa or pure sensation is here evidently admitted vijñapti is the ākāra of vijñāna. The form, or even simple awareness, means Sthiramati, are always contained in the perceiving mind; external matter can be only ὕλη and ὕλη is nothing, since the primary as well as the secondary qualities of Matter (bhūta-bhautika) are subjective constructions of the Mind. — saṃvedana is translated as samyag-vedana. Cp. LVP, p. 124, but MAV, 22.7 ākāra is evidently savikalpaka.

[93] Lit. 16.12—19 „Its object does not exist" this means because the images (projections) of things and living bodies do not exist (don med ces-bya-ba-ni don daṅ sems-can-du snaṅ-ba-rnam-pa-med-pa-daṅ), and because the image of an Ego and of sense-intimation

is a wrong image", i. e. because both the projections of things and of living bodies can impossibly represent wrong images, since they appear as the apprehended (objective) part, just their imagelessness is the cause of the non-existence of the object. (16.15) But others maintain that since they appear as the apprehended (objective) part, not their imagelessness, but just also (this their) wrongness of projection is the cause of the non-existence of the objects. An image indeed is the manner in which an object is apprehended, e. g. as non-eternal. This they dont have, since they appear in the form of objects. This means that imagelessness is the fact of not being the apprehender. Or the image is the feeling (of the presence) of the object (in the ken). This they dont have. Thus imagelessness is absence of the object".

[94] 16.23—25. Lit. „Thus this, although there is no own reality of a different thing, produces an idea projecting different things etc. from its own seed which has, every one, a strictly determined place in the respective life-continuity". Cp. LVP, p. 422.

[95] Read 17.3 — bhūmim... pūrṇām, Tib. sa-la... gaṅ-bar mthoṅ.

[96] The Tib. has thob, i. e. prāptivat, in the place of śrutyādivat in 17.10, evidently for thos. Put a cheda after arthasyābhāva in 17.9.

[97] Lit. 17.11 „Indeed moreover an „intimation" is devoid of the essence constructed by another intimation, such is the established principle". S. Y. calls attention (p. 19, n. 7) to the parallel passage in the Viṃśatikā-vijñaptimātratā, p. 6.19. It means that Sthiramati is opposed to the theory which introduces into the principle of Pure Awareness a second Pure Awareness, so as to make a doulbe Pure Awareness and divide every idea in two parts, the objective part (nimitta-bhāga) and the subjective part (darśana-bhāga). Thus Pure Awareness (vijñapti) is „devoid "of every duality, i. e. it contains only Absolute Reality, that one which the Buddhas alone directly perceive, anabhilāpyena yo buddhānām viṣayas tena ātmanā (paramārtha-satā) na śūnyā vijñaptiḥ. cf. LVP, p. 416 ff.

[98] Lit. 17.12 „Therefore namely, just as for the ideas of things and living bodies, there is for the Ego- and intimation-ideas also no object". Read 17.12 — artha-sattva-pratibhāsasya instead of artha-pratibhāsasya, Tib. don daṅ sems-can-du snaṅ-ba bźin-du.

[99] The Tib. corresponds to vijñāpayati iti vijñānam = rnam-par-rig-pas-na rnam-par śes-pao, or vijñaptir iti vijñānam.

[100] Read 17.14 — vijñātṛtvam api, instead of vijñānam tad api, Tib. rnam-par-śes-pa-por mi-rigs-te.

[101] Read 17.15 — vijñātṛtvena eva or vijñātṛtva-mātreṇa = rnam-par-śes-pa-po-kho-nar.

[102] There was a great strife among the second generation of the Vijñāvādins on the partition of „the idea" (vijñāna) into two, three and even four parts. Sthiramati is known as the advocate of the indivisible idea. According to him real transcendentally (paratantra) is only the self-conscious (svasaṃvitti) moment. Its splitting into an objective part (nimitta-bhāga) and a subjective one (darśana-bhāga) is the work of imagination and therefore objectively unreal. Sthiramati also maintains that in the eighth vijñāna, i. e. in the Mind-store the existence of the two parts is quite imaginary, the sva-saṃvitti part is alone real, i. e. it is paratantra, connected by transcendental causality. According to Dharmapāla both parts have a trancendental reality. According to ācārya Nanda every idea has an objective, apprehended part and a subjective, apprehending part, both parts are paratantra, i. e. transcendentally real. This ācārya also

does admit of no purely parikalpita idea, according to him there always is in it some paratantra part. Diṅnāga and with him the logical school admit three parts, called prameya, pramāṇa and pramāṇa-phala (the vijñāna is here pramāṇa), the third part is nīla-saṃvedana, it is the pramāṇa-phala, cf. Nyāya-bindu and my Buddhist Logic, II, 384 ff. However the logical school maintained the substantial unity of these three aspects. They have been also adopted by the Prābhākara school of the Mīmāmsakas in their celebrated tri-puṭī theory. Finally Dharmapāla establishes four parts. He argues thus: the pramāṇa-phala-nīla-saṃvedana must be cognized by some instrument of knowledge (pramāṇa) and this can be only a further sva-saṃvitti, the saṃvitti of the former saṃvitti; pramāṇa then corresponds to the darśana-bhāga, prameya to the nimitta-bhāga, pramāṇa-phala to sva-saṃvitti, and a second degree of sva-saṃvitti is needed in order to cognize the first, just as pramāṇa is needed to cognize prameya. The siddhānta which Sthiramati mentions MAV, 17.12 is evidently his personal view and the view of the school founded by him. According to the schools admitting the division, the first and second categories of ideas will have no object, but the third and fourth will have an immanent object. The whole classification has been accordingly dropped by the later schools. Cf. Fan yi ming yi tsi, trad. Chavannes, p. 153 ff., LVP, p. 416 ff., 522 ff., 717 ff.

[103] Lit. V. 3. a. 3. „otherwise neither the bondage nor purification would be firmly established, there would be the fault of denying the saṃkleśa (phenomenalizing oppressors of pure reality) and the vyavadāna (thorough purification)":

[104] The reading svayam asad api can be retained only in accepting the following interpretation, Lit. „(The phenomenal world) although in itself unreal, mere illusion is the form in which it appears, like a magical vision", i. e. just as a magical vision which is itself unreal has a real producer, the magician, just so the phenomenal world being in itself an illusion has a real producer in the the shape of our Mind, which is a kind of Thing-in-Itself behind the phenomena. The reading proposed by S. Y., p. 21.2, natu... sā bhrāntir ucyate, means just the contrary of what we should expect, besides there is no trace of a negation in the Tib. Read therofore svayam sad api. Lit. 18.5—9. „And here, in the four modes, there is no adequate apprehender, because of formlessness and because of wrong-projectedness. And because everything is devoid of an essence constructed by another intimation there is no apprehended (object). And not in every respect non-Ens. „Since mere illusion is produced, not in every respect non-Ens". This (means), although by its own (essence) existent, the form in which it appears is illusion like magic", i. e. it is real in its own essence, as the fact of an illusion. Instead of sarva-śūnyatvād read sarvasya or sarvasyāḥ (sc. vijñapteḥ), śūnyatvād, cf. above, p. 17.11. vijñaptyantara is contrasted with vijñapti-mātratā; only the quite pure sensation is the final reality, every other mental construction is bhrāntimātram or māyā, the immanent object is also māyā.

[105] paśvādi, Tib. phyugs-yan-chad.

Part I, Chapter III

[1] Tib. (V. 3. a. 4)... kun-tu-rtog-pa-tsam-du zad-na-... parikalpa-mātre kevale. This must be understood so that while in Hīnayāna sarvam jñeyam is classified in 75 different ultimate realities, dharmas,

the Yogācāras distinguish in every single sanskṛta-dharma three different essences or essential aspects. According to the Dharma-dharmatā-vibhaṅga (kārika 2) two essences must be distinguished in every dharma, its own dharma-essence, (i. e. the thing by itself, the paratantra) and its dharmatā-essence, (i. e. the Absolute, the same thing sub-specie-aeternitatis). The parikalpita-essence, the image of the thing, is omitted, evidently because it is no essence at all, not a reality, but imagination.

[2] artha here means the object of all the four categories of ideas, cf. 14.22, 15.11, 16.11. Wheresoever there is an object there necessarily must be a subject and this division of the unique concrete reality in two parts, the one grasping the other, is a construction of our productive imagination, it does not represent ultimate reality.

[3] Lit. (stanza 1.5) „The quite imagined, the on-other-dependent and also the quite real it is (so) called from object, from the Constructor of the not-quite-real, and from the absence of duality".

[4] Lit. (V. 3. a. 5) „Among these the object is the quite-imagined essence; the universal Constructor of the not-quite-real is the on-other-dependent essence; the absence of grasped and grasper is called the quite real essence" (niṣpanna-siddha).

[5] Read 19.5 with S. Y., — saṃgraha eva lakṣaṇam (bsdu-ba-ñid mtshan-ñid-do).

[6] Lit. 19.5—6. „The inclusive essence is being taught, inclusion itself is the essence, or that (Constructor) owing to whom the inclusion is made essential that is the inclusive essense", i e. samgrahalakṣaṇam is either karma-sādhana (=yaḥ saṃgrahaḥ sa lakṣyate) or it is karaṇa-sādhana (yena saṃgrahaḥ sa lakṣyate).

[7] Read 19.10 — abhūta-parikalpa-mātre kevale (=yaṅdag-pa-ma-yin-pa-kun-tu-rtog-pa-tsam-du zad-na).

[8] dravyato'san contrasted with vyavahārato'sti.

[9] This is one of the main points of dissention between the Mādhyamikas and Yogācāras. For the Mādhyamihas a thing which is produced by causes and conditions, is relative, dependent and ultimately unreal, āpekṣika=paratantra=śūnya MV, XV, cp. Rocznik, XI, p. 13. For the Yogācāras the reality which is produced by causes, (just this „pure" reality, but not the image produced by constructive imagination) is ultimately real; the paratantra (causally dependent) is not śūnya, but paramārtha-sat, whereas the āpekṣika (logically „dependent") is śūnya, i. e. for them causal relativity is real, logical relativity is logical, or only mental. We must therefore in every Ens distinguish its logical contents from its point of reality. Hence the reality which the Yogācāras admit is trans'ogical, transcendental, it is the Thing-in-Itself.

[10] Read 19.17 — aklptaḥ (or na klptaḥ or akalpaḥ, cp. MSA, XI, 31) instead of kalpitaḥ, the reading of the Peking Tanjur brtags-min is right, brtags-yin is an emendation of the editors which is not necessary. paratantra can however also be designated as vikalpita in the sense of a substratum for the constructions of imagination, tatra rūpa-vikalpaḥ kriyate, cp. S. Y.'s ed., p. 139. 6. and ibid., p. 138.20.

[11] Lit. 19.18—19. „Unimagined (akalpa) produced from conditions, in no way utterable (= non-connotative), on-another-dependent own-reality, whose domain is pure (but yet) wordly". This means that paratantra is paramārthasat, but not paramārtha-satya, cp. LVP, p. 101. It belongs

to saṃvṛti-satya (laukika). On the other hand, pariniṣpanna is both paramārtha-sat and paramārtha-satya. The first is moreover vastu-svalakṣaṇa, the second is not vastu, but sāmānya-lakṣaṇa. Both are anabhilāpya „unutterable (by a connotative term)".

[12] Lit 19.20. „The universal fact (=suf. -tā) of being devoid of duality in the Constructor of the not-quite-real this is the quite-real own-essence, because not being dependent on causes by being immutable, it is quite real (the non plus ultra of reality)".

[13] avikalpa-jñāna p. 19.23=mi-rtog ye-śes; jñāna in the sense of absolute knowledge of the saint is rendered by ye-śes. Two varieties of pariniṣpanna are mentioned below, p. 20.5—nirvikāra-pariniṣpatti and aviparita-pariniṣpatti. Thus Absolute Reality and Absolute knowledge here coalesce, it is prajñā-pāramitājñānam advayam sa Tathāgataḥ, i. e. the personification in Buddha, cf. BB, my Introduction to Abhisamāyālaṃkāra.

[14] Lit. 19.22—23. „Quite perfect own-essence is absolute devoidness of imagined own-essence; it is the domain of non-discursive highest knowledge". — The cognition of the Absolute by the Bodhisattva is always direct, by nirvikalpaka-pratyakṣa, it becomes discursive or conceptual only in the intervals between trance (pṛṣṭha-labdha).

[15] Read 19.25—artha iha, Tib. don-ni ḥdir.

[16] Read 19.26—ātmā vijñaptayaś ca (with S. Y.).

[17] Read 20.1 — vikalpo nirvikalpakaḥ-Tib. rnam-rtog rnam-par mi-rtog ni.

[18] Lit. 20.1—2. Imagination is not imagined,
By another imagination (when) imagined
This own-essence of him does not exist,
The by-another-imagination-imagined.

Vikalpa has the meanings of dilemma, dilemmatic construction or splitting in two, also imagination, creative imagination or construction. vikalpa is itself nirvikalpaka. It can be synonym of vijñapti and vijñāna. But it can become savikalpaka when vitarka and vicāra begin to operate, already partly in subliminal consciousness. It then begins to distinguish the subject from the object. In logic the implications of vikalpa are quite different, there is no nirvikalpaka-vikalpa in logic, cf. my Buddhist Logic, I, p. 204 ff. In logic it means conceptual thinking as opposed to pure sensation. In the early Vijñānavāda (āgama-anusārin) it can be synonymous with vijñapti and also with paratantra and can mean pure sensation as well as idea. All the three significations of imagination, construction and splitting in two are implied in the aphorism. We therefore can also translate —

The Constructor (vikalpa=abhūta-parikalpa) is not constructed,
By another construction being constructed
This own-essence of him does not exist,
The by-another-construction-constructed.
or,
The dichotomizer is not being dichotomized
By another dichotomy being dichotomized
This own-essence of him does not exist, (i. e. is not absolute reality),
The by-another-dichotomy-dichotomized.

On the dichotomy of vijñāna cf. MAV., p. 17.9—19, translation and note. The three translations are arrived at by isolating the three shades of meaning. By combining them a synthetic translation can be arrived at. On vikalpa cf. besides my Buddhist Logic, I, p. 212 f. ff. Triṃś., 17; LVP, p. 433 and 515 ff.

[19] The saint (ārya) reaches a direct intuition of the Absolute during a moment of transic enlightment and also a conceptual knowledge of it as a consequence of his former experience in trance. Thus among the two parinişpatti's the one is samāhita and nirvikalpaka, the other is pṛṣṭha-labdha and savikalpaka. Cp. below, kārika 1.15 and LVP, pp. 658, 749.

[20] Read 20.12.—abhūta-parikalpādyat parijñeyam prahātavyam sākṣāt kartavyam ca vastu pradarśitam bhavati, cf. Sūtrālamkāra VI. 13 where the three lakṣaṇas are likewise characterized as jñeya, heya and viśodhya (viśodhya-sakṣātkārya). In Gauḍapāda, kārikā IV. 88 the division is fourfold—jñanam, jñeyam, vijñeyam and turīyam. Neither the Tib. nor the sanscrit text seem to be correct.

[21] asal-lakṣaṇam-med-pai mtshan-ñid.

[22] rnam-par-rig-pa-tsam-du-dmigs-pa-la-vijñapti-mātra-upalabdhau, for vijñapti-mātratā-upalabdhau.

[23] Lit. V. 3. a. 6 ff. „Now (read da-ni instead of de-ni) the essence of the expedient of entering into the essence of the non-existence of that very Constructor of the not-quite-real will be thoroughly shown—

> Basing oneself on perception
> Non-perception is produced,
> Basing oneself on non-perception
> Non-perception is produced.

Basing oneself on the perception of pure intimation non-perception of objects is produced, basing on non-perception of objects, non-perception of pure intimation arises. Such is the entrance into the essence of the apprehended and the apprehender".—Vasubandhu in his imitation of this kārikā adds „When both (the object and the subject) have disappeared, appears the Omnipresent (all-embracing Whole)". Cp. Trisvabhāva-nirdeśa, 36—37, as quoted by the editors of MAV, I, note 230.

[24] Lit. 20.14—15 „Indeed the Constructor of the not-quite-real, not thoroughly known, endowed with non-existing essences, exists for the sake of 1) the universal oppressors of kleša (kleša-saṃkleśa), 2) (the universal oppressors) of karma and 3) (the universal oppressors) of a rebirth (janma)".—On the twelve great oppressors or universal oppressors (saṃkleśa=nidāna) cp. below, MAV, p. 29.13 ff. Saṃkleśa is the phenomenal world, the world of Appearance as a process of ever reverting twelve phenomena, beginning from prenatal forces up to death and rebirth. It is a synonym of the twelve nidānas; saṃkleśas are of three kinds—1) kleśa-saṃkleśa, 2) karma-saṃkleśa and 3) jāti- or āyuḥ-saṃkleśa, cf. below, p. 29.13 (text).

We here translate kleśa-saṃkleśa by Illusion (resp. Transcendental Illusion), because among the „phenomenalizers", i. e. the factors converting the pure reality of the Absolute into phenomenal Appearance, it (avidyā) represents the chief, the root factor, lit. kleśa-saṃkleśa would mean „the oppressor among general oppressors"; avidyā is thus the oppressor κατ'ἐξοχήν.

[25] Lit. 20.18 „Its expedient (means) that after which he enters into its non-existing (or negative) essence".

[26] Read 20.19. — sarvatragārtha-prativedha-prayoge niḥśraya-viśeṣa-kauśalyam dvividham, Tib. kun-tu-ḥgro-bai don rab-tu-rtogs-par-bya-ba-sbyor-ba-na gnas-kyi khyad-par mkhas-pa rnam-pa-gñis-so. Lit. „This expedient is a double proficiency of abiding (getting a firm footing) in a special condition of being trained (in the fact that) everywhere all objects are penetrated by (merged in, cognised as) the Absolute, (the Element of the totality of all Elements)". This refers to the upāya-kauśala-prayoga being the action, skillful and free of effort, of the Bodhisattva on the last three stages, in which he gets rid of the prejudice of believing in the reality of an external world and of an intellect grasping it. Cf. Haribhadra's Ālokā, p. 94 (ed. Tucci) — sarvātmanā dharmatāyāḥ prativedhe'pi niścayotpādanāpekṣayā sarvatragārthena prativedhāt sarvadharma-niḥsvabhāvatā-sakṣātkāri spuṭataram jñānam utpadyate. tadā bodhisattvaḥ samyaktva-nyāma-avakrāntito darśana-mārgam pratilabhate. Cf. also Obermiller, Pr. P., p. 53. The sarvagatārtha-pratisaṃvedha is the name of the first moment of the Mahāyānistic Path of Illumination (darśana-mārga), cp. Obermiller, IHQ, v. IX, p. 175.

[27] Read 21.5 — ucyeta (= Tib. źes-bya-o źes-bya-bai rnam-par śes-pai bya-ba-gźan med-do). This is the known principle of Dependent Origination or Functional Interdependence (pratītya-samut-pāda) of the Elements (dharma). All Elements are „doing nothing" (akiṃcitkara), they are „unemployed" (nirvyāpāra), they only appear for a moment in order to disappear at once, cf. LVP, pp. 123, 420, 430, AK, IX, 280, my Buddhist Logic, v. I, p. 121.

[28] Lit. 21.6 „Thus the production of the representation is not owing to (in Tib. we would expect dmigs-pai rkyen-can for the bahuvrīhi) the objective cause, the over-hypothesis is senseless, the perception of a present object would contradict the instantaneous evanescence". Cf. Berkley's considerations on the connection between idealism and instantaneous reality, Principles, § 45. On simultaneity of cause and effect cp. LVP, pp. 116, 122.

[29] Read 21.7 ...na vijñānotpattiḥ, vyartham tat parikalpyate, vartamāna-ālambana-grahaṇe kṣaṇa-bhanga-bādhaḥ syāt (or with S. Y... pratyayo na vijñānotpādakaḥ).

[30] Read 21.8 insert pūrvavat before vijñānena (with S. Y.).

[31] For 21.8—11 the Tib. has — raṅ-bźin-bye-brag-tu-gyur-pa-yaṅ med-pas sṅa-ma-bźin-te rnam-par-śes-pas dmigs-pa-ḥdzin-par mi-ruṅ-ṅo, ḥon-te dmigs-pa-ḥdzin-pai dus-na de-la raṅ-bźin-bye-brag-tu-gyur-par ḥdod-na, de-ltar-na yaṅ raṅ-bźin-bye-brag-tu-gyur-pa-gźan-ñid-du snaṅ-bas, byuṅ-ba-gźan-ñid-kyis dmigs-pa-ḥdzin-par thal-bar ḥgyur-ro, i. e. — na ca ātma-atiśaya-abhāve (= svabhāva-viśeṣa-abhāve) pūrvavad vijñānena ālambana-grahaṇam yujyate, atha ālambana-grahaṇa-kāle tasya ātma-atiśaya iṣyate, evam apy ātma-atiśayasya anyatvena darśanād, utpanna-anyatvena ālambanam gṛhṇāti iti prasajyate. This sanskrit text is rendered in my translation. Whether it represents the original phrasing of Sthiramati or whether it has been slightly changed by the translators in order to make it more intelligible it is hardly possible to decide. In any case pūrvavat is omitted in the printed text, ātma-

atiśaya-anyatvena darśanāt is more intelligible than ātma-atiśayasya anyata eva darśanād, and anyad eva utpannam ālambanam gṛhṇāti „he grasps a quite other produced object" can be understood only if subjected to some stress. In the translation of Nyāyabinduṭīkā atiśaya is rendered as khyad-par, svabhāva-viśeṣa as raṅ bźin khyad-par-can, cp. E. Obermiller's Index. — The theory of the Mīmāṃsakas is here probably alluded to, according to which cognition produces at the same moment in the object a new quality called jñātatā „cognizedness". Cp. Nyāyakaṇikā, p. 267.12 (reprint). The knowledge of the Ego is according to this school also inferential, being inferred from the fact of the production of jñātatā, cf. my BL, I, p. 165. That there can be no change of quality on the Buddhist theory of universal momentariness is stated in the Nyāyabinduṭīkā, p. 10.12 — iha kṣaṇika-vastuny atiśaya-ādhānāyogāt.

[32] Read 21.11 — anyo hi manyate = Tib. gźan-ni......sñam-du sems-te, des kyaṅ..., cf. below, 21.18.

[33] The Sautrāntika-Yogācāra theory is here evidently alluded to, according to which a representation is produced from an external object by tadutpatti-tatsārūpyābhyām, cf. my BL, I, p. 204 ff. and II, App. IV. Cf. that theory of Vasubandhu which is expounded by him in the Vāda-vidhi, and was replaced by another theory in his subsequent works. Dignāga rejected it in his Pramāṇasamuccaya, and Väcaspatimiśra in the Tātparyaṭīkā refers to it in detail. Cf. Prof. A. Vostrikov's forthcoming work „The Logic of Vasubandhu".

[34] Read 21.14 — ālambanatvena eva parikalpyate = dmigs-pa-kho-nar kun-tu brtag-graṅ-na. — Cp. the same argumentation in the formulation of Hiuan Tsang, LVP, p. 43, cp. ibid, p. 185.

[35] Read 21.18 — yo py' anyo manyate = gaṅ gźan yaṅ... sñam-du sems-pa, cf. above, 21.11.

[36] That a nominal entity — and every universal or every concept is a nominal entity — can never be a cause is a fundamental tenet; only the particular is arthakriyā-kārin, cf. NB., p. 13. The same principle obtains in the Yogācāra school, the parikalpita is asat. Cf. Haribhadra's Ālokā, p. 94 — rāśiś cāpadārthatvān nopādāna-lakṣaṇasya bhāvasya nimittam bhavitum arhati. Cf. Obermiller on Śūnyatā, p. 184. Cp. LVP, p. 43 — l'agglomèration n'est pas une chose réeble.

[37] samudita is rendered in 21.18, 21.19 and 21.20 by sil-bu (samudāya in 21.21 and samūha in 21.23 by ḥdus-pa). The Tib. of 21.18 ff. does not quite agree with the Sanskrit. gaṅ gźan-yaṅ rdul-phra-rab sil-bu-so-so dmigs-pa yin-pa sñam-du sems-pa dei ḥdi-yaṅ dbaṅ-du mi-ruṅ-ste. sil-bu de-ni dedag so-soñid-la dmigs-par ḥdod-gyi, de-dag-gi ḥdus-pa-la-ni ma-yin-no, der rdul-phra-rab so-sor snaṅ-bai śes-pa-ni mi-ḥbyuṅ-gi, ḥdi-ltar de-dag-gi ḥdus-par snaṅ-ba ste = yo'py anyo manyate paramāṇavaḥ pratyeka-samūḥa-ālambanās tasya ayam aparihāraḥ, samuditā api hi te pratyekam eva ālambantvena iṣyante na tat-samudāyena, tathā hi teṣām samudāya-pratibhāsaḥ. „The opinion of that other one who thinks that atoms are perceived in separate groups is no good objection". The Tib. has no na in na pratyekam, and suggests a reading (or emendation?) pratyeka-samūha-ālambanāḥ. — Cp. on the different renderings of samūha LVP, p. 44.

[38] nimitta.

[39] rūpa-citta-viprayukta-saṃskāra, cf. CC, pp. 22,105.

[40] Read 22.5 — abhāva-nirodhayoḥ = Tib. med-pa daṅ dgag-pa. Lit. 22.4 „Neither the nascent nor the produced representation apprehends the mark, because its non-existence and disappearance has been formerly taught" (S. Y. abhāvasya nirodhasya ca pūrvoktatvāt).

[41] According to the Yogācāras vijñāna is sākāra, according to the Vaibhāṣikas it is nirākāra. The subject is then pure consciousness, the object is ākāra, nimitta, pratibhāsa or saṃjñā. This partly explains the insistence of the Vaibhāṣikas that there is some external reality even in dreams. For the Yogācāras reality is a dream, for the Vaibhāṣikas a dream corresponds to some subtle external reality, cf. Santānāntarasiddhi, where Dharmakīrti ridicules the Vaibhāṣikas. For the Vaibhāṣikas the ākāra of vijñāna is vijñapti, i. e. it is nirvikalpaka or, in the Sautrāntika phrasing, nirākāra, cp. above, ch. II, note 92; LVP, p. 124.

[42] Read 22.11 — apratigha (instead of anya-pratigha).

[43] avijñapti-rūpam is a bodily, physical subtle feature, compared with a shadow. Being the consequence of a moral or immoral deed it finds expression in the body. It is assumed as a dharma only by the Vaibhāṣikas and included in rūpaskandha. In the āyatana classification however it is not included among the material āyatanas, but in the āyatana № 12, called dharma-āyatana, cp. my CC, pp. 6, 7, 99.

[44] Read 22.12 — apare tu - Tib. gźan-dag. Cp. Locke's Essay, II, 9, § 8.

[45] Read 22.14 — na hi ātyandhaḥ svapne rūpam na gṛhṇāti.

[46] Lit. 23.3—7 „Again why does he not at the very beginning establish the non-existence of the (pure) intimation itself? Indeed, since the apprehender depends on the apprehended, when there is nothing which were a possible object, the reality (vastu) having the essence of a disappeared object, he easily enters. Otherwise he would make a denial of reality, since the apprehended and the apprehender are (would be?) mutually independent". — The Bodhisattva realizes the ideality of all external objects gradually on his Path of Accumulating Merit (sambhāra-mārga) and his Path of Training (prayoga-mārga) and finally in the first moment of his Path of vision (dṛṣṭi-mārga), when he in a mystic trance perceives the unique substance of the universe (sarvatraga-dharma-dhātu). The unreality of the apprehending subject, i. e. of the cognizer (vijñātṛ), is realized by him only in the subsequent higher stages of his Path. The question is here asked that, since the apprehender depends upon the apprehended just in the same degree as the latter upon the first, why does the Bodhisattva not start by declaring that unreal is consciousness itself and after that deduce the unreality of the external world. That is the method of the Mādhyamikas. They begin by doubting the reality of knowledge and they thus admit no vastu at all. The Yogācāras deny only ālambana-rūpa-vastu, but not vastu eva, cp. 23.6 — vastuno' pavādam eva in the sense of vastuna eva apavādam, denial of all reality whatsoever. The point of Sthiramati is that it is easier for philosophy to familiarize with a spiritual universe, than with the idea of a non-existing consciousness. It must be emphasized that the Mādhyamikas are not Nihilists (abhāva-vādinas), but Relativists svabhāva-śūnyatā-vādinas = parasparāpekṣatā-vādinah. But they denied the independent reality of consciousness, it was for them just as relative (śūnya) as the external world. Nevertheless the Yogā-

cāras always accused the Mādhyamikas of being Nihilists, they imputed on them the principle sarvam sarveṇa nāsti, i. e. total Nihilism, cp. B. bhūmi, p. 43. Sthiramati argues in this place that" otherwise, (i. e. if the unreality of knowledge itself were admitted from the start, all reality (whatsoever it might be) would be denied, because, says he, „there would be no relativity of subject and object", i. e. there would be no relativity in the Yogācāra sense. The Yogācāra theory of Relativity consists in maintaing that both horns of the relation are unreal (=relative) separately (dravyataḥ asat), but real on a higher plane when they merge in a unique reality. This is the higher reality or the merger of both unreal relative counterparts. It could seem that there is some fluctuation in Sthiramati's terminology, inasmuch as he has stated that Pure Awareness vijñapti-mātra, resp. -mātratā is realized as being unreal by the Bodhisattva, but vijñapti-mātra is a synonym of paratantra and of abhūtaparikalpa which are declared to represent Absolute Reality and it is emphatically declared that abhūta-parikalpa, i. e. Mind in the role of the Creator of Illusion, exists, is real „in itself", cp. above, kārika I. 2. But although vijñapti-mātra is not real, paratantra (=vikalpa, parikalpa) and śūnyatā are real, cp. LVP, pp. 420, 426.

[47] sambhāreṣu=sambhāra-mārge.

[48] uṣma-gata. Lit. 23.7—9 „And thus when he takes his stand on this mere-intimation, the mental realization (bhāvanā) of the absence of colour etc. appears to his face, being the essence of the first beginning (ādi-svabhāvaḥ) (leading) to the trans-mundane Path, being the trance called „warm gone" with its satellites". Read bhāvanā, Tib. bsgom-pa-ni (instead of bhāvanāto).

[49] lokottara-mārga here evidently in the sense of the Path „leading" to the transcendent world, because the lokottara-mārga proper begins with the first moment of darśana-mārga. The preceding stages up to the laukikāgradharma belong to the Path of Training (prayoga-mārga) whose highest condition is the laukikāgra-dharma (not lokottara) as indicated in 23.14; therefore it is better to read in 23.10 instead of prathamam svarūpam—rūpādy-abhāva-bhāvanā... ārambha-svabhāvā, Tib. thog-mai raṅ bźin.

[50] mūrdhan.

[51] Lit. 23.12—13 „Immediately after it because of non-perception of (all) apprehended (objects) without any residue the trance called Steadfastness (kṣānti) which is propitious to the non-perception of the apprehending (subject) (is faced by him)". On the meaning of ksānti cp. above, ch. I, note 27.

[52] Lit. 23.13—15 „Immediately after this on the basis of non-perception of objects, when creating by meditation (bhāvayataḥ) a non-perception of pure awareness (vijñapti-mātra), the trance called the „Highest Mundane Qualities" (laukika-agra-dharma) associated with prajñā and its satellites „is faced by him". — We must carefully distinguish between vijñapti-mātra „simple, i. e. indefinite presence of something in the ken", and vijñapti-mātratā which is the Mind as the monistic Absolute, cp. my article in the Rocznik Orjent., X. The difference is the same as between śūnya and śūnyatā, dvaya-rahita and dvaya-rahitatā, abhūta-parikalpa and śūnyatā etc. With the Yogācāras the negation of vijñapti-mātra means the assertion of vijñapti-mātratā, however the tā suffix is sometimes dropped, cf. note 54, vijñapti-mātra or vijñāna-mātra is not „une entité reelle au sens absolu", LVP, p. 80.

[53] The apramāṇa-feelings of maitri, karuṇā, muditā and upekṣā are also characterized as advaya (cf. M. Vyut. § 69 — advayena cittena adhimucya), but they are adhimukta=mos-pa, not tattva-jñāna.

[54] pratyātma-vedyatva 23.21, or pratyātma-vedanīyatva, is a process of searching and finding the Absolute introspectively in the depths of one's own consciousness when plunged in the deepest transic meditation. The Mādhyamika finds by applying this method his śūnyatā, i. e. mere Relativity (dīrgha-hrasva-vat). The Yogācāra, on the other hand, finds by applying the same method a different šūnyatā, i. e. the principle of the Monistic Absolute Reality. On pratisaṃvid cf. Sandhinirmocanasūtra (Lamotte), pp. 98—105.

[55] The punctutation in 24.4—5 should be the following one. — yasmād upalabdhir anupalabdhi-svabhāvā tasmāt samatā, tulyatā jñeyā, arthānupalambhasya vijñapti-mātra-upalambhasya ca asattvād viśeṣābhāvāt=ḥdi-ltar dmigs-pa-ni mi-dmigs-pa-ṅo-bo-ñid-du ḥgyur-te, dei phyir mñam-mo. don-mi-dmigs-pa daṅ rnam par-rig-pa-tsam-du dmigs-pa yaṅ med-par bye-brag med-pai-phyir mtsuṅs-pa-ñid-du śes-par-byao (vijñapti-mātra in 24.5 stands for vijñapti-mātratā). — On the equipollency between phenomenal non-perception and absolute perception cp. MSA. ad XI. 47 — parama upalambhasya yo vigamaḥ (muktiḥ). LVP, p. 607.

[56] Read 24.7 — abhūtārtha-pratibhāsatayā tasya upalabdhir ity ucyate. Lit. „It is called perception in its quality (-tayā) of being a projection of the unreal". But it really is non-perception, cp. LVP, p. 607. — „Le Nirvikalpaka-jñāna est qualifié anupalambha.

[57] Read 24.12 (wich S. Y.) — abhūtārtha-pratibhāsatayā upalabdhir ity ucyate, instead of abhūtārtha-pratibhāsatayānupalabdhir.

[58] The expressions apanīyate and prakṣipyate 24.22—23 allude to Asaṅga's stanza quoted on the next page from the Abbisamayālankāra, V. 21.

[59] Cp. Abhisamayālankāra, V. 21; cp. also Suzuki's Ašvaghosa, p. 95, where a similar idea seems to be expressed.

[60] abhūta-parikalpa-mātram 25.9 refers here to a purely mental creation of phenomenal worlds in the three spheres (dhātu) of existence. It is evidently assumed as a fundamental principle that Mind cannot create Matter, just as it is assumed that Mind cannot „grasp" or cognize Matter. The idea of an interaction between Mind and non-Mind must needs be an illusion, a coarse metaphor. The sphere of gross bodies is therefore only the sphere of gross desires (kāma-rāga-dhātu), the sphere of ethereal bodies only the sphere of gentle desires (rūpa-rāga-dhātu), but the realm of amorphous beings is also a purely imagined world; all are abhūta-parikalpa.

[61] Lit. 25.7—12 „Just the division is the essence, division-essence, because by this division the universal constructor of the unreal is essentially characterized. Why again is this essential division explained? Since the mere universal construction of the unreal does not apply to the realms of desire and of forms, that division in saint individuals etc. will not be possible which comes from a division of obstructions and antidotes through a division of realms, thus a great calamity for the religion will be the consequence; thus in order to repudiate this objection the essential division is explained". —

This is a very curious reason for explaining the necessity of assuming a series of worlds, of gross and subtle Matter, of hells and heavens etc. The higher stages of a Bodhisattva's career are situated in the heavens. His progress requires enormous efforts during fabulously long periods of time. An easy salvation is quite impossible for the ordinary man. Every theory which would entail easy salvation is eo ipso condemned from the point of view of religion, cf. MAV, p. 11.15—16. „This would be, says Sthiramati, a great calamity for religion" (mahāñ śāsana-upaplavaḥ). Buddhism is thus conceived by him as the doctrine of the different classes of beings bound by their seeming materiality, all striving with the greatest efforts to Nirvāṇa through different degres of vimokṣa. Thus it is that Berkley deamed idealism a support for religion against materialism; Sthiramati, on the contrary, thinks that extreme idealism might prove a danger to religion!

62 Lit. 25.12—13 „Or where there is running through (vitarka) and fixing (vicāra), this alone is the Constructor of the not-quite-real, but no other." — The new alinea should begin 25.12 with athavā. On vitarka and vicāra, cf. LVP, pp. 385—392 my CC, p. 104, and AK, Index. They are deficient in the higher spheres of existence in trance.

63 The primary qualities of Matter are four (mahā-bhūtāni). Matter reduces to qualities (dharma) already in early Buddhism. These primary qualities are: repulsion (pṛthivī), attraction (ap), temperature (tejas) and motion (samīraṇa). They are all varieties of the tangible (spraṣṭavya). The tangible sense-data are alone divided in primary and secondary. All other sense-data are only secondary (bhautika) „Form" which according to Locke is a primary quality, is placed by the Buddhists among the secondary one's as saṃsthāna, because it evidently cannot be separated from colour (rūpa), which is secondary. Thus it is clear that Matter as ὑλη reduces in the Buddhist system (like with Berkley) to a sensation of opposition to pressure (spraṣṭavya), and Mind reduces to a primary pure sensation (viṣaya-prativijñapti).

64 aprahīṇa=ma-spaṅs-pa, avidhūta=ma-bral-ba.

65 Lit. 25.26—26.2. Lit. „According to others kāma-dhātu are those who are developed from attachment to kāma's; rūpa-dhātu are those who are developed from attachment to rūpa; ārūpya-dhātu are those who are developed from attachment to ārūpya". — anuśayita is explained in AK, I. 14 as anusevita. In our passage it is rendered in Tib. by rgyas-par-ḥgyur-ba-rnams=vistara-bhūtāḥ; anuśaya is sometimes rendered as phra-rgyas „developing germs". The explanation seems to imply that there are three kinds of existence because there are three different kinds of germs or seeds from which individual life develops like a plant out of a corresponding seed, with the implication that every life is the realization of an attachment or will (cetanā=karma). The seed is hetu, karman is adhipati, cp. LVP, p. 437. The amorphous beings of ārūpya-dhātu are evidently constructed on the pattern of ākāśa, ātma and other ubiquitous substances. They are created by the different „desires" or, as we may put it,by necessities in the struggle for life, cf. the legend of the origin of food (kavalī-kāra-āhāra) through its necessity for the living beings descended from the rūpa-heavens where there was no necessity (or desire) for it.

66 They consist only of the dhātu's №№ 6,12 and 18.

67 Lit. 26.7—8 „Among all these explanations which are the best ones? Necessarily to be mentioned are only (the Constructors) named in the first explanation. Just supplementary (of one another) are these explanations". —

katama is here accorded with parikalpāḥ (25.15) or with a to be supplemented prabhedāḥ. Otherwise we must correct the text and read — pūrvam vyākhyānam eva vaktavyam, yataḥ... - Tib. thag-mar bśad-pa-las brjod pa-ñid bsñad-par-bya-ba-ste, ḥdi-ltar...

[68] The repetition of the term abhūta-parikalpa in stanza I. 8 is a failure against the strict sūtra style, since being the adhikāra of the section it is understood in all the following kārikās of this section by implication. Sthiramati finds an excuse for Asaṅga in the fact that the abhūta-parikalpa exposition has been interrupted by an explanation of anupalabdhi in the preceding stanza.

[69] Read (punctuation!) 26.12 — katham kṛtvā? parikalpya-vastunaḥ svabhāva-viśeṣa-parikalpanayā citta-caittānām pravṛttatvāt. artha-svarūpa-viśeṣa-dṛṣṭiś citta-caittā...

[70] Read 26.14 — abhūta-parikalpaś ceti paryāya-, Tib. yaṅ-dag-pa-yin-źes-bya-ba-ni rnam-graṅs...

[71] Lit. 26.10—14 „And the synonym-essence"; he thus proclames the synonym-essence of the Constructor of the unreal by indicating the Mind and different mental evolutes. By telling what? Because the Mind and the mental phenomena are active through the construction of the own-essence and of the qualities of the thing which is to be constructed (parikalpya-vastu). Perception of the thing itself and of its qualities is the Mind and mental phenomena and the Constructor of unreality (also), thus they arrive to be synonyms".—Instead of parikalpya-vastunaḥ the Tib. reads abhūta-parikalpa-vastunaḥ which can possibly represent a slight emendation of the text by the translators. — svabhāva-viśeṣa is here used as a dvandva compound, - Tib. ran-bźin daṅ khyad-par. Otherwise svabhāva-viśeṣa as viśiṣṭa-svabhāva can also mean the empirical object, the object characterized by its qualities, cf. Nyāya-bindu-ṭīkā, II. 14 (p. 22).

[72] vijñāna 26.22, - prativiṣaya-vijñaptiḥ.

[73] LVP, p. 497 and 414.1, cp. Vācaspati, Tāp., p. 454.19 (Vizian.)— nānā hi citram ucyate, tat katham ekam iti..., yad āhuḥ (Dignāga) —

citram tad ekam iti cet,
aho citrataram mahat!

[74] Read 27.3 — na sarvathābhāva ity ukteḥ, Tib. med-min; reference to kārikā I. 4.

[75] Read 27.6 — prāptir, instead of saṃyogo, Tib. phrad-par On prāpti cf. AK, II. 179—195; LVP, p. 54.

[76] Lit 26.24—27.7. „The mental evolutes (caittāh) are just special minds, this is intended by some one's. Just such a mind arises variegated, representing such sort of thing etc., just as those of a peacock's tail. Indeed many marks are admitted in common life as one variegated (thing) in order that a unity should not possess many essences. This fault could be, if the own-essence of a dharma would be absolute reality (pariniṣpanna), but when it is mere illusion, there is no such fault, because it is said „neither so (nor) non-existence in every respect". This is not so! because of contradiction with the sūtra; „what is feeling, what is idea, what is volition, what is pure sensation, these dharmas are united, not disunited". Union namely is simultaneous appearence (prāpti) of (different) realities. Indeed that

one who does not admit that dharmas are absolute realities (parinişpanna) for him this sūtra is not suggestive of such meaning". — This passage excellently illustrates the mutual position of the Sarvāstivādins and Vijñāvādins. The first party maintains the ultimate reality of the 75 dharmas into which all reality is analyzed (sarvam asti). Here only the 46 (resp. 51) caitta-dharmas or the four mental skandhas are the subject of the controversy. The ātma-theory, alias sat-kāya-dṛṣṭi, the theory of the reality of an assemblage of dharmas is the main enemy. The Psyche does not exist, it is split in mind-dust, it is a multitude of interconnected mental Elements of four different kinds (skandhas). The pure mind is but pure sensation (prativijñaptiḥ), one of the Elements, existing on the same level as all other Elements. For the second party the only ultimate reality (parinişpanna) is this pure sensation or the pure Mind alone. It is the only „Thing" (ekam dravyam). Notice the use of the term parinişpanna, as well as of the term dharma=sat, and of the term prāpti which mean according to the abhidharma of the Hīnayāna that all mental phenomena are separate realities (dharmas) connected by causal laws, not by inherence in a thinking substance. Mental phenomena are united by samprayukta-hetu in contrast to sahabhū-hetu which is mutual causation of two or more simultaneously appearing Elements as e. g. the four fundamental qualities (mahābhūta) of Matter. The samprayukta-hetu thus points to a more intimate connection than simple simultaneousness the mental phenomena are united by a force called prāpti in four respects, cp. above, p. 26.21, but they are still separate realities, dharma (=sat). In the Yogācāra system they represent one concrete unity, one dharma=dravya=sat=kşaṇa=saṃskṛta-dharma=paratantra, the difference being abstract (ākāra=kalpita=parikalpita). Thus samprayoga means prāpti in Hīnayāna and tādātmya=samatā in the Yogācāra system. Cp. LVP, p. 395 ff.

Part I, Chapter IV

1 ḥjug-pai mtshan-ñid=pravṛtti-lakşaṇa.
2 pratyaya-vijñāna=ālaya-vijñāna.
3 aupabhogika, lit. „referring to (actual) enjoyment or experience".
4 vedanā.
5 samjñā.
6 cetanā.
7 anubhava.
8 pariccheda.
9 preraka.
10 Lit. (kārikā I.9) „The one is cause-sensation, the other refers to experience; enjoying, cognizing, stimulating are the mental evolutes". — Enjoying refers to feeling, pleasant or unpleasant. Cognizing (pariccheda) refers to ideas, representations or concepts (saṃjñā). Stimulating (preraka-ḥjug-byed) refers to the will (cetanā) and includes all other faculties (citta-sampruyakta-saṃskāra), moral and immoral forces whose catalogue includes in the system of the Sarvāstivādins 46 items and 51 items in the system of the Yogācāras, cf. Rosenberg, Problems, p. 128—130.

11 The fundamental change which Asaṅga has introduced into Buddhism or, what is the same, into the anātma=dharma theory, was, according to his own confession, the establishment of a „common foundation" for all the

Elements of Existence (the dharma's). It is called ālaya-vijñāna which means „all-conserving Mind" or a „magazine of ideas", a „Mind-Store". Its implication is first of all the denial of the external world which is replaced by ideas. It is also a step towards the reintroduction of the dethroned Soul. Uddyotakara (p. 69) and Vācaspatimišra (Tātparya, p. 145, Vizianagram) reject it as a poor substitute for their substantial Soul. It is kṣaṇika, i. e. a staccato run of discrete point-instants, nothing of a substance. This, sacrifice Buddhism could not make. The anātma-vāda could not become ātma-vāda. The whole system of dharma's has been retained, their number even was enlarged from 75 to 100 and the ālaya received a place in it. Buddhism continued to be a pluralistic dharma-theory, but a monistic subway has been added to it. The theory of the ālaya is very elaborate, cp. LVP, p. 94—220. It is beginningless (anādi) and everlasting (dhruva, not nitya) through all reincarnations up to Nirvāṇa. It is the source of all ideas and the receptacle of all passed experience, hence the source of memory. It replaces both the external (nimitta-bhāga) and the internal (daršana-bhāga) worlds. But it is not a substance, it is a process, it runs underground of actual experience. Since we have in the European languages no adequate term for a running Soul we must either leave the term ālaya untranslated (like the terms nirvāṇa and karma) or resort to the term Psyche which is yet unengaged in Buddhist philosophy. We must of course keep in mind its difference not only from the Greek psyche but also trom the vedic ātman (which was likened to the Greek psyche by Prof. H. Jacobi), from the Vedāntic jiva, from the transmigrating liṅga-šarira of Sānkhya, not to speak of the ātman of Nyāya-Vaišesika. But that it is a substitute for an individual's surviving Soul is clear from the words of Uddyotakara and Vācaspati.

[12] Read (probably) 27.8 — hetu-phala-prabhedo na vijñāyata iti.

[13] It is clear from this passage that abhūta-parikalpa and paratantra as well as saṃskṛta-dharma are synonyms, although in different systems these terms carry different implications. Thus it is clear from 27.9 that the saṃskṛta of Hīnayāna appears to the Yogācāra as a kind of pariniṣpanna, whereas for him there is between them a great difference inasmuch as saṃskṛta is paratantra, but pariniṣpanna (=pari-siddha, yoṅs-grub) is asaṃskṛta.

[14] Read 27.10 — pravṛttir eva lakṣaṇam iti pravṛtti-lakṣaṇam. Thus the point-instant (kṣaṇa) is the „dependent".

[15] Lit. 27.11. Lit. „The process of the consecution of moments is that owing to which there is the phenomenality (phenomenal „great oppression" — saṃkleśa) of the experience of the present moment" (saṃkleśa-duḥkha=anityatā)". — ādhipatyena points to adhipati-pratyaya-mātram (28.21), general condition. Lit. 27.12 „And the movement towards another birth through which we will have in future the great impediments (saṃkleśa) of the Oppressors (kleśa), of Retribution (karma) and of Life-duration (āyuḥ)". On the saṃkleśas cf. below, text p. 30.5 ff. and LVP, p. 214 ff.

[16] Read 27.13 — atra kṣaṇa-paramparā-pravṛttiḥ pravṛtti-lakṣaṇam uktam=Tib. ḥdir-ni skad-cig-rgyud-mar ḥjug-pa ḥjug-pai mtshan-ñid-du bśad-pao. Lit. „Here the essence of the process which is a process of consecution of (single) moments has been explained. In the sequel (adhastāt=Tib. ḥog-nas) he will explain the motion towards a future life (in twelve consecutive stages) as having the essence of the great oppressors", i. e. the twelve consecutive stages of life and rebirth

will be interpreted as so many oppressors or „phenomenalizers" of pure absolute Reality.

[17] hetu-pratyaya corresponds to the first five items of the hetu-classification, it means that the ālaya-vijñāna is not adhipati-pratyaya (=pratyaya-mātram) alone, a remote cause, a general condition, but a real, efficient, immediate cause, cp. LVP, p. 116 ff.

[18] i. e. the five kinds corresponding to the five outer senses, the inner sense and the Ego (kliṣṭa-manaḥ), together seven kinds of sensation, the Mind-Store sensation being the eighth.

[19] prayojana.

[20] In the Vaibhāṣika system vijñāna (pure sensation) and sukha-vedanā (feeling of pleasure) represent two realities, two pariniṣpanna-dharma (27.2), but connected by samprayukta-hetu. In the Yogācāra system they are one reality, the second (sukha) being bhrānti.

[21] Read, 27.24 — vijñānaikayogakṣematvāt, „because identical with vijñāna"; cf. S. Y., 33.6 — vijñānatvād(?) ekayoga kṣematvāc ca.

[22] Read 27.24—25 — ālaya-vijñānam hi vijnānāntarāṇām hetu-pratyaya iti pratyaya-vijñānam ity ālıyante...= Tib. kun-gźi-rnam-par-śes-pa-ni rnam-par-śes-pa-gźan-dag-gi rgyui-rkyen yin-pas rkyen-gyi rnam-par-śes-pao-źes-bya-ba-la.

[23] Lit. 28.1. „Because it intimates (the presence of) the living bodies and of the receptacle world, by making them appear it is sensation". Allusion to the definition of vijñāna as viṣaya-prativijñaptih, cf. my CC, p. 10, 63; my Buddhist Logic, I, 150 ff.

[24] Lit. 28.2 „And because it is exclusively retribution, it is neutral". ālaya is ekānta-vipāka, this means that it neither is vipāka-hetu (=savipāka), nor vipaka-ja, but „pure„ vipāka, it is the non-active residue of former life, purely a consequence of former good or bad deeds, but itself it is neither good nor bad, neither associated with kušala-dharmas nor with klešas, but only with sarvatraga-dharmas. It represents, so te speak, a „subway" for the passage from one life into another of the seeds left back by former deeds to be fructified in some future rebirth. Being a mere subway equally for seeds good and bad it can naturally be itself neither good nor bad. Cp. LVP, p. 98—„vraiment et par excellence vipāka-phala par opposition aux dharmas vipāka-ja". Ibid., p. 197—„il constitue, pour un temps déterminé une série perpetuelle at homogène; c'est lui qn'on désigne sous le nom de „pensée à la conception", „pensée à la mort;" cp. ibid., pp. 60, 92, 190, 192 and passim.

[25] Read 28.3 — sarva-sāsrava-dharma-bıjānubaddhānām anyeṣām ca.

[26] Read 28.8—9 tasmāt paripuṣṭa-bījāl labdha-pariṇāma-višeṣāt punas... Lit. 28.6—10 „Indeed an actual idea having started out of the Mind-Store develops (perhaps better poṣayati instead of vistārayati) in that Mind-Store a seed, the producer of a not yet produced (new) homogeneous actual idea. From this developed seed which has reached a special evolution again a homogeneous actual idea (experience) is produced and thus it is that the actual sensation arises as having its cause in that (Mind- Store)". Cp. LVP, p. 50.

[27] Lit. 28. 10—18 „But does it not follow that the Mind-Store-Sensation is also an experience (of former deeds) and an actual sensation its cause-sensation, because it is the place where a feeling neither pleasant nor unple-

asant is being experienced and because the Mind-Store-Sensation is charged (besmeared, anointed) with a biotic force (vāsanā). There is no other force-anointment than being a cause".

28 Lit. 28.21—25 „Indeed, the Mind-Store-Sensation, since it is the (remote) ruler-cause over good and bad Elements encloses the forces which (produce) the maturation-and outflow-results; and since it is the ruler-cause over indefinite Elements, (it encloses) the forces producing the outflow-results. Therefore the Mind-Store-Sensation is the efficient cause of all the Elements of phenomenal life, but actual sensation is a (remote) ruler-cause, not the (immediate) efficient cause. Thus it does not follow that actual sensation is the efficient cause of the Mind-Store-Sensation". On this reciprocal causation cp. LVP, p. 107, cp. also pp. 60, 92—93.

29 Read 28.22—vipāka-phala-vāsanāḥ (drop niṣyaṇḍa).

30 Read 28.23—niṣyaṇḍa-phala-vāsanāś cety ālaya-...

31 Read 28.24—pravṛtti-vijñānam tv adhipati-pratyayo, na hetu-pratyaya iti nāsti... The Tib. (Pek. T.) has—ḥjug-pai rnam-par-śes-pai, like the printed pravṛtti-vijñānasya, but it must be corrected into ḥjug-pai rnampar-śes-pa-ni.

32 Read 28.26—triprakārāpy upabhujyate, anubhūyata ity arthaḥ; = Tib. (Pek. T. f. 30. b. 1) rnam-pa-gsum-char yaṅ ñe-bar-spyod-pa-ste, myoṅ-bar-byed ces-bya-bai tha-tshig-go. Lit. „And being threefold it is savoured (eaten), thus it is experienced".

33 Read 29.1—bhava-rasa-āsvāda-sāra-anurūpā vedanā-srid-pai ro-bro-bai-sñiṅ-po-ḥdra-ba-ni tshor-ba-ste. Lit. „Feeling conforms with the quintessence of savouring the juice of mundane existence". saṃvedanayā=samyag-vedanayā=kun-tu-myoṅ-bas.

34 In Nyāya-Vaiśesika „cognition" (buddhir, upalabdhir, jnānam, NS, I. 15) embraces both pure sensation (nirvikalpaka) and definite cognition (savikalpaka). In early Buddhism pure sensation (cittam, mano, vijñānam) is the pure Mind itself, the heir of the Sānkhya puruṣa, the central Element of cognition, it is characterized as an internal organ (indriya) and the mental phenomena are its corresponding mental objects (viṣaya). But in the Yogācāra system this Mind becomes Mind-only (vijñāna-mātram), the unique Reality, with regard to which the manifold of ideas and feelings are mere phenomena and represent a Transcendental Illusion. Who the anye are which are quoted in 29.3 it is impossible to state, but they evidently are charged with the fault of confounding the absolute character of the pure Mind or pure sensation with the phenomenal, empirical character of feeling. If we adhere to Locke's and Berkely's terminology, which for the Vijñānavāda system is convenient in many cases, we would call pure sensation, i. e. the mere sensation of the presence in the ken of something quite indefinite, also feeling, but in the abhidharma we must make a strict difference between pure sensation (nirvikalpaka), feeling (vedanā) and a more or less definite, connotative cognition (saṃjñā); otherwise we would share in the mistake of the Pali scholars who could not find out the difference between saṃjñā-skandha and vijñāna-skandha.

35 Read 29.5—vedanā-paribhogaḥ. Lit. „An idea is thorough experience of feeling by making it to consist (ātmaka) of abstracting the peculiar characteristic of pleasure etc". Vasubandhu has simply upabhogo vedanā, paribhogaḥ saṃjñā. The usual definition is nimitta-

udgrahaṇam „abstraction of the mark" or a cognition containing some abstraction. Sthiramati's explanation is an attempt to unite both definitions.

[36] Read 29.7—cetanā-manaskāra-, (sems-pa=cetanā, sems=citta).

[37] Lit. 29.9—10 „Idea is definiteness because it circumcuts the mark of the object, (the mark) which is the foundation of (our) dealing (with that object)".

[38] Read 29.11—cetanādyādhipatyāt (sems-pa=cetanā).

[39] The twelve ever reverting stages in the phenomenal existence (of reincarnations) in a beginningless continuity of the life of a Psyche are the following —

1. Transcendental Illusion (avidyā), the ruling general condition of the whole series with the removal of which there are no more incarnations, i. e. no phenomenal life.
2. Prenatal Biotic Forces (saṃskāra=karma).
3. Intermediate existence of consciousness (vijñāna) in an ethereal incarnation (gandharva).
4. The embryo (nāma-rūpa=5 skandha's) with undeveloped sense-organs.
5. The embryo with developed sense-organs (ṣad-āyatana).
6. Sensation (sparśa).
7. Feeling (vedanā).
8. Sexual desire (tṛsṇā).
9. Attachment to life (upādāna).
10. Fully developed life (bhava), responsible activity (new karma).
11. Old age and death (jarā-maraṇam).
12. Reincarnation (jāti).

These twelve members are called „great oppressors" (saṃkleṣa) or „phenomenalizers" which convert the pure reality of the Absolute into the phenomenal impurity. Of them the №№ 1, 8 and 9. are called kleśa-samkleśa or phenomenalizers κατ'ἐξοχήν. The Transcendental Illusion, Sexual Desire and Attachment to life are the origin of phenomenality. The first of them, i. e. Transcendental Illusion, is the most important, the „ruling" cause of phenomenal life, with its extinction phenomenality disappears. The №№ 2 and 10 are called karma-saṃkleša. They determine the happy or unhappy existence in accordance with the former good or bad deeds. The remaining seven members are called jāti-saṃkleša or āyuḥ-saṃkleśa, the phenomenal life proper, i. e. an individual life which has been produced by Transcendental Illusion and shaped according to its moral antecedents arrives in seven stages from a prenatal condition through an embryo to conscious life, old age death and then to a new rebirth and so on ad infinitum, up to Nirvāṇa. From different view-points these twelve items can be rearranged in two, in three, or in seven groups. The arrangement in three groups (saṃkleša) is the most important, it points to 1) the origin, 2) the shape (man or beast) and 3) the course of life of the individual.

[40] Read 29.14 kleśa-karma-janma-saṃkleśā.

[41] Read 29.15—drop the cheda after bhavanti and insert one after lakṣaṇam.

[42] anātmakam, „contains nothing substantial".

[43] prajāyate, rendered in Tib. by rgyas-pa, which in 31.1 corresponds to āpyāyana.

[44] Lit. 29.23—24 „Indeed perception of reality is not produced when concealed in the domain where perception is overpowered, because the essence of illusion is non-perception".

[45] prādhānyena.

[46] Read — lokottarā prajñā, Tib. ḥjig-rten-las ḥdas-pai śes-rab-bo.

[47] pṛṣṭha-labdha, cf. E. Obermiller, Pr. P., p. 20. There is a twofold cognition of the Absolute. The one is samāhita-jñāna and is nirvikalpaka, it is a mystic Gnosis, a direct supernatural intuition of the Saint. The other is pṛṣṭha-labdha-jñāna and is savikalpaka, it is a logically constructed explanation of what has been perceived in trance, as far as it is capable of logical explanation.

[48] Read (probably) 29.25—30. 3. — bhūta-darśanam punaḥ prādhānyena lokattarā prajñā, tat-pṛṣṭhodbhavatvāt tat-pṛṣṭha-labdham ca, tad-avabodhāt, tat-prayojakam api śruta-cintā-bhāvanā-mayam bhūta-darśanam ity ucyate. The Peking T. has sbyoṅ-bar-byed-pa (viśodhaka instead of sbyor-bar-byed-pa=prayojaka, and this seems to be the right reading. Lit. „(Direct) intuition of the real is mainly a trans-mundane intuition, (but) its subsequently attained (conceptual knowledge), because it is attained subsequently on it, as well as its preparation containing study, consideration and meditation, are also termed (indirectly) intuition of the real".

[49] Read 30.6 — vijñāne karma-vāsanāyāh. — vijñāne=ālaye.

[50] Read 30.8 — iti saṃskāraḥ drop the word sa.

[51] For a full list of saṃskāras according to the Sarvāstivādi and to the Yogācāra schools cf. O. Rosenberg, Probleme, pp. 127—131.

[52] The word ādhipatyāt p. 30.9—10 points to a remote, fundamental cause — adhipati-pratyaya, cf. also 30.12.

[53]. I. e. by adhipati-pratyaya and hetu-pratyaya together, the hetu-pratyaya here includes samprayukta-hetu (cf. 30.14) and the sahabhū-hetu (p. 30.16—17). On the hetu-pratyaya theory cf. AK, II. 299. Avidyā is thus, on the one side, the adhipati-pratyaya of phenomenal existence, on the other side, it also is its hetu-pratyaya which here includes sahabhū-hetu and samprayukta-hetu. In other words it is not only the fundamental, remote cause creating the phenomenal worlds as a general Transcendental Illusion corresponding to the mukhyā bhrānti of Vedānta, it also is the constant, simultaneous inherent companion of all phenomenal ideas or of phenomena in general. One avidyā is the first bhavāṅga, the other is included among saṃskāra, cp. LVP, p. 279.

[54] sāmānya-pratyaya here means „cumulative cause" in the sense of a double cause. The main division being into adhipati-pratyaya and hetu-pratyaya (which we may for sake of clearness translate roughly as remote cause and proximate cause), sāmānya-pratyaya will be a force (saṃskāra) which is both the fundamental condition of karma and all phenomenal life and also its immediate efficient cause. We find the following explanation of the theory of the double dependence of saṃskāra on avidyā in the work Rten-ḥbrel-gyi rnam-bźag-luṅ-rigs ban-mdzod of the celebrated Labrang lama Rje-guṅ-thaṅ-bstan-pai sgroṅ-me (1762—1823), cf. his complete works (gsuṅ-ḥbum, v. III, f. 13. b.3) — ḥdu-byed-kyi rkyen chags-sogs-kyaṅ yod-na, ma-rig-pa-ñid bstan mi-rigs-so sñam-na; ma-yin-te. gtso-boi rkyen-

gyi dbaṅ-du byas-pai-phyir-te. chags-sogs kun-ḥbyuṅ-ba-yaṅ ḥdii rkyen-gyis yin pas, des bskyed-pai las-gñis-kyi gtso-boi rkyen-yaṅ ḥdis byed-pa mi-ḥgal-bai-phyir-te, blon-pai bran-yaṅ rgyal-pai dbaṅ-du-ḥgro-dgos-ma bźin, ḥdi-las ñon-de gnis-kai spyii rkyen yin-pas gñis-kar dbaṅ-byed-pai phyir. This means literally — „If you think that it is not right to indicate avidyā alone while rāgādi is also the cause of saṃskāra, it is not so! because it is referred to as the ruler-cause; and because, since the origination of rāgādi is also produced by this cause, it is not contradictory that the double karma produced by it is also produced by this ruler-cause; and because just as the agent of the minister is also obliged to act according to the will of the king, it being the „common" cause of both karma and kleśa; in both of them it exercises its influence". This can be paraphrased in the following way — „Phenomenal life is conditioned by a Transcendental Illusion which conceals from us the eternal Absolute. But it is not right to point out this Transcendental Illusion (avidyā) as the exclusive cause of a new life (rebirth), because it is only its general and remote condition. Its immediate causes are those subconscious phenomenalizing agencies (kleśas) which call forth the creative force of former deeds, the double karma, i. e. the moral or immoral antecedents for which a given existence is going to be the pleasant or unpleasant retribution. Some philosophers therefore think that it was not right to mention Transcendental Illusion alone as the cause of the double karma. That is not so! Transcendental Illusion remains the fundamental condition of all phenomenal life. It is the cause of all phenomenalizing forces (kleśa) and also ot the force of former moral and immoral deeds (karma). This double causation does not prevent to mention Transcendental Illusion (avidyā) as a cause of karma, i. e. of the influence on a new life of its moral antecedents. Just as the agent of a minister must also execute the will of the king, just so the force of former deeds (karma=saṃskāra) obeys in first line to the phenomenalizing forces (kleśa) and in the second line — to Transcendental Illusion (avidyā)". — According to the opinion of lama Guṅ-thaṅ avidyā is the cause of kleśa and kleśa is the cause of karma, but this does not prevent us from asserting that avidyā is the cause of karma also. According to Sthiramati's formulation there is a double avidyā, a so to speak, root-avidyā (aveṇikī avidyā?) which is the adhipati-pratyaya and another avidyā which is the sahabhū-hetu and the samprayukta-hetu of cetanā (-karma). The latter is therefore not adhipati-pratyaya, but hetu-pratyaya. The expression sāmānya-hetu=sphii-rkyen thus refers to a combination of adhi-pati- and hetu-pratyaya. Cf. the following diagram —

A. (avidyā) A (avidyā)
B. (kleśa) ↓ ↘B (kleśa)
C. (karma) C (karma)

Thus avidyā is both the indirect and direct (= simultaneous) cause of saṃskāra, cp. LVP, p. 279.

Read 30. 14—15 — yathā kleśa-samutthānasya sāmānya-samutthāna-pratyayas tathā tat-samutthitānām cetanā-nām api.

35 ānejya or āniñjya, Tib. mi-gyo-ba. Lit. 30. 17 „also of immovable arising from a view to quit such bhūmi". Cf. on this theory LVP

Morale, p. 77 ff. The Saint (ārya) who ascends to the immaterial heavens (ārūpya) has liberated himself from karma. His existence nevertheless comes from a bīja or germ produced by a concentrated (samāhita) mental act or prayer of absolutely certain, immovable (āneјya) retribution. Cp. LVP, p. 474.

[56] Lit. 30.9—19. „And it is capable of composing a new birth through the sovereignty of avidyā, not through its mere existence; thus the saṃskāra's have avidyā as cause, thus it is said. Indeed they can compose the rebirth of that one who has not attained vidyā, but not of that one who has attained vidyā (30.12). And avidyā is the cause of the saṃskāra's not by mere sovereignty, since there also is samutthāna by the cumulative cause. Indeed since avidyā is associated with all kleśa's, (therefore), just as it is the cumulative cause of the rising of all kleśa's just so it is the cause of the cetanā's (=samskāra=karma) which arise through them". (30.16). „Even good saṃskāra's which are associated with a desire for some mundane enjoyment have simultaneous avidyā as their cumulative cause when they arise". (30.17). „Even with āneјya's which arise at the consideration of parting with a bhūmi an avidyā simultaneous with this production is a cumulative cause. Thus the causal dependence of the saṃskāras is stated".

[57] Asaṅga gives in Mahāyāna-saṃgrahal a series of reasons establishing that it is indispensable to admit the existence of a Psyche (ālaya) as an enduring subconscious Mind-Store. Cp. LVP, pp. 182—220. The pravṛtti-vijñānas have interruptions, ibid., p. 184.

[58] The ālaya-vijñāna is dhruva „enduring", it is not nitya „eternal" since eternality would imply absence of change, immobility. The ālaya-vijñāna of a given personal continuity (saṃtāna) is beginningless and endures in an uninterrupted stream of moments up to Nirvāṇa. Cp. Triṃś., d. 21—22 and LVP, p. 156 ff.

[59] This is one of the reasons why the existence of ālaya-vijñāna must be admitted. It alone, being itself morally indifferent, can contain all seeds of future events, happy and unhappy, morally good and morally bad. Neither a kuśala-citta nor a kliṣṭa-citta can contain seeds of a contrary character. But ālaya is similar to a stuff which can absorb freely a bad as well as a good odour. kuśala-dharma such as alobha, adveṣa, on the one hand, and kliṣṭa-dharma such as lobha, dveṣa, on the other, could not enter at once into the same saṃtāna. Therefore a vāsanā-bīja could not be thrown into a running stream of consciousness having a definite moral character, good or bad. Thus only ālaya-vijñāna which always is avyākṛta can contain bija's or vāsanā's of both kinds, like an inodorous piece of cloth which is ready to absorb bad as well as sweet odours without changing them. Cp. LVP, p. 152.

[60] Read 30.25 pariṇāmena.

[61] According to the Tib. we should read 31.1. tena prathamasyaiva tad-bījasya āpyāyanam=des thog-ma-kho-nai savon-de rgyas-par-byed-pa.

[62] Lit. 31.1. „Indeed on no impure Element nor on a pure one any new (apūrva) seed can be placed". The Tib. has sa-bon sṅon-ma bskyed-pa-med-de. The remark probably refers to the theory that ālaya-vijñāna is sarva-bījaka. Therefore neither an old seed (sṅon-ma) can be created (bskyed-pa); nor, as the sanscrit text has it, a new (apūrva) can be added (ādhiyate). Therefore the „throwing" of the seed must be understood as the beginning of its development.

63 Read 31.5 — sampreṣaṇād iti karma-prabhāvita-vijñāna-saṃtāna-pravṛttyā...

64 Lit. 31.6—8. „By the run of the uninterrupted continuity, which is consciousness controlled by karma, from the place of death to the place of rebirth the force which constitutes the germ of a new life is conveyed, is lead. Only considering this it is shown that the cause (as far as it is) intermediate consciousness is not the saṃskāra, but the consciousness of former life alone possesses saṃskāra-causality", i. e. is charged with bīja.

65 Read 31.8 — evam kṛtvā pratisaṃdhi-vijñānam pratyayo, na saṃskāraḥ, pūrvakālīna-bhava-vijñānam eva saṃskāra-pratyayam iti pradarśitam bhavati; cf. Tib. de-ltar byas-na ñiṅ-mtshams-sbyor-bai rnam-par-śes-pa rkyen-ni, ḥdu-byed ma-yin-gyi, sṅon-gyi dus-kyi srid-pai rnam-par-śes-pa-ñid-kyi rkyen ḥdu-byed-par rab-tu bstan-pa-yin-te.

66 nāma-rūpa.

67 sam-pari-grahāt=kun-ḥdzin-phyir.

68 tshe-phyi-mar lus-so (ātma-bhāva=lus).

69 Lit. „in the (undeveloped) name and form".

70 kalala-arbuda-ghana-peśi the embryo in the 1st, 2nd, 3d and 4th week of its development are rendered in Tib. as nurnur-po daṅ, mer-mer-po daṅ, nar-nar-po daṅ, gor-gor-po, but praśākhāvasthā is translated rkaṅ-lag-ḥgyur-pai dus.

71 Read 31.17 — evam vāsanā-viśeṣeṇa sabhāga-nikāya-antareṣu... (bsgo-ba=vāsanā).

72 Read 31.18 — tasmiṃś cotpanne.

73 Drop the cheda before manuṣya in 31.18.

74 Lit. 31.18 „Also it includes just the whole individual existence up to death, because from the beginning everything is determined (in the embryo) in the condition of cause".

75 Lit. 31.21 „Or without difference also by Mind-Body the own existence is totally embraced, thus its division is taught, just as all saṃskṛta is included in the five skandhas".

76 Lit. 31.24 „Therefore the fact that name-form depends on consciousness, must be conceived according to possibility. Cf. above, 31.12. Cp. LVP, p. 486.

77 Read 32.4 — yady api ca tasyām avasthāyām kāyāyatanam asti tathāpy aparipūrṇam eva, āśritāśraya-paripūry-abhāvāt. In note 408 at the end read yoṅs-su-ma-rdzogs-pa-.

78 Lit. 32.5 „as place and placed it is not quite complete".

79 Read 32.6 — āśrayaḥ=gnas, instead of āśritaḥ.

80 Read 32.11 — evam for eva and drop the cheda before it.

81 Read 32.10 — paripūraṇāt paripūrṇam bhavati.

82 Lit. 32.13 „By treble definition. The words «the living world is oppressed» must be connected. „Treble" is the meeting of sense-organ, object and consciousness, through it a treble modification of the organ which is favourable to the production of a pleasant or other feeling; this is its definition, a contact".

83 Read 32.15 — ata eva ya indriya-vikāras tad-ākāra-sādṛśyena spṛśatīti sparšaḥ=de-bas-na dpaṅ-poi gyur-pa-gaṅ-yin-pa dei rnam-pa daṅ ḥdra-bar reg-par byed-pas reg-pa źes-bya-ste. Lit. „just therefore the modification of the sense-organ is contact, since by the similarity of its procedure it (quasi)

touches". Cp. MAV, p. 16.16—ā k ā r o g r a h a ṇ a - p r a k ā r a ḥ, cp. LVP, pp. 124, 492.

[84] Lit. 32.17 „Or conditioned by the six senses contact produces a threefold modification of the sense-organ which is favourable to the feeling of pleasure etc", i. e. three are the causes, three the v i k ā r ā s of i n d r i y a and threefold the feelings. —The translation of s p a r ś a as „contact" is misleading, since it is clearly stated that it is a process m e t a p h o r i c a l l y so called, because of its similarity with a tactile sensation. In the a b h i d h a r m a the organ of touch is called k ā y e n d r i y a and a tactile sensation is s p r a ṣ ṭ a v y a - v i j ñ ā n a. By analogy with r ū p a - ś a b d a - g a n d h a - r a s a we would expect the 11th ā y a t a n a to be called s p a r ś a, but it is always called s p r a ṣ ṭ a v y a. In the classification of mental phenomena s p a r ś a belongs to the c a i t t a - class, hence to the s a ṃ s k ā r a - s k a n d h a, whereas a tactile sensation (s p r a ṣ ṭ a v y a - v i j ñ ā n a) belongs to the c i t t a - class and therefore to the v i j ñ ā n a - s k a n d h a. With the Y o g ā c ā r a s this difference becomes immaterial, since all Elements belong ultimately to the v i j ñ ā n a - class, hence s p a r ś a instead of s p r a ṣ ṭ a v y a becomes possible, as in MAV, p. 16.2. The T r i ṃ ś., p. 20 (Jacobi's transl., p. 15) contains the same definition of s p a r ś a with the additional remark that it represents rather a modification, or effect, on the object than on the sense-organ (v i ṣ a y a - v i k ā r a - p a r i c c h e d a - ā t m a k o p i i n d r i y a - v i k ā r a - p a r i c c h e d a u k t a ḥ). J a c o b i's translation of p a r i c c h e d a as cognition (Erkenntniss) must be understood in that sense that s p a r ś a belongs to the noetic class of phenomena (p r a j ñ ā - m a t i), but it is unconscious (a s a m v i d i t a), subliminal (a n a t y ū h a - a v a s t h ā). B u - s t o n says (P h a r - p h y i n., ch. V) „The ṣ a ḍ - ā y a t a n a - condition lies between the evolution of the senses and the meeting of organ, object and consciousness; the s p a r ś a - condition — between this meeting and the „recognition" (ṅ o - ś e s - p r a t y a b h i j ñ ā) of the cause of the threefold feeling; the v e d a n ā - condition — between this recognition during the time (the child) is yet sexually incapable etc". The Chinese K o u e i - k i explains here p a r i c c h e d a as „pattern" of a future feeling, cf. LVP, p. 144 „découpure". It is the foundation (s a n n i ś r a y a) of feeling and all other mental phenomena which arrive in its track. The similarity is between a physical contact and a mental sensation, not between i n d r i y a and s p a r ś a, as supposed by J a c o b i, op. c., p. 15 note. The similarity or conformity mentioned by me on pp. 56, 57 of CC is the solution of a quite different, epistemological, question, i. e. the „objectness" (v i ṣ a y a t ā) or object-conformity (v i ṣ a y a - s ā r ū p y a). It is asked that, if the object is defined as the cause of its cognition, the definition will be wrong, since the organ is also a cause of it. On this s ā r ū p y a cf. my B u d d h i s t L o g i c, v. I, p. 204 ff, v. II, App. IV. Hence in the subliminal consciousness we must distinguish between 1) v i j ñ ā n a itself which is ā l a y a, 2) v i t a r k a and v i c ā r a a n a t y ū h a - a v a s t h ā y ā m, they are modifications of c e t a n ā which accompanies ā l a y a and 3) s p a r ś a. Only the next following degree, v e d a n ā, is self-conscious. Cf. the excellent account of s p a r ś a by LVP, p. 143 ff. It must be added that s p a r ś a can also have the meaning of a „feeling of the Absolute" (d h a r m a t ā - s p a r ś a), cf. D h a r m a - d h a r m a t ā - v i b h a n g a, kārika 22.

[85] Drop 32.22—the cheda after ā p y ā y a n ā t.

[86] According to the T r i m ṣ., p. 20 v e d a n ā „feeling" is the direct apprehension (a n u b h a v a - s ā k ṣ ā t - k a r a ṇ a) of that essence (s v a r ū p a) of the object which has an emotional character, is pleasant or unpleasant, but

not of that its essence which serves to distinguish it from other objects, this latter operation of distinction being achieved by samjñā. The second explanation — experiencing of former deeds — is inadmissible, thinks Vasubandhu, because if vedanā is the experiencing of the results of former good or bad deeds it should always be either pleasent or unpleasant, but ālaya-vijñāna is accompanied always by an indifferent feeling. Therefore, says he, vedanā can be characterized as the experiencing of the consequences of former deeds only conditionally or metaphorically (vipākopocāraḥ). Cf. LVP, p. 149. Saṃjñā and other caitta's are not mentioned in the twelve membered formula, but we must keep in mind that from the beginning, i. e. from the embryonic condition, all the five skandhas are present in each individual life. It is not the aim of the formula to give a full account of the evolution, but only to pick out the chief stages in the development from prenatal biotic forces to birth and death, and then again to a new rebirth.

[87] Read 33.1 — vijñane.

[88] The end of the phrase (33.3) in Tib. is yaṅ-srid-pa ḥbyuṅ-bar ñe-bar-sbyor-ba ñes-par-ḥjog-pa-gaṅ-yin-pa de-ni sdud-pao-punarbhava-utpādam upanibadhya yad utpāda-vyavasthāpanam sa saṃgrahaḥ. The phrase is awkward, its construction seems to be — saṃskārair vijñāne punarbhava-bija-paripoṣaṇena ākṣiptasya punarbhavasya udaka-kalpayā tṛṣṇayā ārdrīkaraṇena... yad vyavasthāpanam sa saṃgrahaḥ. The words — sarva-gatiṣv aviśeṣeṇa ātmabhāva-abhilāṣa iti (žes-bya-bas) are a subordinate clause. Lit. „Through the forces in the consciousness (vijñāna), by fostering the seed, for the casted new existence, by passion resembling water, by moistening, since every living kind without difference strives for (its) own existence, after having composed a new existence (its) determination is (its) summing up". Bu-ston, op. cit. has simply las-kyis btab-pai yaṅ-srid bsdud-pas sred-pa=saṃskārair ākṣipta-punarbhava-saṃgrahāt tṛṣṇā. The idea of tṛṣṇā is always associated vith the idea of that moisture which is indispensable for the seeds to grow. Here it is interpreted as summarizing or binding (sdud-pa) with which, the next bhavāṅga, the upādāna, is also associated, cp. LVP, p. 495 — „Les klešas lient, c. a. d. mouillent la renaissance", cp. also ibid., pp. 358, 382, 401, 409, 456, 480, 484—5, 488—9 etc.

[89] Read 33.6 — chanda-rāga-, (desire, predilection, inclination), LVP, p. 309.

[90] On difference between tṛṣṇā and upādāna cp. LVP, p. 488.

[91] Lit. 33.10 „Because the deeds done in a (former) existence are made to turn their face (become manifest) towards giving retribution in a new existence".

[92] Read 33.11 — yathā nibandhanam vijñanasya-pūrvakṛtam karma, paunarbhavikam vāsanāvastham vipākaphalam iti pravṛtti-lābhena, bhavanād bhavākṣepa-siddhaye'bhimukhībhavati, tathā bhavena... yathā should be separated from nibandhanam (-rgyu), bhavo before bhavākṣepa as well as the cheda before tathā must be dropped, the phrase marked by iti is a subordinate clause (just as the phrase ending with abhilāṣa in 33.2). — Lit. „Just as the formerly done deed being the cause of consciousness, by taking its course, since it is a retribution-result of a new existence in a potential condition, through «becoming,» is turning its face towards the

realization of the forcasted existence, just so by turning the ace through (full) existence the living world is tormented".

According to this comment the tenth stage (b h a v a) represents the realization of that existence which has been forcasted in the embryo and by former deeds. This is also the definition of B u - s t o n, op. cit. - l a s - k y i r n a m - s m i n y a ṅ - s r i d - p a r ḥ b y i n - p a r m ṅ o n - d u - b y e d - p a s s r i d - p a. But in the sequel p. 36.1 S t h i r a m a t i gives an alternate (a t h a v ā) explanation according to which b h a v a also consists of willful deeds which will be retributed in a next following existence. Cf. on the difference between the k a r m a of the second and the k a r m a of the tenth n i d ā n a p. 34.23. According to H i u a n T s a n g (LVP, p. 484) — „Réunis la T ṛ ṣ ṇ ā et l'U p ā d ā n a „mouillent" les b ī j a s ā k ṣ e p a k a et... ā k ṣ i p t a. Dès lors ils... prennent le nom de B h a v a, parcequ'ils sont tout proches du futur b h a v a, de la future existence". And ibid., p. 500 „le k a r m a n comprend... une partie du Bhava, le Duḥkha comprend les b ī j a s mouillés". It follows that the b h a v a comprises two parts, the one is realization of former deeds, the other is projection of a future life.

[93] Tib. — ź u - b a - d a ṅ - m a - ź u - b a i g n a s - k y i b a r - n a ḥ g r e - l h o g - p a s, lit. „by being rolled in the intermediate place (between the places) for undigested and digested food".

[94] Tib. k h a - z a s d a ṅ s p y o d - p a - ñ a m - ṅ a - b a d a ṅ y a - ṅ a - b a - m a - s p a ṅ s - p a s - k y a ṅ... The dictionary of Tse-ring-dpaṅ-rgyal gives for ñ a m - ṅ a - b a — k ṣ a m ā, s a ṃ k a ṭ a, ā t a ṅ k a t ā, s a m b ā d h a, and for y a - ṅ a - b a - m i - s p o ṅ - b a v i ṣ a m a - a p a r i h ā r a, we probably must read — p i ṇ ḍ a p ā t a - u p a b h o g a - ā t a ṅ k e n a s a ṅ k a t a - a p a r i t y ā - g e n a c a. In note 441 correct y a - ṅ a - b a instead of y a ṅ - b a.

[95] Read 33.24 — ā j a v a - j a v ī - b h ā v e n a.

[96] Lit. 33.25 „Tormented not purified, thus others (maintain)".

[97] This word has not been found by the editors, cf. their note 450. It is found in the text of Vasubandhu (V. f. 4. a. 3 of the Aga edition) at the close of the full kārikā I. 12. The editors apparently have expected to find it in 4. a. 6 where only half the stanza is repeated.

[98] Read 34.8 — s a m u c c a y a - v i p a r y ā s a - a r t h a k a ḥ. The Tib. — sanscrit dictionary (B a c o t) g o - b s n o r - p a - v i p a r y ā s a (probably v i p a r y a y a). S. Y. 40.19 — p a r i v a r t a š c a.

[99] The members are twelve, but the ā k ā r'a s eleven (34.2), because the two last members (birth and death) have the same ā k ā r a, namely d u ḥ k h a. In a sense still more general d u ḥ k h a is synonym of s a ṃ k l e ś a and embraces all the twelve members of p r a t ī t y a - s a m - u t p ā d a.

[100] Put 34.20 a cheda before t r e d h ā.

[101] Lit. (34.23) „s a ṃ s k ā r a is real k a r m a, b h a v a, is (potential) k a r m a in seed-condition". The sense is that real k a r m a are only past deeds, the deeds of the current existence can be so called only metaphorically. Cp. above, note 92.

[102] Embryo and sense-organs for the Y o g ā c ā r a are naturally only „ideas" in the B e r k l e y a n sense of the term. Therefore since the first explanation is open to objections S t h i r a m a t i proposes another one.

[103] Lit. 36.1 „Or love, attachment and existence are the pulling cause since through desire they are turned directly to the force (v ā s a n ā) of one of the two k a r m a's agreeing with (one's) inclinations".

[104] Lit. 36.9 „three segments, of the former end, of the other end and of the middle part".

[106] Read 36.21 — v i j ñ ā n e v ā s a n ā...

Part I, Chapter V

[1] śūnyatā.

[2] abhi-sambandha.

[3] vyavadāna.

[4] saṃkleśa.

[5] dharmatā.

[6] dharma. To this problem of the relation between dharma and dharmatā Maitreya-Asanga has devoted a special treatise Dharma-dharmatā-vibhanga. Taking it roughly dharma is saṃskṛta-dharma and dharmatā is asaṃskṛta-dharma, but as para-tantra=abhūtaparikalpa the first is at the same time bhrānti bhrānty-āśrayaś ca (=ḥkhrulpa-daṅ ḥkhrul-gźi as Jamyan-źadpa puts it). Therefore dharma is the foundation of saṃsāra, and dharmatā the foundation of nirvāṇa.

[7] Read 38.7 — śūnyatayā=stoṅ-pa-ñid-kyis. Lit. 38.7 — „Here essence consists of denial of a Reality and an Unreality". — Just as abhūta-parikalpa is the foundation of a phenomenon and the phenomenon itself, the latter being included in this foundation, just so śūnyatā is the non-relative Absolute and the Relativity included in it, cf. below the sixteen varieties of the Absolute, which are not the varieties of the Absolute, — since the Absolute, being unique, can have no varieties, — but they are the varieties of that Relativity, whose subjacent counterpart is absolute Reality.

[8] Read 38.8—9—yathārthānuguṇa-paryāya-pravṛtti-nimittam, the Tib. corresponds to a reading paryāyānuguṇa-paryāya-pravṛtti-nimittam, in any case the pravṛtti is anuguṇa, but not the nimitta.

[9] Drop the cheda after laksaṇatvāt in 38.9.

[10] nirvikalpatva-abhinna-lakṣaṇatva.

[11] The term upakleśa is not used here (38.10) in the sense of the ten upakleśas entered in the list among the citta-samprayukta-saṃskāra, cf. my CC, p. 102, it simply means „small oppressors" or „insignificant impurities", insignificant because they cannot invalidate the pure essence of the Absolute. It here embraces kleśa and upakleśa, cp. LVP, pp. 259, 343, 362.

[12] Drop iti in 38.11; it is not rendered in Tib. and seems superfluous.

[13] Lit. 38.11 „And something else. By a difference of imputation of pudgala and dharma a sixteen-fold division".

[14] sūnyatā as both Relativity and the subjacent Absolute.

[15] viśuddhy-arthin-bodhisattva-ārya-yogiṅ.

[16] viśuddhy-ālambana is that transcendent, pure, eternal world which remains as the pure object of Omniscience, when all other subject-object relations have been set aside, cf. MAV, p. 10.21.

[17] Read 38.11 — paryāyārthāvabodhe śūnyatāyā viśuddhy-ālambanatvena nirdiṣṭatvāt. Tib. rnam-graṅs kyi don khoṅ-du chud-par gyur na, stoṅ pa ñid la rnam par dag pa'i dmigs-pa-ñid-du ṅes-pa'i-phyir.

[18] Lit. 38.15—17 „When the meaning of synonyms is known, for the sake of limitation of the very pure objectivity to śūnyatā, according to the meaning of synonyms (it must be known). When the «great oppressors» are removed, its great purity appears; thus in order to produce an effort for the final extinction of the great oppressors, according to its division (it should be known)".

[19] Lit. „Neither an Ens nor a non-Ens". The Ens has here the meaning of assertion.

[20] Read V. 5—a.—5-tha-dad-pa-yin-na-ni chos-las chos-ñid gźan yin-par mi ruṅ-ste, instead of chos-la chos-ñid gźan-ma-yin-par mi-ruṅ-ste, cf. MAV, 40.7. In early Buddhism dharma is a momentary interconnected ultimate reality, a point-instant of reality, it is kṣaṇa and svalakṣaṇa, an extreme concrete and absolutely particular Ens, it is vastu and parmārtha-sat. In the idealistic system, where all reality is mental, it retains the meaning of an extreme concrete and particular point-instant of mental reality. The dharmatā „Elementness" is the absolute sum-total of all the particular point-instants of reality, its synonym is tathatā. All Universals are constructions of productive imagnation (parikalpita) and therefore in themselves quite devoid of concrete reality (svabhāva-śūnya), but dharmatā is moreover „absolutely pure" viśuddha, it is transcendent (lokottara) in regard of the phenomenal worlds; it is tathatā-paramārtha-satya, it is universal, but not abstract, since for the contemplation of the Omniscient Saint, it is a concrete object, a reality, therefore in this sense it is also paramārtha-sat. Thus it is both paramārtha-sat and paramārtha-satya, but not svalakṣaṇa, not the particular Thing-in-Itself. The dharma, on the other hand, is not transcendent lokottara, but it is the „pure" object (viśuddha), it is śuddha-laukika, it belongs to saṃvṛti-satya, to the phenomenal world as the condition of the existence of particular phenomena; it is transcendental, but not transcendent (to use Kantian terminology), paramārtha-sat, but not paramārtha-satya. Cf. Maitreya-Asaṅga's Dharma-dharmatā-vibhanga, where this problem is specially treated.

[21] Cf. the same example of anitya and anityatā quoted in Triṃś., p. 40.

[22] It is sometimes very much misleading to translate duḥkha as „misery" in philosophy, it is duḥkha-satya-saṃsāra-saṃkleśa. It includ es empirical joy, as well as pain, it is anityatā-duḥkha, cp. LVP, 480.

[23] The constructor (parikalpa-vikalpa-paratantra) represents the Absolute in its function of constructing phenomena. The constructor is the particular, transcendental, Thing-in-Itself, the Absolute is the universal transcendent Thing-in-Itself (if we be allowed thus to adapt Kantian tepminology).

[24] śūnya without the generalizing suffix means svabhāva-śūnya, devoid of absolute reality or relative, it is just the opposite of śūnyatā meaning absolute, non-relative reality, cf. notes to my translation of a passage of MV in Rocznik, X, p. 19.

[25] Lit. 39.8 Lit. «The fact (-tva) of śūnyatā having the essence of „own-existence of non-existence" is thus quite established, not the essence of the form of existence».

[26] Read 39.6—dvayābhāvaḥ instead of dvayabhāvah, Tib. gñis-kyis dṅos-po med-pa.

[27] Lit. 39.6—8 „The non-existence of duality is the essence of śūnyatā", if this were separately (prati-) specified (nir-diś), the independence of the two (cases) of non-existence would follow, just as the non-existence of (two) horns on the head of a hare, but not dharmatā like duḥkhatādi". — The Tib. translators have completely changed the phrasing for the sake of clearness, Pek. T. f. 47. a. 2—dṅos-po-med-pa stoṅ-pai mtshan-ñid-do źes de-tsam-źig bśad-na, gtso-gñis-

kyis dṅos-po-med-pa-ñid-du ri-boṅ-rva dṅos-po-med-pa daṅ ḥdra-bar khoṅ-du chud-de, sdug-bsṅal-la-sogs-pa-ltar chos-ñid-gyi ṅo-bor mi-ruṅ-ṅo; Lit. „If it were said that the essence of the Absolute is non-existence, (i. e. if the Absolute were a negative concept), we would understand that non-existence is asserted in two chief, (i. e. independent) cases, similar to the non-existence of the (two) horns of a hare, which is impossible, in the manner of dharmatā like duḥkhādi". —This example proves clearly that the Tib. translators do not scruple completely to change the phrasing when this is required by the sense.

[28] Lit. 39.8—11 „Therefore it is said so: śūnyatā is non-existence of duality and the presence of this non-existence in the Constructor of phenomena. Because the term sūnyatā envelopes non-existence in (the compas of) existence, it is very clearly shown that its essence is dharmatā".

[29] Read 39.12—ity atyantābhāva, Tib. gtan-med-par, instead of ity antābhava.

[30] Read 39.15—bhāvasya abhāva...

[31] paramārtha in the sense of paramārtha-sat. Thus śūnyatā-tathatā-pariniṣpanna is both paramārtha-sat and paramārtha-satya, but not vastu; it is paramārtha-sat only for the saint who perceives lokottara and viśuddha-ālambana, paramajñāna-viṣaya (=ye-śes-dam-pai yul). The abhūta-parikalpa-paratantra, on the other hand, is paramārtha-sat=svalakṣaṇa and vastu, the Thing-in-Itself, but not paramārtha-satya; it belongs to the phenomenal world, to saṃvṛti-laukika, although it is pure. (śuddha), cp. above, note 20.

[32] api ca in 38.19 is rendered in Tib. by de-lta mod-kyi da-tathā syād api idānīm...

[33] abhāva-rūpatva = abhāva-svarūpatva = abhāvasya bhāvaḥ. The word tasya in 39.19 should not be underlined since it is not found in V. 5. a. 3.

[34] The śūnyatā-dharmatā is the general attribute of abhūta-parikalpa-paratantra and abhuta-parikalpa is the „possessor", the dharmin, of this attribute, cf. above, p. 153, n. 6.

[35] Read 39.24—25—eva syān nā... (syādannā... is evidently a missprint).

[36] duḥkha means what is repulsive to the Saint, i. e. the phenomenal world, cp. MAV, p. 168.21 and LVP, p. 480—„tout ce que les Aryas considèrent comme pénible". The words 40.1-2—bhāvo'pi na bhavati abhāvo'pi na bhavati should be printed sublined, since they are intended as a quotation from Vasubandhu.

[37] Read 39.23—40.2—dvayābhāvo hi (in Tib. read med-pa-ni for med-na-ni) na dvayābhāva-svabhāvābhāvaḥ. tad-abhāve dvaya-bhāva eva syān, nābhutaparikalpa-dharmatā, yathā-nityatā duhkhatā ca, sattva-viparyāsa-samāropita-nitya-sukha-vastu-svabhāvatvād bhāvo'pi na bhavaty abhāvo'pi na bhavati. Lit. „The absence of duality is not absence of the own-existence of the absence of duality. If the latter were absent, there would be just the presence of duality, but not the principle of a construction of the unreal. Just so are the principles (-tā) of Impermanence and of (phenomenal) Misery neither an Ens nor a non-Ens, because their essence is the (real) absence of things eternal and blissful constructed by the wrong imagination of living beings". — Dharma is related to dharmatā like anitya to anityatā, duḥkha to duḥkhatā etc. Dharma as

saṃskṛta-dharma is a synonym of abhūta-parikalpa or paratantra, and dharmatā is a synonym of asaṃskṛta-dharma-tathatā-pariniṣpanna-svabhāva. Cp. Rocznik, X, p. 19.

[38] Read 40.5 — bhāva eva abhāva-pratiṣedhātmaka eva- Tib. dṅos-po kho-na dṅos-po med-pa-dgag-pa-bdag-ñid khonao.

[39] Read 40.10 with S. Y. — tasyāpi punar dharmāntaram anveṣṭavyam iti anavasthā-prasaṅgah.

[40] Lit. 40.8—10 „The dharmatā by having an essence separate from dharma becomes just another dharma, like a dharma other than it. But one dharma cannot be the dharmatā of another dharma; there will be necessity of finding another dharma for it also, thus there will be anavasthā (no end)".

[41] sūnya means „void" in the sense of „devoid" of absolute reality — sva-bhāvena-śūnya, or „relative" as the „long and the short", dirgha-hrasva-vat, but śūnyatā is the general attribute of all things relative, it is not itself śūnya or relative, it is that unique foundation of non-relative, absolute reality which underlies all relative particular things. From this point of view śūnya means „relative", śūnyatā the „non-relative foundation of all things relative. This meaning is given to śūnyāta only in the Yogācāra system. Cp. my article in the Rocznik, X, p. 19. In the Mādhyamika system, as already stated, the śūnyatā means Relativity, absence of every absolute reality in itself, denial of the Thing-in-Itself, denial of the absolute Particular as well as of the absolute Universal.

[42] athavā.

[43] Lit. 40.19—21 „Or the object is a pure object, because it must be purified. The things own-essence being object-made does not bring purity, because of the absurdity of the purity of all living beings". — Pure means clear of phenomenal impurity, traascendent or absolute.

[44] Read 40.22—23—yo .. tattva-anyatvam na vyākaroti = Tib. de-ñid-dam gźan-du luṅ-mi-ston-pa gaṅ-yin-pa (Peking T. has gaṅ lin-pa).

[45] Lit. 40.21—24 „If unutterable as to being other or non-other, how is it that the Jaina theory is not resorted to? Indeed that one who does not determine the thisness or otherness of a thing, of a reality, he takes his stand on Jainism. The śūnyatā is not a thing, therefore there is no such fault". The Jainas maitained that the Absolute — avadhikṛta-vastu — being the Universal Thing-in-Itself includes also a Universal (vairūpyam), cp. TS, p. 488.

[46] Read 40.25—abhāva-svabhāva-lakṣaṇā ca advaya-lakṣaṇā ca, Tib. dṅos-po-med-pai ṅo-bo-ñid kyi mtshan-ñid daṅ mi-gñis-kyi mtshan-ñid-de.

[47] Lit. 40.24—26 „And thus this śūnyatā has an essence of non-existence, and an essence of the reality (subjacent to this) non-existence and an essence of non-duality (of object and subject) and it is thoroughly illucidated as having the essence of being quite free from thisness-otherness".

[48] The difference between the two varieties of the omniscience of a Buddha (sarvajñatā and sarva-ākāra-jñatā, gźi-śes and rnam-śes) on one side, and the omniscience of a Saint or Bodhisattva in the last stages of his career, on the other, is insignificant, cf. MAV, p. 5.15. Therefore the Saint here also means the Buddha.

[49] Read 41.4 (according to E. O) — prasiddhiḥ instead of kirtana, Tib. grags-te.

[50] Read 41.6—pañcakam yathā pradhānam, as in the MS and Tib. ji-skad-mos-pa. Lit. 41.6—7 „Just as these five synonyms, the principle ones, have been mentioned in metrical form, just so other synonyms also, here unmentioned, can be added from scripture".

[51] Read 41.8—anirodho instead of nirodho, Tib. mi-ḥgag-pa-ñid.

[52] Read 41.9—10—naite'rthābhinnatve'pi śabdā gauṇāḥ, the translators into Tib. have simplified, as if the text had been na te śabdāḥ kalpanikāḥ. The translation of kim tarhi is included in ma-yin-kyi.

[53] Lit. 41.9—10 „There being a difference of sense, these words are not metaphors, but what? they agree in the (general) sense". — The editors had no right to change the reading of the MS so radically. The general meaning of śūnyatā is „one undifferentiated Whole of the Universe" or Monism. Just as the abhūta-parikalpa = paratantra Element represents the „extreme concrete and particular", the Thing-in-Itself (svalakṣaṇa-paramārtha-sat), just so śūnyatā represents the extreme abstract and universal (sāmānya-lakṣaṇa, paramārtha-satya). But although being abstract, śūnyatā is, so to speak, a „concretion" (to use Berkley's expression) of the Totality of the particulars of the Universe and in this sense it also represents a concrete thing. It is consequently both paramārtha-sat and paramārtha-sātya, whereas abhūta-parikalpa or paratantra is paramārtha-sat without being paramārtha-satya. (The Jainas accused the Thing-in-Itself of the Buddhists of being also an abstraction, cp. TSP, p. 488, the non abstraction would thus be also an abstraction, just as there is a śūnyatā of śūnyatā in the sense of Relativity of Relativity (cf. my CN, p. 49). The term paryāya expresses both synonym and homonym (artha-abhinnatve sati śabdo bhinnaḥ, śabda-abhinnatve sati bhinno'rthaḥ), but synonym alone is here meant. However there is also a difference of meaning between the five synonyms, but a slight one. They are artha-bhinnatve saty anvarthāḥ, i. e. expressing the same general meaning. They are yaugika-names, i. e. the analysis of the names themselves reveals their identity of meaning, since they are anvarthāḥ, not gauṇaḥ, not metaphors as e. g. the moon and the damzel's face agree only metaphorically, as a rūpaka-figure, the tertium comparationis being their refreshing action, the moon by itself does not mean a damzel's face. The 4th and 5th synonyms put a stress on the meaning of transcendent (lokottara), but this is also a yaugika meaning implied in the meaning of „one undifferentiated Whole". Thus samartha here means the identity of the general meaning, artha-bheda its different shades. The editors were not justified in changing gauṇa into kālpanika, even although the Tib. translators had done it. This is an eloquent example of how misleading a retranslation or restitution of a text can sometimes be. Translators uniformly translate e. g. such a term as dharma-chos, but phrases are usually translated according to their sense, the translation being at the same time an interpretation.

[54] bhūta usually means „what has happened" as well as a „living creature"; here it means „true", it is rendered in Tib. by yaṅ-dag-sanscrit samyag. koṭi means „highest point" and also crore. Cp. LVP, p. 745 ff. In poetical works and sūtras it can have the meanings of both „highest truth and „crores of living beings", the one will be direct, the other a metaphor. I do not think there is much difference between tathatā and bhūta-tathatā, if we reject the metaphor; the interpretation bhūtatā ca tathata ca is of course also possible, but I doubt whether it is always necessary.

[55] Read 41.18—19—jñeyāvaraṇa-viśuddha-jñāna-gocaratvāt (better than viśuddher).

[56] jñāna, Tib. ye-śes (not śes-pa).

[57] Read (with the MS)—ananyāropa instead of asamāropa, the meaning is the same and the Tib. translators have translated according to sense.

[58] viparyāsa-vastu „a point of mistake" is the same as viparyāsa simply, therefore viparyāsa-avastutvāt is the same as viparyāsa-abhāvāt. The Tib. translation is according to sense. On the identification of logic with error cp. Bodhicaryāv., IX. 2.

[59] Read 41.22—nirodhāt instead of virodhāt.

[60] Read 41.23— nirodha instead of virodha.

[61] It is nevertheless called asaṃskṛta in 41.8; the Hīnayāna realistic conception of saṃskṛta and asaṃskṛta is evidently aimed at in 41.24.

[62] jñāna-ye-śes.

[63] samyag-dṛṣṭi evidently refers here to the Hīnayāna theory of real dharmas.

[64] Read 42.5.—samyag-vimokṣa, Tib. rnam-par-thar-la instead of samyag-vimukti (E. O.).

[65] samyag-vimokṣa and jñāna are a dvandva-compound, jñāna-ye-śes absolute knowledge, „direct, mystic intuition of the transcendent Absolute", „Omniscience".

[66] vibhāvayan-pradarśayan, Tib. bstan-pa.

[67] It is clear from that passage that ālambana means hetu and hetu is used in the sense of samavāyi-kāraṇa.

[68] Cf. AK, I.20. The Vibhāṣā gives eleven etymological explanations of dhātu of which the principal mean „family, lineage" and „mine". A polymetallic mine is evidently understood, since Vasubandhu speaks of a place in which many „families" of metals, iron, brass, silver and gold are found. Just so the human individual is composed of Elements of many families, physical, mental etc. Every dhātu is at the same time a dharma „Element". The 75 dharmas of the Sarvāstivādins are distributed in 18 dhātus. vijñāna (=citta=manas) is one item in the dharma-classification, but it is divided in seven items in the dhātu-classification; the dharmāḥ are one item in the dhātu-classification and include 64 dharmas of the dharma-classification. The usual definition of dharma is svalakṣaṇa-dhāraṇād dharmaḥ and sva-svabhāva-dhāraṇād dharmaḥ. The definition of a dhātu is similar. Indeed, e. g. rūpa-dharma „Element colour" and rūpa-dhātu „family-component of colour" would be similar. But here dhātu is defined as the point of reality supporting its own particularity and the secondary qualities of Matter (upādāya, bhautika), the primary qualities of Matter (mahā-bhūtāni) are evidently also included.

[69] Lit. 42.14 „The Constructor of phenomena is Universal Oppression; when it is rejected, there is purity".

[70] Read 42.14—15—saṃkleśa-viśuddhy-avasthayor api śūnyatām vihāya nāsty anyad yat saṃkliṣyate viśuddhyate vā. The Constructor of unreality—abhūta-parikalpa—is here equalled to saṃkleśa or phenomenal apperance. In other passages, e. g. in stanza I.2, it is declared that it has no duality (dvayam tatra na vidyate), it therefore represents the Absolute. This is because, according to the accepted terminology, it is both bhrāntiḥ and bhrānter āśrayas ca, it can be both impure and pure (aśuddhaḥ śuddha

eva ca=dag-ma-dag), just as śūnyatā is both Relativity and Absolute, i. e. the superimposed Relativity and the subjacent Reality.

[71] Read 42.16 — tasmāt saṃkleśa-viśuddhy-avasthā-dvaye'pi śūnyataiva... lit. „Therefore in order to show that in both conditions, of oppression and purification, there is śūnyatā alone which is being oppressed and purified, he says"...

[72] Read 42.21—samalā vimalā ca yā. S. Y.'s emendation is in conflict with versification.

[73] āśraya-parāvṛtti-gnas-gyur-pa.

[74] Lit. 43.2—4 „Thus in regard of śūnyatā the view of (being) oppressed or pure is relative, since being resplendently pure by nature, it is impure not by itself". The Labrang commentary (f. 12.b. 2.) says „it is resplendently pure, because it includes all dharmas and elicits Dharma-kāya and Dharmatā".

[75] Read 43.16—17 ...vyavasthāpayati tasya svabhāvāntara-vikāra-vikāri-dharma-nivṛttir nāsti, yasya tv āgantukam tad-ubhayam tasyāpi nāsti. Tib. ... rnampar hjog-pa-de-ni raṅ-bźin-gźan-du-gyur-pas gyur-bai chos bzlog-par-ma-(ḥ)gyur-gyi, gaṅ-la de gñi-ga-yaṅ glo-bur-yin-pa (de)-la-ni ma-yin-te.

[76] Lit. 43.16—17 ... „(that one who) establishes (this), for him there is no cessation of the changing dharma through its change into another essence, but for that one for whom both (saṃsāra and nirvāṇa) are accidental, for him also there is no (cessation, i. e. no nirvāṇa)". — One of the main tenets of Hīnayāna is that nirvāṇa is transcendent to saṃsāra; against this Mahāyāna maintains that saṃsāra is immanent to nirvāṇa, the first is an accidental impurity upon the latter.

[77] vikāra-dharmatā in 43.18 evidently means the same as vikāra-dharmiṇītva in 43.6, lit. „Therefore this (śūnyatā) does even not touch the possession of the quality of change", or „does not touch the dharmatā of change".

[78] Read 43.20—aparo'pi prabhedaḥ=Tib. gźan-yaṅ rab-tu-dbye-ba; V. 6. a. 1 gźan-yaṅ.

[79] A passage is found in the Pañca-viṃşati-sāhasrikā Prajñāpāramitā-sūtra, but neither in the number of items nor in their definition does it agree with the sixteen items of MAV, cf. Obermiller in JHQ, IX, p. 172 ff.

[80] śūnyatā means with the Yogācāras both the phenomenal Relativity of every separate Element of existence and the absolute Reality of its foundation. The first four varieties refer to things, the remaining ones are varieties of cognition, cp. below, p. 44.18.

[81] Read 43.25—śūnyatā instead of śūnyatāyāḥ, Tib. chos-thams-cad gñis-med-pai ṅo-bo-ñid-kyi-phyir stoṅ-pa-ñid-ni spyi-mtshan-ñid-de.

[82] Lit. 43.25 „The śūnyatā is a universal essence, since all the dharmas have an essence of non-duality".

[83] vibhāvayitavya 44.2=gźig(s)-par-bya-ba.

[84] Read 44.3—4—buddhatva-siddhi-vimokşa-prāpti-. It is advandva compound = Tib. saṅs-rgyas-sa ḥgrub-pa daṅ rnampar-thar-pa-thob-pai. The eight vimokşas, cf. MVyut., § 70.

[85] Read 44.5—tad-anantaram tad-adhiṣṭhānasya... Tib. dei ḥog-tu... dei gnas.

[86] The cheda in 44.6 before bhoktur should be dropped or replaced by half a cheda; in the Tib. translation the two following compounds are included in the forgoing phrase.

[87] śūnyatā meaning both phenomenal relativity and the subjacent non-relativity.

[88] Read 44.8 with S. Y. — ādhyātmikāyatanair ārabdhā - Tib. naṅ-gi skye-mched-rnams-las brtsams-so.

[89] The Hīnayānists are referred to despicably by this designation, because, as is seen from the context, although they do not admit the reality of a Soul they replace it by the ultimate reality of the Elements (dharmas), they are pudgala-nairātmya-vādins, but not sarva-dharma-nairātmya-vādins.

[90] abhimāna.

[91] Read 44.12—bāhyānām iti (bhāṣya and ṭīkā). Tib. has phyi-rol-gyi-rnams-so.

[92] rūpa-āyatana (āyatana № 7) is constituted by colours and shapes (or lines), varṇaḥ samsthānam eva ca.

[93] dharma-āyatana, āyatana № 12, „non-sensuous objects".

[94] Read 44.13 — te viṣaya-bhāvena (bhojyāḥ).

[95] Read 44.13 — bhujyante - Tib. bzaḥ-bar-bya-ba.

[96] Read 44.16 after śūnyatā insert adhyātma-bāhya-śūnyateti. The Tib. ṭīkā Peking ed. omits these words, but the bhāṣya has them.

[97] Read 44.16 — sarvathā sattva...-thams-cad-du sems-can... instead of sarva=sattva.

[98] Read 44.17 — pratiṣṭhā-vastu instead of āśraya-vastu.

[99] Lit. 44.19—21 „Thus to this meditator, the Bodhisattva, whose attention is directed by a discursive (savikalpaka) mental act of attention (directed) upon the Relativity-Reality (śūnyatā) of the fourfold cognizable things, to him another objectivizing prejudice arises".

[100] Lit. 44.21—26 1) „By what śūnyatā-knowledge these outer and inner bases are being intuited as šūnya, the (presence) in it of the object-subject habit and 2) just this idea (vikalpa) having here the ultimate form, namely „in what manner by śūnyatā-jñāna it is intuited", by minutely investigating these two varieties of idea which are the illusive object in the yoga-stages, the śūnyatā-śūnyatā and the paramārtha śūnyatā are respectively specified, by dropping the words jñāna and ākāra" — i. e. śūnyatā-śūnyatā instead of śūnyata-jñāna-śūnyatā and paramārtha-śūnyatā instead of paramārtha-ākāra-śūnyatā. The 5th the and 6th varieties of Relativity-Reality refer 1) „to the knowledge which cognizes Relativity, i. e. to the Relativity of the cognition of Relativity and 2) to „the manner in which it is cognized", these words referring to the fact that the cognition of śūnyatā represents the Highest Truth (paramārthākāra=paramārtha-satya), but it is the Highest Truth only when realized in direct mystic intuition. When considered abstractly in discursive thought it again becomes relative as affected by the subject-object relativity. Cf. my B. Nirvāṇa, p. 49.

[101] Read 45.2 — yathā dṛṣṭam...

[102] Read 44.26—45.1 — tad-grāhya-gryhaka-bhāvena, instead of grāhya-grāhaka-abhāvena, Tib. gzuṅ-ba-daṅ-ḥdzin-pai-dṅos-po-de stoṅ-pa-ñid-ni.

[103] Lit. 44.26—45.1 „Or knowledge is here called Relativity (śūnyatā), because šūnyatā is its object; the devoidness from this object-subject-relation is śūnyatā-śūnyatā".

[104] Lit. 45.1—3 „And the inner bases, etc. how perceived by this śūnyatā-knowledge this is here the Highest Thing, thus the śūnyatā in respect of this form is the śūnyatā of the Highest Thing".

[105] pratipadyate-sgrub-pa.

[106] Read a cheda before yadartham in in 45.6 and drop it before tasya.

[107] vibhāvanā-gźig(s)-pa minutely critically to examine and repudiate, „wegdenken", „weginterpretiren" (?).

[108] 45.11 prabhāvayati-pratipadyate-bhāvayati-bsgom-pa-bsgrub-pa; bhāvanā and abhyāsa-karma-vāsanā-saṃskāra are very closely related notions, goms-pa daṅ sgom-pa, lam-la sbyar-na don-gcig yin.

[109] The degrees of sanctification or purification imply parijñāna, prahāna and viśuddhi, i. e. thorough comprehension of phenomenality, liberation-rejection of the bonds of phenomenality and Final Deliverance or Transsubstantiation which implies the attainment of miraculous powers.

[110] The asaṃskṛta or Nirvāṇa is here characterized as relative, evidently not in the Mādhyamika, but in the Yogācāra sense, as an ultimate transcendent reality in which the unreality of the phenomenal worlds is immanent.

[111] This is the bodhi-citta-utpāda-sems-bskyed, „creative effort for Enlightment (as E. Obermiller translates). The consequence of such a vow is life (notwithstanding the annihilation of all karma) in the highest immaterial heavens and transcendent existence for the weal of all living creatures in apratiṣṭhita-Nirvāṇa.

[112] The MS reads 45.18—śrāvaka-bodhau, the Tib. corresponding to śrāvaka-bhūmau, the meaning is the same.

[113] Lit. 45.17—18. „Indeed he does not reach enlightment when he forsakes saṃsāra, he remains permanently in the śrāvaka-bhūmi. His šūnyatā is šūnyatā without bottom and top".

[114] Read 45.23—kuśala-mūlam na kṣatavyam mayā nirupadhi-śeṣe nirvāṇe'pi.

[115] Drop the cheda after sidhyati and put one after abhāvāt. Read 46.1—2—sāsrava-dharma vipākābhāvāt. Instead of vipākakāyasya read simply vipākād. According to S. Y. the word kāya is found in the MS, according to Tucci it is absent. kāya would be sku not lus in Tib. There is no word at all corresponding to atītānām in Tib. The editors have perhaps mistaken the ḥdas-rnams-kyi of bcom-ldan-ḥdas-rnams-kyi for a separate word.

[116] Read 46.2—buddhānām bhagavatām anāsrava-bhāvasya dharma-kāyasya nirupadhišeṣa-nirvāṇa-dhātāv api saṃtānānuccheda iti siddhāntaḥ. Lit. 46.2 „It is (our) established dogma that the immaculate Reality, the dharma-kāya of our Lords the Buddhas is not interrupted in its continuity even in the Nirvāṇa in which there is no rest (of the skandhas)".

[117] Read 46.15—16—śūnyatā lakṣaṇa-śūnyatety ucyate.

[118] prapadyate is apparently here synonym to pratipadyate (both are rendered by sgrub-par-byed) and to bhāvayati-bsgom-pa „realize or create mentally", to make the „citta-utpāda"

[119] Read 46.23—tasya śūnyatā sarva-dharma-śū.nyatety ucyate; put a cheda before tasya.

[120] The Tib. here has śes-pa not ye-śes which usually corresponds to jñāna in the meaning of a mystic vision of the Absolute, but the tran-

slators evidently assumed that bar-chad-med-pai śes-pa is just ye-śes.

[121] Lit. V. 6. b. 6 „What is here śūnyatā? The unreality of pudgala and of dharmas is here śūnyatā. Of this unreality the reality is a śūnyatā different from it". There are thus two śūnyatā's (-pariniṣpanna's), pure and impure. The first is Absolute Reality, the other the unreality (phenomenality, relativity) immanent in the first and concealing its purity. In the same sense there are two paratantra's, pure and impure.

[122] The first (pudgala-śunyatā) is Hīnayāna, the second (sarvadharma-śūnyatā) is Mahāyāna. The third variety (sadbhāva-śūnyatā) is Vijñāna-vāda.

[123] dṅos-po-med-pa=svabhāva-abhāva.

[124] apavāda-skur-ba-ḥdebs-pa.

[125] It should not be forgotten that the Individual is constituted by the run of those separate Elements (dharmas) which together constitute its subjective and objective Elements. The external world of the Individual, his „receptacle" world is also included in him. Hīnayāna denies the concrete separate reality of the assemblages of such Elements, their „concretion" (to speak with Berkley), but maintains the reality of the separate Elements themselves. The Mahāyāna makes a further step, lays stress upon the Relativity (pratītya-samutpāda) of all these Elements without exception, interprets their interdependence (pratītya-samutpannatva) as their Relativity (dīrgha-hrasva-vat), as their ultimate Unreality. The Mādhyamikas abide by this Relativity, without admitting any subjacent ultimate Reality. The Yogācāras establish the reality of the subjacent Absolute which being spiritual leads them to a denial of Matter, to subjective Idealism and strict Monism (advaita).

[126] Read 47.7—8—teṣām madhye dvividhā śūnyatā kuto'nte vyavasthāpitā-Tib. de-dag-gi naṅ-nas stoṅ-pa-ñid-rnam-pa-gñis cii-phyir tha-mar rnam-par-bźag ce-na. It is not clear wherefrom the adhyātma, p. 47.8, comes; it could be a misinterpretation of naṅ-nas, which I find in my copy of the Peking T., v. 48, f. 52. b. 6, but the editors in note 638 read gaṅ-nas in the place of my naṅ-nas; gaṅ-nas however is possibly a missprint. Lit. „Whatfore are the two varieties of śūnyatā, (i. e. the 15th and 16th variety) established at the conclusion among these, (i. e. in addition to the fourteen preceding varieties)?" The question has a foundation inasmuch as these two last varieties are, properly speaking, no varieties at all, but only a repetition of the general definition of śūnyatā as layed down in stanza I.13, a definition moreover which is split in two parts, a negative one and a positive one. Thus the two last varieties represent something which is implied in every one of the fourteen preceding ones. Vasubandhu explains that this is done in order to emphasize the general trend of all the system of the varieties of the Absolute. Like the whole treatise it is directed against the exagerated scepticism of the Mādhyamikas and the exagerated realism of the Sarvāstivādins and Sautrāntikas. In establishing a new classification and a new interpretation of the modes of the hidden Absolute in accordance with its new definition Asaṅga in the two last modes repeats only the general definition which embraces all the modes. This corresponds to the old Indian method of counting in a system the general and particular items together as if they were all on the same level.

[127] nir-deśa, the Tib. has simply bstan-pai-phyir.

[128] śūnyatā.

[129] ucyeta=nir-diśyeta.

[130] śūnyatā, lit. „that the śūnyatā would be mere non-existence". The Yogācāras always accuse the Mādhyamikas of nihilism, according to them they maintain that sarvam sarveṇa nāsti, cf. Bodh. bhūmi, p. 43, but the Mādhyamikas energetically protest, they say that they are maintainers of general Relativity, not nihilists, śūnyatā-vādinas, na tv abhāva-vādinaḥ. śūnyatā is relativity, as the long and the short, and the Mādhyamika's absolute is all-embracing Relativity, without any subjacent reality of the Absolute.

[131] Lit. 47.16—19 „Here, among the internal bases, which in their essence are maturity-consciousness (and) which simpledons agree (to take as) the Enjoyer; the non-existence in them of the Enjoyer, of the concrete Individual (pudgala), and of the eye, etc. which have the essence of things constructed by imagination; (this non-existence) and the ultimate reality (subjacent to) this non-existence, are the subjective śūnyatā".

[132] Under rūpādi, āyatana № 7, included is also dharmāytana, āyatana № 12; cf. 32.2 and 16.1—2.

[133] Lit. 47.19—21 „The non-existence in the external bases, which in their essence are appearance of intimations of colours, etc., which simpledons agree to (call) „enjoyed objects", (the non-existence in them) of one's own food, of the colours, etc., which in their essence are constructed by our productive imagination, and the reality (subjacent) to this non-existence is the objective śūnyatā".

[134] Read 47.22 (with S. Y.)—tasya sarīre dehe bhoktuḥ=Tib. dei lus-te, khog-pa-la za-bai..., cf. above, 44.15. It is not clear on what foundation the word abhyantare has been introduced into the text, the Tib. has no equivalent.

[135] Lit. 47.22—24. „The non-existence in the body, in the corpse, of the Enjoyer, of the Individual and of the sense-data imagined by simple people, just as of the body (itself) and the ultimate reality (subjacent) to that non-existence is the inner and outer śūnyatā".

[136] I. e. the conceptual knowledge of Relativity is also relative as well as Relativity itself and its subjacent ultimate Reality. I do not find in Hiuan-Tsang this exceedingly important confession, cp. LVP, p. 658, 743 ff., cp. the following note.

[137] Read 47.25—48.2—šūnyatā-jñāne paramārthākāre cāpi jñātrā ākāra-grāhaka-pudgalena ca parikalpita-lakṣaṇayoḥ šūnyatā-jñānasya paramārthākārasya cābhāvas= stoṅ-pa-ñid-śes pa daṅ don-dam-pai rnam-pa-la-yaṅ, śes-pa-po-daṅ, rnam pa-ḥdzin-pa-poi gaṅ-zag-daṅ, kun-brtags-pai mtshan-ñid stoṅ-pa-ñid śes-pa daṅ, don-dam-pai-rnam-pai dṅos-po med-pa-daṅ... Lit. „The absence in the cognition of šūnyatā and in the concept of paramārtha of the cognition of šūnyatā and of the concept of paramārtha in their imagined essence, (imagined the first) by the cognizer, (the second) by the individual realizing the concept"... In other words, „the conceptual cognition of the Absolute is itself relative and the concept of the non-relative Absolute is also, as a matter of fact, relative, as long as they are ideas constructed by abstract thought and not things intuited directly in a mystic experience".

[138] saṃskṛta=paratantra.

[139] The predicate nirdiṣṭah is at 48.11.

[140] Read 48.5—sādhana-prayojaneṣu=bsg rub-dgos-pa-rnams-a (instead of siddhi=grub-pa).

141 Read 48.8 — saṃskṛte vā or saṃskṛto vā, Tib. ḥdus-byas-kyaṅ (saṃskṛta=paratantra).

142 Read 48.8—9 — parikalpita ātmaiva nāsti=kun-brtags-pai bdag-ñid med-do. In this passage ātman=svabhāva, cf. MV, p. 437.4 The first clause refers to pudgala-nairātmya, the denial of the Soul as a separate Element, the second to dharma-nairātmya, the denial of ultimate reality (ātma=svabhāva) in every saṃskṛta-dharma. The first implies the ultimate reality of all dharmas, sarvāsti-vāda or Pluralism. The second denies their ultimate reality altogether and without exception, it is the radical scepticism of the Mādhyamikas, śūnyavāda.

143 Lit. 48.4—11 „Now for which aim the Bodhisattva realizes (creates in thought), in them, in the Dependent etc. up to in all the Buddha attributes, whose aim is to create the Bodhisattva, the non-existence of the pudgala and of those dharmas which are parikalpita-lakṣaṇa and the existence of this non-existence (are indicated) in due order as saṃskṛta-śūnyatā up to sarva (buddha) dharma-śūnyatā. Indeed there is no owner, or propelling individual, for the saṃskṛta; nor is there in saṃskṛta any real (eva) ātman which is imagined (parikalpita) by stupid people; in short for an antidote against all grips of thought-construction and for the revelation of the intention of all sūtras these sixteen śūnyatā's which are not common with the śrāvakas have been described for the Bodhisattvas".

144 Read 48.12 — pradarśitam, Tib. rab-tu-bstan-to.

145 Read 48.16 — niḥsaraṇātmaka-jñānotpādanārtham=ṅes-par-ḥbhuṅ-bai bdag-ñid-du śes-par-byed-pai-phyir-ro; I presume that this is here said in the sense of ye-śes-bskyed-par-byed-pai-phyir-ro.

146 Read — sva-parārtha-rūpa-dharma-kāya-sampat-prakarṣaḥ; MS and S. Y. have sva-parātmano...; the Tib. has bdag-daṅ-gźan-gyi gzugsdaṅ-chos-kyi sku... probably instead of bdag-daṅ-gźan-gyi don-gyi gzugs-dan... S. Y. moreover corrects sūnyatā-bhāvanāyāḥ prāpya iti for the simple bhāvanād iti of the MS. Cf. MSA, IX. 65 and Obermiller's Buston, I. 129. — Lit. 48.18—20 „The indication of this has moreover the aim of indicating that from meditation on śūnyatā comes the highest point of perfection of the rūpa-kāya and dharma-kāya for one's own and for another's sake".

147 Read 48.21 — ity anantarokta-adhyātma-śūnyatādiṣodaśa-bheda-ākāro veditavyaḥ=Tib. źes-bya-ba daṅ naṅ-stoṅ-pa-ñid-la-sogs-pa-bcu-drug-dbye-ba-bśad-pa-ma-thag-pa-rnam-pa yin-par śes-par-byao.

148 Read 48.25 — svabhāva-viśuddha-bhāvas ca (separated from the preceding compound).

149 kleśa stands here evidently for saṃkleśa and saṃkleśa is the same as dvādaśa-nidāna.

150 saṃkleśa.

151 bhāvanā „profound meditation" involving the idea of mental creation, just as cittotpāda is mārga-bhāvanā.

152 tathatā=śūnyatā.

153 saṃkliṣṭatā „oppressed" in the sense of „phenomenalized".

154 Read 49.1 with S. Y. — idānīm instead of tatra, Tib. da-ni...

155 Read 49.9 — viśuddhi-prabhedam=Tib. rab-dbye-ba rnam-par-dag-pa, instead of prabhedākāram(?). The editors have

evidently mistaken rnam-par which is the rendering of the particle vi of vi-śuddhi for rnam-pa=ākāra.

156 iṣyate.

157 mokṣa is here 49.16 rendered in Tib. by thar-ba just as in 49.7, whereas mukti of the preceding line is rendered by ḥgrol-ba.

158 pratipakṣa, i. e. mārga.

159 Lit. 49.18—50.1 „Here by taking dharmas of quite-oppression it is quite-oppressed, by taking dharmas of quite-purity it is quite-pure. But śūnyatā is not directly quite-oppressed or quite-pure, since dharmatā is dependent on dharma. Just therefore it is said „saved would be all body-possessors". Here „body-possessors" refers to their substratum. Otherwise, if there would be direct quite-oppression or quite-purification of śūnyatā, what would be the connection with body-possessors? Indeed so by quite-purification a quite-purification of body-possessors and from quite-oppression of śūnyatā (their) quite-oppression".

160 Read 50.4 — sidhyati after iti before katham., Tib. grub-pa...

161 Read 50.4—5 — śuddhi-dvayena śuddher eva prakṛta-gamakatvāt, Tib. dag-pa-gñis-kyis skabs-khon-du-chod-par-byed-pas dag-pa-ñid-de. As to the correction of the Tib. text of the Peking T. v. 48, f. 55. a. 2 it seems better to read ḥdir luṅ-las... ḥbyuṅ-ṅo, instead of ḥdir lus-daṅ...

162 citta, Tib. sems, i. e ālaya-vijñāna.

163 citta-dharmatā, Tib. sems-kyi chos-ñid. The term citta-dharmatā does not differ, with the Yogācāras, from dharmatā simply, it is the same as citta-mātratā, vijñāna- resp. vijñapti-mātratā, śūnyatā, the unique reality of the pure spiritual principle. By using Hegelian terminology we can translate „Absolute Idea."

164 Read 50.7 — mala-lakṣaṇa-tvāt, Tib. dri-mai-mtshan-ñid, „impure", i. e. phenomenal, the ālaya-vijñāna as belonging to saṃvṛti.

165 Read 50.13 — na tv adhamais tat-pratipakṣatvāt, Tib. ḥdi-gñen-poi-phyir ḥog-mas-ni ma-yin-no.

166 Read 50.15 — na kliṣṭety ukte and drop the cheda after ukte. The Tib. suggests na saṃkliṣṭety ukte=kun-nas ñon-moṅs-pa ma-yin-no źes-bśad-pa-la, but the stanza has na kliṣṭā.

167 Read 50.16 — anivṛta-avyākṛta instead of anāvṛta, Tib. ma-sgribs-pai luṅ-du ma-bstan-pa.

168 Read 50.17—evam saiva nākliṣṭety ukte'(a)śuddheti; the Tib. text must be corrected thus — de-bźin-du ñon-moṅs-pa-ma-yin-pa de-yaṅ ma-yin-no źes-bśad-pa-la dag-pa ma-yin-no źes-bya-ba-ni... The kuśala-sāsrava is kliṣṭa (=na akliṣṭa) but śuddha and thus distinguished from śūnyatā in its phenomenal garb when it is both kliṣṭa and aśuddha.

169 Read 50.18—kuśala-sāsravād viśeṣaṇārtham (like in the MS.) = Tib. zag-pa-daṅ bcai-pai dge-ba-daṅ bye-brag-yod-pai-phyir.

170 Lit. 50.18—19 „Indeed the good and influenced is not non-obscured, because it is quite included into saṃsāra and pure, because of a pleasant retribution (or a welcome concoction)".

171 Read 50.20 — sā hi klistāvasthāyām kliṣṭā satī na śuddhaivety uktā, Tib. ñon-moṅs-pa-can yin-la ma-dag-pa-ñid ces-bśad-do.

172 Read 50.21 — evam śūnyatā-prabheda-saṃkleśa-viṣuddhi-nirdeśo'yam, Tib. de-ltar stoṅ-pa-ñid-kyi rab-tu-dbye-

ba-kun-nas-ñon-moñs-pa-dañ-rnam-par-dag-paibstan...

[173] Read 51.1 — bhāva-lakṣaṇasyāpi instead ot bhāva-lakṣaṇatašca. — We thus will have a fourfold division, viz. 1) abhāvataḥ, 2) bhāvataḥ, 3) bhāva-lakṣaṇasyāpi bhāvābhāva-vinirmukta-lakṣaṇtaḥ and 4) tattva-anyatva-vinirmukta-lakṣaṇataḥ.

[174] Put a cheda before tattva in 51.3.

[175] Read perhaps 51.8 — etayā ca catuḥ-prakāra-lakṣaṇādi-nirdiṣṭyā... S. Y. reads nirdistvā (?!).

[176] las=karma 51.9 and ff. evidently in the sense of phalam.

[177] Read 51.10 — yukti-lakṣaṇam instead of gotra-(Tucci) or vidyā-(S. Y.), cp. yukti in 38.12.

[178] Read 51.11 — apṛthag-ekatva. The Tib. also omits the negative particle, cp. however kārika 1.13d, p. 40.6.

[179] Read 51.12 ananyathā-tathatā-karma instead of nimitta tathatā (Tucci) and abhrānti-tathatā (S. Y.), cp. above, 41.13. Cp. on this earliest interpretation of tathatā LVP, p. 743.

[180] Read 51.12 — aviparyāsa-karma, cp. 41.15.

[181] Read 51.13 — sarva-nimitta-nirodha-karma, cp. 41.22.

[182] Read 51.13—14 — sarva-loklttara-jñāna-gocaratvena sthiti-karma, cp. 42.2.

[183] Read 51.14 — ālambane ca (S. Y., p. 264.5 — pratilabdhy-?), in this šūnyatā-ālambana is contained the hetu-bhāva (or hetutva) of the ārya-dharma's, cp. 42.7.

[184] Read 51.15 — paryāpta-grāhakānam instead of vikalpa. —

[185] Read 51.17 — samdigdhānām instead of upabhoktṝṇām.

[186] Read 51.17 — yukti-lakṣaṇam, cp. above, n. 176.

[187] Lit. [50.21] The summarized meaning of šūnyatā should be regarded as a definition (and as its) establishment. As a definition we must here (distinguish) as non-existence-definition and as existence-definition. As non-existence-definition-because it is said „non-existence of two" (1.13). As existence-definition, because it is said „and existence of non-existence" (ibid). [51.1] „neither existence nor non-existence" (ibid). [51.3] As a definition quite beyond from thisness and otherness, because it is said (p. 40.5—6) „And this is the essence of the Absolute... therefore in regard of the Constructor of Unreality it is neither separate nor having the same essence. So is the summarized meaning as regards definition. [51.5] How is the summarized meaning to be regarded in respect of (its) establishment? He says „as establishment, (i. e.) as establishment of synonyms, etc." This means synonyms, their meanings, its division, its proof. [51.8] And through this [175] fourfold indication of definition, etc. as a remedy against four minor vices, own-essence, result-essence, defiling-purifying essence and argument-essence [176] are expressed. [61.10] As a remedy against uncertainty here — own, essence; and this consists in grasping existence, non-existence, them both and non-separateness-unity [177]. [51.11] Having heard the definition of šūnyatā the unbelievers tremble. As a remedy against this, result-essence [178] (is given): unmistaken-suchness [179] result, non-contradiction [180] result; all-marks-forsaking [181] result, supra-mundane-knowledge [182] result, concerning all-objects and the result of the existence on that foundation [183] of the cause of saintly endowments. [51.14] Thus in order to remove the laziness of those lazy persons who have grasped enough [184] by merely hearing the essence and result of šūnyatā, the division-essence (is given). [51.16] In order to remove the doubt of those sceptics [185] who ask how is saṃkleša to be made pure, the argument-essence (is given). [186]

———